D0742343

WITHDRAWN
UTSA LIBRARIES

WITHDRAWN
UTSA LIBRARIES

DE PROPRIETATIBUS LITTERARUM

edenda curat

C.H. VAN SCHOONEVELD

Indiana University

Series Practica, 106

МICHIGAN
U┘SA LIBRARY

WORLDS APART:

Structural Parallels in the Poetry of Paul Valéry, Saint-John Perse, Benjamin Péret and René Char

by

ELIZABETH R. JACKSON

1976
MOUTON
THE HAGUE - PARIS

© Copyright 1976
Mouton & Co. B.V., Publishers, The Hague

No part of this book may be translated or reproduced in any form, by print, photo-print, microfilm, or any other means, without written permission from the publishers.

ISBN 90 279 3394 4

LIBRARY
University of Texas
At San Antonio

Printed in the Netherlands

ACKNOWLEDGMENTS

I wish to express my appreciation to Mme Rouart for her aid in making available to me manuscripts from her private collection of the Valéry documents and for her personal kindness.

Similarly I am grateful to Professor Henri Peyre and Professor Edith Kern for their attentive reading of my manuscript, for their suggestions and for their encouragement.

And to René Char I extend my thanks for giving me a glimpse of a poet's view, a world shared.

PREFACE

"Language is a labyrinth of paths. You approach from one side and know your way about; you approach the same place from another side and no longer know your way about."*1 The paths of French poetry have led far since Baudelaire introduced the perspective of a poetic imagination, a combined function of "les sens et l'esprit", which is both analytic and synthetic, which invents analogies, metaphors and which in effect "governs" the world. Considering the complexities of this endeavor it is no wonder that the buildingstones of the route, the multiple components of language, were reshaped, regrouped. The result has been a variety of poetic idioms, each delineating a unique world, distinct from the worlds of other poets and all, in turn, distinct from the domain of objective reality. They are doubly "worlds apart".

The unity of the present study is methodological. My aim is to develop a type of analysis, rigorous from a scholarly point of view but flexible enough to preserve the organic individuality of each author's work, a method which will also reveal characteristics common to all, such as the relationship of the modern poetic imagination to reality, such as recurrent differences between the language of esthetic communication and the language of every-day communication. So I have chosen four first-rate poets whose work represents intentionally different periods, different styles, and personalities. Paul Valéry is a direct descendant of the symbolist group and his main poetic production dates roughly from 1912 to 1920; it is a mythological domain whose boundaries are delicately and carefully traced and whose inhabitants breathe an air which is rarefied but charged with immediate psychic intensity. Saint-John Perse remains independent of any particular literary group. His mature poetry, dating from the twenties, encompasses a true universe reflecting the breadth, the unbounded all-pervasive vigorous spirit of his life, articulated with mastery and unselfconscious invention. Benjamin Péret is one of the lesser-known but one of the finest stars in the surrealist constellation. His work radiates that emotional and linguistic freedom, that fairy-tale realm of possibilities which epitomized the great ideal of the surrealist quest. René Char, first influenced by the surrealists in the thirties, then developing his own poetic goals, reintegrates ethical tensions in a personal poetic domain - earthy, fluid, human and harmoniously taut. The variety of these poetic temperaments is clear.

However, they have one common denominator, representative also of the main current in France, which is most important. Their creations reflect the structure of intimate human consciousness rather than the structure of practical thought and reactions to immediate situations rather than the logic of discursive presentations in poetry or prose. Tristan Tzara, as spokesman for the Dada movement, lucidly formulated this essential feature. In what amounts to a reaffirmation of Baudelaire's definition, he proclaimed that poetry is not a form of expression but rather "activité de l'esprit".*2 Thus, while the raw materials of poetry - sense-perceptions - which are equally raw materials of our mental life, have their source in the common outside world, and while in a certain sense poetry remains expressive of ideas and feelings, the focus of interest for the poet and for the reader is the self-sufficient world created by the play of the mind. If a particular scene (event or experience) is the starting point for a poem, it is transformed, so imbedded in the balance of a spiritual schema that we no longer "see" the original scene, nor should we try to. As in music, and in nonrepresentational painting and sculpture, the configurations of sound and rhythm, line, color, or surfaces suffice to hold one's attention.

Similarly, if one can sometimes perceive ideas (thoughts which can be formulated discursively) in a poem, they cannot be abstracted or isolated permanently from the web of the whole without distorting the sense. The content of a poem cannot be reduced simply to an idea nor to a symbolic abstraction. Essentially this poetry is not comment but the consolidation of mental events. It forms rather than reflects, says Gaeton Picon.*3

This being the case, several conclusions can be drawn concerning effective means of analysis. For one thing it is important to resist any tendency to consider intellectual content as more clear, more certain, perhaps more basic or substantial, than emotional content. Although our linguistic habits enable us to express ideas more clearly than emotions, our emotions are certainly neither ambiguous nor peripheral to our mental life - quite the contrary - thus it is natural that they should form the very core of poetry. So, when seeking the deepest sense of a poem it is essential to look for all the tonal elements: the patterns of emphasis and imagery which add up to a particular emotional coloring, the sets of such patterns which complete or react upon each other, the progression and variation of tone in the development.

It is equally important to avoid the arbitrary distinction between "forme et fond". Although it is often useful to examine the formal aspects of poetry separately - sound, rhythm, rhyme, imagery - this should be done bearing in mind that the meaning of the poem will probably be shaped and defined by them. Also, all the deviant elements of a poet's language (distorted syntax, grammatical quirks, even the proliferation of nonsense characteristic of the surrealists) would have a positive rather than a negative weight. Instead of representing simply an attempt to be original, or to establish a language distinct from prose, they may be crucial to elaborate the intrinsic sense, a potential structure necessary for the process of crystallization. Far from being vague or even obscure, this language is in fact more precise, although difficult.

Interestingly, both Breton and Aragon, ardent apologists of disrespect in all areas including that of grammatical conventions, invite technical analysis of their poetry. In that revolutionary document, the First Manifesto of Surrealism (1924), Breton says quite clearly that a rigorous logical and grammatical analysis could clarify certain characteristics of his texts. And Aragon, a few years later, while advocating a radical violation of grammatical rules for the poet, opens the door brusquely to the critic: "I ask that my books be criticized with greatest rigor by knowledgeable people who, versed in grammar and logic, will seek in the steps of my commas the lice of thought in the head of my style."*4 Thus, these poets speak of meaning in those very texts which superficially appear nonsensical to the extreme. One would conclude that meaning may be revealed by considering precisely those nonsensical, deviant elements.

Finally, a few words about the organization of this present study. In each section, I have sought initially some clue, in the author's own words, as to the direction to follow in exploring his creative domain. These frequently point out his sense of structure and also illustrate typical esthetic urges and attitudes. Then, in order to examine first an esthetic microcosm, I analyze a series of particular poems (or extracts from poems). The choice is designed to reflect a range of subjects and styles characteristic of the given poet. My technique is basically the traditional explication de texte, which I find indispensable for a clear and precise understanding of poetry, but with special emphasis on tonal patterns and on linguistic traits. The final step in each section is a synthesis, a free-style essay portraying and examining the salient features of each poetic world. More abstract considerations, of a philosophical and linguistic nature, are treated in the "postface", since at that point it is possible to consider parallels between the works of all four authors. As is often the case with this sort of speculation, the questions raised may be as interesting as the questions solved. Such is the open-ended satisfaction of literary criticism.

NOTES

*1 Ludwig Wittgenstein, Philosophical Investigations, trans. G.E.M. Anscombe, 2nd ed. (New York, 1967), 82.

*2 "Dénonçons au plus vite un malentendu qui prétendait classer la poésie sous la rubrique des moyens d'expression. La poésie qui ne se distingue des romans que par sa forme extérieure, la poésie qui exprime soit des idées, soit des sentiments, n'intéresse plus personne. Je lui oppose la poésie activité de l'esprit..." Tristan Tzara, "Essai sur la situation de la poésie", Le Surréalisme au service de la révolution, n. 4 (déc.1931), 15-23.

*3 Gaeton Picon, L'Usage de la lecture (Paris, 1961), 289.

*4 "Je demande à ce que mes livres soient critiqués avec la dernière rigueur, par des gens qui s'y connaissent, et qui sachant la grammaire et la logique, chercheront sous le pas de mes virgules les poux de ma pensée dans la tête de mon style." Louis Aragon, Traité du style (Paris, 1928), 46.

TABLE OF CONTENTS

PART ONE

VALÉRY: CETTE FORME PENSIVE

Formally, Valéry's poetry leaves the reader with an immediate impression of structure. Each poem is an entity: self-sufficient, complete, resounding with internal echoes. But further perusal is apt to result in a number of apparently paradoxical and inevitably puzzling discoveries. Themes and a manner of expression which are highly intellectual exist sometimes intermingled with and sometimes dramatically contrasted with their forcefully sensual counterparts. Similarly, the careful wording, the elegant finish of the prosody, the involved but accurate syntax create oddly a total effect of vagueness, a disturbing transparency of meaning. How then does one integrate such disparate elements, follow the thread of meaning throughout an opaque narrative development? The poet himself suggests a perspective which embraces details and oppositions within the pattern of the whole.

> Il faut que l'oeil parvienne à la structure mais n'y parvienne que par le détour d'un ensemble de mouvement d'incidents et d'égarements qui finissent bien et le conduisent au but non brusquement mais comme un système de biefs et de canaux conduisent l'eau de la montagne à la mer, ayant été toute [sic] utilisée.*1*

The structure is thus not static but fluid, consisting of events and even seemingly unconnected distractions, constantly moving towards a goal. So the substance of the poem, indistinguishable from the form, consists of movement and intelligible change.

NOTE

*1 Paul Valéry, Cahier VI, 1916-1918 (Paris, 1958), 119.

"LES PAS"

Les Pas

Tes pas, enfants de mon silence,
Saintement, lentement placés,
Vers le lit de ma vigilance
Procèdent muets et glacés.

Personne pure, ombre divine,
Qu'ils sont doux, tes pas retenus!
Dieux! ...tous les dons que je devine
Viennent à moi sur ces pieds nus!

Si, de tes lèvres avancées,
Tu prépares pour l'apaiser,
A l'habitant de mes pensées
La nourriture d'un baiser.

Ne hâte pas cet acte tendre,
Douceur d'être et de n'être pas,
Car j'ai vécu de vous attendre
Et mon coeur n'était que vos pas.*

Clear in tone, light in touch, "Les Pas" is typical of Valéry's short
poems which despite their brevity contain a full measure of intricate
patterns of meaning. To suggest initially a succinct description, one
might say that is a model of anticipation, a state of mind in which
waiting and undistracted attention are surrounded with a diaphanous
atmosphere of pleasure. Valéry admired Rimbaud because he rendered
perceptible such infinitely delicate phenomena. This is exactly what
characterizes "Les Pas".

The first verse sets the stage with a bare minimum of character and
scene. There is a bed, an anonymous narrator, silent and alert, and
disembodied footsteps. The relation between the two human elements
is close, familiar since the narrator uses the familiar form of address
"tes" and since he tenderly pronounces the word "enfants". Yet he conceives a physical distance between himself and the steps as he speaks
of their approach. "Tes pas": these monosyllables are the phonetic
equivalent of the steps. Their initial consonants themselves have the
short, staccato but muted quality which is later described as "muets
et glacés" and the vowels are equally delicate and ephemeral.

These lines show particularly well the careful blending of suspension
and movement, sustained throughout the whole poem. We see suspen-

sion in the narrator's expectancy, in the slow placing of the steps ("saintement, lentement placés"), in the lengthening of the rhythm through those adverbs. Also, the three phrases separating the subject and verb check the forward place. One is an apposition ("enfants de mon silence"); the second and third ("Saintement, lentement placés", "Vers le lit de ma vigilance") are adverbial phrases and the latter would normally follow the verb. All of these are "correct" grammatically and represent a typical poetic sequence,*1 but the accumulation in this case seems to have a particular function, that of orchestrating the theme of delay. However, movement, final and definite, is unambiguously announced. "Procèdent", the first word in the last line, is a word for which not only the narrator but we, the readers, too have waited. Also, the rhyme scheme (silence, placés, vigilance, glacés) swings from one line to the next, from a contained sound suggesting rest to another perhaps suggesting a slight forward movement through its sharper quality. In addition, all of the s and l sounds together with the many interior vowels, variants of a sounds, form the tonal nucleus of the stanza - attentive calm.

This calm disappears in the second stanza. The narrator is swept with an intense pleasure of which the overtones are mystical. In fact, the mystical theme is one of the main patterns of the poem, judging from the number of reinforcing words. "Saintement" is the first hint, broadened and brought to a high pitch in the second tanza: "Personne pure", "ombre divine", "Dieux!" To these one can add "devine" by virtue of one meaning given by Littré: to discover by supernatural means. Exclamations, ecstasy. A final line then continues the forward movement of the first stanza and adds a new note of sensuality thus intensifying the tone of excitement and anticipation:

...tous les dons que je devine
Viennent à moi sur ces pieds nus!

In the third stanza, the tension is sustained and, for the narrator, infused with desire. "Si, de tes lèvres avancées, / Tu prépares... / La nourriture d'un baiser." All four rhymes in e maintain the anticipation as does the form in which the thought is presented. "Si" introduces the sentence and the supposition remains unresolved until the next verse. The inverted phrase, "de tes lèvres avancées", emphasizes it still further. This stanza is the most physically concrete: lips, a kiss, a near future embrace imagined. Here, as in the preceding stanza, that pure person seems very close, fused in the line of thought.

So the final verse appears as both a surprise and a resolution. Instead of continued forward movement, fulfillment of the expectation and the desire, there is a brusque negative reaction which slows down the current, suspends satisfaction. "Ne hâte pas cet acte tendre...", suddenly forbids the voice. Throughout these four lines resounds the negative monosyllable, "pas", recurring in the rhyme and as homonyms repeating in echo the footsteps. This is certainly what Valéry meant by "resonance": the sound patterns in poetry which are essential to their esthetic success, where words which are homonyms multiply their physical and intellectual impact.

The ultimate pleasure, it appears, is the attentive grasp of that tenuous state, "Douceur d'être et de n'être pas", reminiscent of Gide's Nathaniel in <u>Les Nourritures terrestres</u> who seeks and prolongs a symbolic thirst. A new lucidity accompanies this state. The pure person recedes. In the final lines she is addressed formally, "j'ai vécu de <u>vous</u> attendre", and thus the psychological distance between her and the narrator widens. So that the last remark follows smoothly, a straight-forward explanation of the momentary trance. The rhythmical steps were really heartbeats. The tone becomes calm once again (<u>a</u> sounds reappear within the lines as well as in the rhymes). The last line is none other than a direct restatement of the first: the final words, "vos pas", rejoin the first, "tes pas", with the slightly altered nuance of distance.

Seeking the intricacies of structure, one can distinguish several perspectives. First, stanzas one and two consist of direct statements. They set the stage, light the scene, indicate the mental disposition of the narrator and carefully signal the forward movement of the footsteps. The second half of the poem, stanzas three and four, interrupts the motion, poses a problem in the form of a hypothesis creating dramatic tension and then resolves the question, shows the reaction of the narrator, at first instinctive and then elaborated on an intellectual plane. This view of the structure, while accurate, seems to me rather of a cut and dried cast. It adds little to real comprehension. Another perspective, more illuminating, discloses two parallel lines of motion: that of the pure person, whose role suggests all the physical action, and that of the narrator, who is immobilized on his bed but whose mind wanders - literally and figuratively. This line is the most revealing since it includes the enunciation of thought and the manifestation of a complete cycle of feeling: attentive calm leading to thrill of anticipation, then full excitement with a quick return to controlled and lucid repose. Valéry, in his life-long life reflection on mental activity, posed as a fundamental phenomenon a pattern consisting of deviation from a certain equilibrium which, after a period of variation, would return to the initial state.*2 This pattern is typical of numerous aspects of human activity such as fear, anger, sleep, hunger, love. "Les Pas" is an exquisite poetic equivalent.

Next to consider are the patterns of tone and thought. For they are guides to the sense of a poem equally important as the structural lines. Five main patterns, I should say, stand out in the fabric of "Les Pas": the afore-mentioned mystical complex for one; for another a sensual pattern; thirdly a strong tendency towards "dénuement"; fourth, evidence of waiting, anticipation; and fifth, the intellectual theme of attention.

Sensuality is suggested generally by the stage settings and particularly by the following words all of which have sensual connotations: "doux", "dons", "pieds nus", "lèvres avancées", "nourriture", "baiser", "tendre", "douceur". The sensuality, I think, should be considered the counterpart of the mysticism, the latter dominant in the second stanza and the former suffusing the third. Each typifies a certain sort of pleasure similar in their intensity and certainly not necessarily exclusive, witness the sensual vocabulary of religious mystics and the mystical cast of theories of love from Plato through Petrarch. The "dénuement" provides a stark contrast to the full, concrete nature of sensuality. It is pervasive: the words "silence", "muets", "glacés", "pure", "ombre", "retenus", "nus", "attendre" and the three striking negative statements in the last stanza "ne hâte pas", "Douceur d'être et de n'être pas", and "mon coeur n'était que vos pas". It is something of a poetic triumph to render so vivid a tendency towards nothingness, and even to have that tone stronger than something concrete and sensual. Or perhaps, to be more exact, to have such a life-like sensual image take substance from, be created out of silence and absence.

The patterns of waiting and of attention have fewer verbal indications but are nonetheless clear and central. Waiting is infused in the dramatic progression. The formulated thought, introduced by the word "vigilance" and reaffirmed at the end by "attendre", is sustained by the syntax. Attention is implied in the phrase "enfants de mon silence", explicit in "vigilance", and again implied in "l'habitant de mes pensées". The latter phrase is imbedded rather unobtrusively in the third stanza amidst the image of the evocation of a kiss. Nevertheless, the import of it is such that one has to recognize the surrounding sensual elements as metaphorical in weight, sweet but perishable like the flesh of a peach enclosing the vital potential of the pit.

Interestingly, the psychological forms of waiting and of attention exhibit certain similarities. This is very clear in the French equivalents, "attente" and "attention", whose Latin substratum indicates moving towards, tending towards. One might say, perhaps, that waiting implies more of a direction to the future and some sort of inkling of what one is waiting for, whereas attention is wholly present in its field of activity and the object of attention may be known or unknown, immediate or virtual. Attention, often independent, self-sufficient, would seem also to be a necessary component of expectancy, providing a level of alertness and energy.

Before attempting to synthesize these components of structure and patterns, it will prove helpful to see how Valéry arrived at the final version of "Les Pas", for, typically, this poem evolved very slowly with a surprising shift of length, wording, theme and tone along the way. There were at least three preliminary versions.*3 The initial sketch has the definitive rhythm in octosyllables. Frequently, Valéry sensed first a certain rhythm from which then developed an atmosphere and a subject. The setting of the first version is similar - night, a bed, an expectant narrator. But the pure person is much more in evidence. " Personne pure, ombre divine" are the first words. She is soon named, Psyche, and is not only less of a shadow but also clearly the Muse from whom the poet awaits inspiration. The line "à l'habitant de mes pensées" was originally "A la soif des pures pensées". The sketch is longer than "Les Pas" without division into stanzas and generally amorphous. It also contains suggestions of death.

The second version develops dramatic excitement ("terreurs", "fureurs", "spectre") it also develops to the end as main plot the amorous overtones. Another significant change is that it ceases to name the pure person Psyche; only a marginal note identifies her as a "messagère intérieure". The third sketch eliminates that extra information entirely.

A number of details of the final changes are revelatory. Although the first two stanzas are in position and although the theme of the steps is now clear, the final title is nowhere in evidence and instead three other possibilities, none as original, head the sheet: "Nourrice", "Nocturne", and "Le Lit". Furthermore, at two different points in the margin the author specifies "Danse", once next to what eventually becomes the final verse. Another hint of the dance theme occurs in the early stages of the line "Ne hâte pas la marche tendre" substituting "l'allure" for "la marche" and finally writing in "cet acte". So, at one point Valéry played with the notion of developing the suggestion of the movement of the steps, an ordered dance.

And, not surprisingly, the dance was one of Valéry's particular interests. Degas was an early friend and an artistic idol. In L'Ame et la Danse, a dramatic dialogue written in 1921, he explores at length the esthetics of that art form; and he frequently touches on the subject in his essays and notebooks. The combination of gesture, rhythm and ordered, self-enclosed pattern, all immaterial expression, no doubt appealed to his imagination. Some critics have proposed the dance as a central symbolic theme of "Les Pas" (even without the evidence of earlier versions). Although that theme did occur to the poet at one stage of composition, the fact remains that he eliminated from the final version any direct references ("la marche" or "l'allure" and "C'est mon coeur qui compte ces pas"), so that such an interpretation seems to me to go beyond the evidence.

The final structure and tonal progression are set only at the very last revision. While the first two stanzas are definitively placed in the third version, the final last stanza, "Ne hâte pas...", comes next followed by "Si de tes lèvres avancées...", and then there is a fourth stanza containing the dramatic element which was afterwards abandoned. What appears so clear and perfect as the final last stanza, closing the circle, was the result of a sudden ultimate inspiration. In its position as third stanza in the third sketch, it is very indecisive with many changes of a radical nature and the definitive lines, "Car j'ai vécu de vous attendre" and "Et mon coeur n'était que vos pas", come, separated at the bottom of the page - sudden chance thoughts. One other change is of note. The word "vigilance", so central to the sense, was hesitatingly used throughout the composition. In the first sketch "indolence" is an equal alternative and in the third "silence" is a suggested substitution. Thus, the important undercurrent of attention was similarly a delayed decision.

Now comes the key problem. To what extent can one define a level of symbolic meaning in this poem? Or in any other. How should one use the information gained from knowledge of the early stages of creation? I think extreme care should be exercised in proposing an explicit symbol from an early version, such as the Psyche image, to justify an exclusive interpretation of the final poem. "Les Pas", as one reads it and absorbs it, is not simply and solely a poet in search of inspiration, desiring and sensing the imminence of a creative spark, savoring and prolonging that moment of imminence. But that is the most frequent interpretation proposed. Knowing the history of "Les Pas" and knowing the author's constant interest in the sources and nature of art, one can admit that such a reading is consistent with certain lines. Particularly, the phrases, "le lit de ma vigilance" and "l'habitant de mes pensées" not only justify but spur the search for some such symbolic overtone - a person seeking within the silence of his being for some fruitful thought. But Valéry did eliminate in the end both the name Psyche and the description "messagère intérieure". The final stanza, with its return to a state of calm, its lucid self-contained and self-satisfying grasp of a state of non-being and its last rational revelation, is <u>not</u> the conclusion of the birth of a poem or even of the discovery of an idea. Steps as symbols of poetic rhythm or of dance, the pure person conceived as the poet's intimate Muse, these are indeed pertinent as secondary symbols, resonances on a metaphorical level. Yet the main import lies elsewhere. The combined force of the structural lines and of the patterns of tone and theme, whose impressive action on the reader is dominant and uncontestable, indicates that the direct sense of "Les Pas" embodies a short and sweet, pregnant yet suspended time of willed anticipation. In his <u>Cahiers</u>, Valéry pointing out the dangers of abstract exegesis gives as an example this very poem: "...<u>les Pas</u>, petit poème purement <u>sentimental</u> auquel on prête un sens intellectuel, un symbole de 'l'inspiration'!"*4 "Sentimental?" Certainly, in the exact French weight of that word - as a cool, clear, vibrant model of human feeling in a precise configuration.

NOTES

*1 Several interesting studies have shown to what extent poetry, by nature, distorts ordinary language patterns. Jean Cohen in his book, <u>Structure du langage poétique</u> (Paris, 1966), analyses the many ways in which poetry appears as "antiprose"; and Pierre Guiraud, using a statistical approach in <u>Langage et versification d'après l'oeuvre de Paul Valéry</u> (Paris, 1958), shows the extent and nature of deviants from the linguistic norm in Valéry's work compared with that of predecessors.

*2 The law of thermodynamics suggested to Valéry certain analogies with this aspect of mental activity, particularly the idea of closed cycles. Judith Robinson discusses this matter in <u>L'Analyse de l'esprit dans les Cahiers de Valéry</u>, 64-69.

*3 For an excellent presentation of the genesis and final form of this poem (as well as the others in the same collection), see James Lawler, <u>Lecture de Charmes</u> (Paris, 1963). There, he gives the full text of the first version (from the first notebook of sketches of <u>Charmes</u>) and mentions the significant changes to be found in the second version (from the second notebook). I found a third version, a separate original typed copy with handwritten corrections and changes in the margin, in the collection of the Bibliothèque Doucet; on this worksheet many of the significant final changes appear.

*4 <u>Cahier</u> XXVIII, 427.

II

"LE CIMETIÈRE MARIN"

<u>Le Cimetière marin</u>

Μή, φίλα ψυά, βίου ἀθάνατου
σπεῦδε, τὰν δ᾽ ἔμπρακτου ἄντλει μαχανάν.

Pindare, <u>Pythiques</u>, III

I

Ce toit tranquille, où marchent des colombes,
Entre les pins palpite, entre les tombes;
Midi le juste y compose de feux
La mer, la mer, toujours recommencée!
O récompense après une pensée
Qu'un long regard sur le calme des dieux!

II

Quel pur travail de fins éclairs consume
Maint diamant d'imperceptible écume,
Et quelle paix semble se concevoir!
Quand sur l'abîme un soleil se repose,
Ouvrages purs d'une éternelle cause,
Le Temps scintille et le Songe est savoir.

III

Stable trésor, temple simple à Minerve,
Masse de calme, et visible réserve,
Eau sourcilleuse, OEil qui gardes en toi
Tant de sommeil sous un voile de flamme,
O mon silence! ... Edifice dans l'âme,
Mais comble d'or aux mille tuiles, Toit!

IV

Temple du Temps, qu'un seul soupir résume,
A ce point pur je monte et m'accoutume,
Tout entouré de mon regard marin;
Et comme aux dieux mon offrande suprême,
La scintillation sereine sème
Sur l'altitude un dédain souverain.

V

Comme le fruit se fond en jouissance,
Comme en délice il change son absence
Dans une bouche où sa forme se meurt,
Je hume ici ma future fumée,
Et le ciel chante à l'âme consumée
Le changement des rives en rumeur.

VI

Beau ciel, vrai ciel, regarde-moi qui change!
Après tant d'orgueil, après tant d'étrange
Oisiveté, mais pleine de pouvoir,
Je m'abandonne à ce brillant espace,
Sur les maisons des morts mon ombre passe
Qui m'apprivoise à son frêle mouvoir.

VII

L'âme exposée aux torches du solstice,
Je te soutiens, admirable justice
De la lumière aux armes sans pitié!
Je te rends pure à ta place première:
Regarde-toi! ... Mais rendre la lumière
Suppose d'ombre une morne moitié.

VIII

O pour moi seul, à moi seul, en moi-même,
Auprès d'un coeur, aux sources du poème,
Entre le vide et l'événement pur,
J'attends l'écho de ma grandeur interne,
Amère, sombre et sonore citerne,
Sonnant dans l'âme un creux toujours futur!

IX

Sais-tu, fausse captive des feuillages,
Golfe mangeur de ces maigres grillages,
Sur mes yeux clos, secrets éblouissants,
Quel corps me traîne à sa fin paresseuse,
Quel front l'attire à cette terre osseuse?
Une étincelle y pense à mes absents.

X

Fermé, sacré, plein d'un feu sans matière,
Fragment terrestre offert à la lumière,
Ce lieu me plaît, dominé de flambeaux,
Composé d'or, de pierre et d'arbres sombres,
Où tant de marbre est tremblant sur tant d'ombres;
La mer fidèle y dort sur mes tombeaux!

XI

Chienne splendide, écarte l'idolâtre !
Quand solitaire au sourire de pâtre,
Je pais longtemps, moutons mystérieux,
Le blanc troupeau de mes tranquilles tombes,
Eloignes-en les prudentes colombes,
Les songes vains, les anges curieux !

XII

Ici venu, l'avenir est paresse.
L'insecte net gratte la sécheresse;
Tout est brûlé, défait, reçu dans l'air
A je ne sais quelle sévère essence...
La vie est vaste, étant ivre d'absence,
Et l'amertume est douce, et l'esprit clair.

XIII

Les morts cachés sont bien dans cette terre
Qui les réchauffe et sèche leur mystère.
Midi là-haut, Midi sans mouvement
En soi se pense et convient à soi-même...
Tête complète et parfait diadème,
Je suis en toi le secret changement.

XIV

Tu n'as que moi pour contenir tes craintes !
Mes repentirs, mes doutes, mes contraintes
Sont le défaut de ton grand diamant...
Mais dans leur nuit toute lourde de marbres,
Un peuple vague aux racines des arbres
A pris déjà ton parti lentement.

XV

Ils ont fondu dans une absence épaisse,
L'argile rouge a bu la blanche espèce,
Le don de vivre a passé dans les fleurs !
Où sont des morts les phrases familières,
L'art personnel, les âmes singulières ?
La larve file où se formaient des pleurs.

XVI

Les cris aigus des filles chatouillées,
Les yeux, les dents, les paupières mouillées,
Le sein charmant qui joue avec le feu,
Le sang qui brille aux lèvres qui se rendent,
Les derniers dons, les doigts qui les défendent,
Tout va sous terre et rentre dans le jeu !

XVII

Et vous, grande âme, espérez-vous un songe
Qui n'aura plus ces couleurs de mensonge
Qu'aux yeux de chair l'onde et l'or font ici?
Chanterez-vous quand serez vaporeuse?
Allez! Tout fuit! Ma présence est poreuse,
La sainte impatience meurt aussi!

XVIII

Maigre immortalité noire et dorée,
Consolatrice affreusement laurée,
Qui de la mort fais un sein maternel,
Le beau mensonge et la pieuse ruse!
Qui ne connaît, et ne les refuse,
Ce crâne vide et ce rire éternel!

XIX

Pères profonds, têtes inhabitées,
Qui sous le poids de tant de pelletées,
Etes la terre et confondez nos pas,
Le vrai rongeur, le ver irréfutable
N'est point pour vous qui dormez sous la table,
Il vit de vie, il ne me quitte pas!

XX

Amour, peut-être, ou de moi-même haine?
Sa dent secrète est de moi si prochaine
Que tous les noms lui peuvent convenir!
Qu'importe! Il voit, il veut, il songe, il touche!
Ma chair lui plaît, et jusque sur ma couche,
A ce vivant je vis d'appartenir!

XXI

Zénon! Cruel Zénon! Zénon d'Elée!
M'as-tu percé de cette flèche ailée
Qui vibre, vole, et qui ne vole pas!
Le son m'enfante et la flèche me tue!
Ah! le soleil...Quelle ombre de tortue
Pour l'âme, Achille immobile à grands pas!

XXII

Non, non! ...Debout! Dans l'ère successive!
Brisez, mon corps, cette forme pensive!
Buvez, mon sein, la naissance du vent!
Une fraîcheur, de la mer exhalée,
Me rend mon âme... O puissance salée!
Courons à l'onde en rejaillir vivant!

XXIII

Oui! Grande mer de délires douée,
Peau de panthère et chlamyde trouée
De mille et mille idoles du soleil,
Hydre absolue, ivre de ta chair bleue,
Qui te remords l'étincelante queue
Dans un tumulte au silence pareil.

XXIV

Le vent se lève!... Il faut tenter de vivre!
L'air immense ouvre et referme mon livre,
La vague en poudre ose jaillir des rocs!
Envolez-vous, pages tout éblouies!
Rompez, vagues! Rompez d'eaux réjouies
Ce toit tranquille où picoraient des focs!

"Le Cimetière marin" is as bathed in light and sheer explosive energy
as "Les Pas" is restrained and opaque. It is the most easily accessible
of Valéry's three long poems. The other two, "La Jeune Parque" and
"Fragments de Narcisse", are nocturnal, shadowy, subtly sinuous,
introspective and therefore difficult though rich. It is also the best-
known of Valéry's work and justifiably so: the sun, the sea, the narrator's alert spirit are irresistibly engaging. Wallace Stevens' "Cre-
dences of Summer" has much of the same spirit - the sense of enthusiastic pleasure, of enrichment, of direct contact with a place and moment and also a similar elevated lucidity.

Valéry considered that "Le Cimetière marin" represented his most
authentic type of poetic expression.*1 Born in Sète, a small Mediterranean coastal town, he grew naturally with an early passion for the
sea, for swimming, for ships, for the stimulating activity of a port;
and he preserved that spirit throughout his life. When he was nineteen,
he wrote to Gide of an ambition to write a "marine symphony". Many
early poems have a similar setting and spirit and even contain some
of the same imagery.*2 Unlike the rest of his poems, this one is based
on a real location (that cemetery exists), and the raw materials for
the spirit come from the poet's experience. However, the drama is
fictional; the initial point of inspiration, according to the author, was
a certain rhythm in ten syllables,*3 which was accompanied by memories of tone and physical sensations.

Although the impact of the poem is direct and unequivocal, many
particular words and phrases are not easy to explain, and one cannot
suggest what the poem conveys simply in one or two words. Seeking a
brief statement which would adequately grasp the essence, I would
say this. It is an interior monologue reflecting the experience of a
given time and a given place - noon and a short period thereafter, in
a cemetery by the sea. The narrator, attracted by the surroundings,
gazes and reflects. He thinks about what he sees, but he also actually
reflects the scene because of his heightened receptivity and sensitivity.
The bonds between the man and the total event are very close, mutually
essential one might say. All the nuances of the moment, the changes,

the possibilities are subsumed in his thought. The period is marked
by the emotional bond between the man and the object of his attention.
The progressive changes in this bond delineate what seems to me to be
the natural structure of the poem. Roughly, the curve has four stages.
First, an initial state where the man is fused in direct spiritual union
with the sea and the sky, emanating a tonal quality of electric rapture,
intoxicating equilibrium. Then, a time when the equilibrium continues
but where the narrator comes down to earth and to himself, conscious
of the plot of land, of the tombs, of his body and the depths of his mind.
A sense of calm and well-being pervades the interval. Next, comes a
shadow of doubt, uneasiness which, pursuing the idea of death, leads
to a climax of irony and helpless anger. Finally, there is a reaction,
reaffirmation of life, return to the immediate - wind, sea, waves - a
renewed intoxicated immersion in the present, in this case to pursue
action.*4

"Ce toit tranquille, où marchent des colombes, / Entre les pins palpite, entre les tombes..." With breathtaking directness, the narrator,
lifting his eyes from his work, shares with us his spontaneous view of
the instant. "Ce toit...," this roof - a demonstrative adjective serves
as a gesture, showing us exactly and closely what is meant.*5 There
is the sea, its calm expanse dotted with sails, resembling at first
glance a roof with doves; then the cemetery, tombs and pines, the sun
at its zenith. There is the narrator's pleasure emphasized by a series
of exclamations sustained through three stanzas. The Mediterranean
heat is suggested too: by the water shimmering beyond the pines, by
"feux", and also by a shade of meaning in "calme" which includes besides rest (composure), a motionless sea and at its base, in the Greek
root, burning heat (kauma). The word "compose" may appear puzzling,
but Valéry surely uses it knowingly - to indicate both a calming effect
and to suggest the sun's effect of ordering and forming nature, as seen
by us. In an offhand reflection, not connected with this poem, he once
said: "Tout ce que nous voyons est composé par lui, et j'entends par
composition un ordre de choses visibles et la transformation lente de
cet ordre qui constitue tout le spectacle d'une journée."*6

This sparkling, dazzling sight, "Quel pur travail de fins éclairs
consume..." has the double effect of activity ("travail" and "ouvrages")
and self-contained peace. The verb "consume" is evasive in meaning;
but perhaps that evasiveness is just what is suggested - the rapid appearance and disappearance of each sparkle of foam. And the last line
of stanza II, "Le Temps scintille et le Songe est savoir", also calls
for explanation. Although the fact that "Temps" and "Songe" are capitalized suggest a symbolic and philosophical meaning, I doubt that one
should follow up the consequences absolutely. But a certain development of thought does seem reasonable. The rapid tiny changes which
form the sparkling in a sense make time visible. "Le Temps scintille..."
Later in the poem the line, "entre le vide et l'événement pur" (stanza
VIII) suggests that a perceptible event, like a pebble breaking the surface of the water in a well would create the necessary visible ripple
and echo to break the apparent emptiness of waiting. For time to be
perceptible, something, however short or small, must happen.

As for the phrase "le Songe est savoir", one's first reaction might be to consider a mystical interpretation. There are, however, a number of considerations which enter into the picture. One is Valéry's explicit views on that subject. His essay on Swedenborg offers a typical synthesis.*7 Here, he purses the nature of the mystical experience and is clearly fascinated by the visions which form the basis of an ordered universe or rather of two interrelated worlds. And he points out that one should not consider mysticism to be the same as delirium since the mystic discerns and emphasizes the boundaries between the two worlds and the two sets of values. His fascination, nevertheless, is tempered by the recognition that the mystics' language is evasive and distorts an experience which might have some real value, but most importantly it excludes critical method and verification, equating the feeling of conviction with knowledge. Another point to bear in mind is the fact that Valéry's use of the word "songe" in general does not correspond exactly to the dictionary or to normal usage. Normally, "songe" has a definite connotation of irrationality, of something unreal, distorted, a figment of the imagination. But Valéry, in contrast, uses it frequently, often as a synonym for "penser" or "réfléchir", with an admixture of rational and irrational. A third consideration is the fact that even in the third of three successive versions of "Le Cimetière marin" neither "temps" nor "songe" is capitalized (that whole stanza is slow to take form) and two surprising alternatives are written in for "songe" – "sommeil" and "calme". Neither of these contains the idea of thought; quite the contrary, the single point in common to all three is a certain restful sense. To conclude, if any philosophical meaning is present, it must be something of a secondary echo; and the mystical quality of "le Songe est savoir" should be considered metaphorical rather than intellectual. The restful, reflective mental cast of the narrator is like knowledge by virtue of its reassuring equilibrium.

The theme of stability is developed in stanza III. It includes not only an extension of the sensation of equilibrium but also an elaboration of the first metaphor, "ce toit tranquille". Valéry pursues these ideas in an astounding series of metaphors, five initially, one following another and tied by a metamorphosis of idea or an imposing visual impression. "Eau sourcilleuse", for instance, combines the moral impression of self-contained pride with a physical characteristic, the lines of the waves resembling that of an eyebrow. And it is the latter image which leads into the next picture, "OEil qui gardes en toi / Tant de sommeil sous un voile de flamme." This stanza is also remarkable, and equally typical, in that there is not a single main verb in the whole succession of statements! In each case the elliptical element would be a form of the verb "to be" or else "to seem". Clearly, the poet felt that the verb was unnecessary and perhaps even that the use of it would falsify his thought. All of the statements are really separate spontaneous acts of perception and in each case there is a spontaneous expression of what the mind senses. Generally, the source of images comes from the notation of a direct impression, noted and expressed before the play of rational judgement corrects or modifies it. In his essay on Leonar da Vinci, Valéry discusses at length the value (for the artist and for anyone with an urge to capture the thrill of "la moindre chose réelle") of looking with the eye rather than with the mind. "La constatation est d'abo subie, presque sans pensée,

avec le sentiment de se laisser emplir..."*8 Proust, too, developed
the same idea and considered it a key for attaining esthetic pleasure
in experience and in art. He called it the importance of "l'impression
première". In his case, the background of this notion included under-
standably the impressionist painters but also the works of Vermeer,
Chardin, Turner, not to mention his own visual experience. Excellent
examples of such theories, the "toit tranquille" and the "masse de
calme" in "Le Cimetière marin" are not in the least artificial poetic
devices, ornaments or even calculated symbols. They are simply exact
perceptions of the human mind.

The last two lines of the stanza show not only Valéry's concern for
precise notation on the part of the narrator but also a quick grasp and
a decisive option of values. "O mon silence!..." is the sudden awareness of that silence and of the fact that the preceding impressions are
a result of that sustained attention. It is the equivalent of "enfants de
mon silence", the footsteps in "Les Pas". "Edifice dans l'âme", then,
is the lucid judgment that the roof, the mass, the temple - all edifices -
are nonetheless mental constructions. "Mais comble d'or aux mille
tuiles, Toit!" reaffirms the value and the beauty and shows the narrator embracing unrestrained the full sensation. The two rhymes, "toi"
and "Toit!" homonyms, double and redouble the two themes, one of
the rooftop and the other of familiarity and tenderness.

Full acceptance, even complete abandoned identification with that
perceptive field, comes to a climax in the fourth stanza. The first line
is a brief, but interesting remark with philosophical overtones. The
sigh may appear strange in the context but actually it can be seen again
as a very exact transcription. Valéry was attentive to all human gestures and physical expressions (laughter, tears...) and suggested the
following interpretation of sighs: "Qu'il est rare de penser à fond sans
soupirer. A l'extrême de toute pensée est un soupir."*9 So, here a
sigh is entirely in keeping with the intense mental activity of the narrator. Furthermore, as with the sparkling of the foam, a sigh would
mark, isolate and define a moment of time - which is just what the
line states.

But the main tone of the stanza is not philosophical but dramatic:
altitude and a concomitant sense of glorious domination. The notion of
limitless dimensions, and in particular of height has already been introduced. "Abîme" (stanza II) has one rather unusual meaning, the
ocean, and of course includes the sense of limitless depths. The roof
gives an extension of height; and "comble", which formerly was a synonym for roof, involves the sense of physical height, a connotation of
summit or crown as well as the idea of an emotional highpoint. "Altitude" used at the end of this stanza also combines meanings of height
and depth since one use of the word in Latin designates the depth of
the sea. So, the sense of the whole stanza, "A ce point pur je monte
et m'accoutume", embraces the narrator's fusion with the expanse and
even the depth of the sea crowned by the height of light, the sun at its
zenith.

The tone of the following stanza, while less expansive, continues the
intense pleasure and the fusion of the soul in the atmosphere ("l'âme
consumée"). Yet, there is a new note of inward sensual enjoyment.

Valéry thought the lines developing the image of the fruit were among
his best. A delightful passage from a letter to Gide parallels the tone
and shows the personal predilection behind the image.

Jeannie a bien reçu vos dattes. C'est moi qui les mange. J'ai un
immense faible pour ce fruit poisseux dont le sucre à demi liquide
et presque charnu est pénétré d'une soie particulière autour d'un
os prédestiné aux bouches.
On devrait classer les fruits comme les lettres de l'alphabet. Il
y en a qui font mal aux dents, les d et les t. Les dattes sont liquides
et labiales.*10*

That concrete sensual image leads up to the climax "Je hume ici ma
future fumée" where the multiplication of sharp vowels y and i reinforce
uninterruptedly the narrator's ecstasy. What he does, what he is conscious of is physical too: he is breathing. The verb "hume" neatly combines eating (suggested in the image) and breathing. Etymological dic-
tionaries (Littré, Bloch and Wartburg) give the original meaning from
a medieval Wallon dialect "avaler en retirant son haleine, des oeufs,
du lait" and the derived meaning, to breathe. Of note also is the ono-
matopoeia patterned on the sharp intake of breath.

Beau ciel, vrai ciel, regarde-moi qui change !
Après tant d'orgueil, après tant d'étrange
Oisiveté, mais pleine de pouvoir,
Je m'abandonne à ce brillant espace...

Noting succinctly the shift of sentiment and of attention, the narrator
introduces a new orientation. He is aware of himself and his gaze
shifts back and forth from the cemetery, from his real position in the
whole scene, to the sea and the sky and to the relations within the total
picture. For nine stanzas (VI-XIII) one clear tone dominates: a state
of well-being, relaxed acceptance, observations about himself and the
place he occupies.
The theme of change mentioned first at the end of stanza V, "Le
changement des rives en rumeur", is picked up immediately, "Beau
ciel ... regarde-moi qui change!" Together with the theme of shadow
these words show how the narrator differs from the noon sun and in
addition how he is aware of the difference, somewhat regretfully. The
sun is seemingly immobile, pure light, while on earth that perfection
is broken by change and by shade. A touch of the narrator's recent
pride remains however. In the seventh stanza, he decisively accepts
the challenge. "Je te soutiens, admirable justice...Je te rends pure à
ta place première..." The mercilessness of the noonday sun, "lumière
aux armes sans pitié" recalls that sun in Camus L'Etranger, also mer-
idional with its combined attack of heat and light which has such a dis-
astrous effect on the hero, Meursault, contributing in a sense to his
act of violence. The narrator of "Le Cimetière marin", standing up to,
facing with direct gaze the real antagonist, proves himself momentarily equal to the situation. He parries the onslaught of light. In earlier
versions the image of a mirror was explicit; but in the final poem it is

only suggested - "Je te rends pure à ta place première / Regarde-toi !... "
The eye of the narrator reflects thus the rays of the sun.

The following verse, totally inward, is a surprise because of the
contrast of tone and because there is no apparent connection of theme
or idea, although the tone of calm acceptance is still consistent with
the rest. It too had a history in the many stages of creation. Throughout the early versions, the narrator was clearly a poet and the theme
of poetic inspiration was pronounced. While sitting by the sea, he was
waiting for a poem to take shape, expecting some suggestion from the
ocean. Here is a line from the longest and latest sketch: "Un premier
signe, un spectre de poème / Naît d'un regard repris aux bleus bassins!"*11
The final form seems to me to be an improvement. The introspection
here, transposes the image of the body of water into an obscure, resonant spiritual well. And the narrator awaits some indication of self -
a thought, a feeling - searching in the same direction, in the same area
of consciousness where poetry is born. The poem mentioned is now an
image rather than a subject.

Shifting his attention outwards again, the narrator addresses the sea
familiarly, questions it in stanza IX. And he names it in another striking series of spontaneous, accurate images: "fausse captive des feuillages", "golfe mangeur de ces maigres grillages", "Sur mes yeux clos,
secrets éblouissants..." His frame of mind manifests a new negative
suspicious cast, reflected in his questions and in the form of the first
two images ("fausse", "mangeur") and in his discreet mention of death,
his "fin paresseuse". But the following stanza returns to direct sensations and to an unequivocal statement of pleasure - "Ce lieu me plaît."
The cemetery is composed and rendered visually, as in a painting. Indeed, the scene and the atmosphere recall vividly Van Gogh - stone,
shadows, trees (cypress no doubt) whose outlines resemble by their
shape and by their dissolving edges those of a candle, a vibrant light
which infuses all forms and makes them tremble.

Picking up the description of the sea in the last line, "mer fidèle",
stanza XI develops into a complex metaphor what is suggested by the
adjective "faithful". This time the idea was born from an emotional tie
with the sea, a sense of security, rather than a visual impression.
Interestingly, the whole verse came to being as an enlargement of the
image, "chienne splendide", combined with that of the shepherd. In the
margin of version B, the following group of words is noted:

Chienne splendide écarte
l'idolâtre
...pâtre
haleine
laine
moutons mystérieux
troupeau

One concludes that for this verse the basic source is a combination of
image and rhyme. As the sea becomes the faithful dog, the tombs are
transformed into sheep, and the narrator into a shepherd. What, one
wonders, is the menace to be chased away ("les prudentes colombes,
les songes vains, les anges curieux")? Two interpretations have been

proposed. Either that the narrator is dismissing false comforts of religion in which case the doves would be a symbol of an immortal soul. Or that he is rejecting the images and speculations with which he has just been preoccupied. "Colombes" does echo the very first image and "songes" an important earlier theme. But because of the religious inference of "idolâtre" and "pâtre" and the cemetery, I should judge that the aim is mainly to clear the air of vain hopes of immortality and to protect the peace of the present.

At any rate the present is full and forceful in stanza XII. These lines provide an admirable example of poetry which is highly alogical, but where the poetic sense is unmistakable. "Ici venu" affirms succinctly the here and now. Probably the grammatical function of this phrase is that of an ablative absolute, referring to the narrator. But its proximity to "l'avenir" adds a note of ambiguity which is continued in the rest of the sentence. The future, by virtue of being an abstract noun and by virtue of its meaning, time to come, can neither have arrived here already nor be the same thing as a moral quality, laziness. Beyond this, the real meaning is clear: the future has no weight and the present holds sway. In striking contrast to his normal practice, Valéry uses the verb "to be" here repeatedly - five times! The total scene - man, earth and air - is.

Other semantic puzzles are similarly unimportant in the long run. "L'insecte net gratte la sécheresse." An insect can scratch; but certainly it can't scratch dryness. And one may wonder in what sense it is "net": clean? distinct? I think it is most likely that the author chose the word mainly for its sound which reinforces the crisp, dry atmosphere. Also, the identity of the insect has been a source of some speculation. Cicada, ant, sand wasp have all been suggested; and when the author was consulted about the latter possibility, he replied: "J'adopte Ammophila hirsuta que vous avez observée sur place, et de l'oeil aigu de l'entomologiste, tandis que je n'ai fait que voir entendre l'insecte net gratter le sol grillé... "*12 Obligingly, the poet adopts a reasonable suggestion, clearly implying all the while that his original view included the idea of a certain anonymity, an unnamed creature and that the main idea was to suggest a sound connected with dry earth. Thus the insect was conceived and remained unidentified; and the dry earth was reduced to its pure quality, dryness, which is abstract as a noun (that is, in language) but concrete as a sensation. The whole sense of the stanza, really, lies in the group of very immediate sensations and these are easy to distinguish. There is one set which marks a movement towards an unbounded immaterial state ("brûlé", "défait", "reçu dans l'air", "essence", "vaste", "absence"). One is tempted to call this a negative movement since it tends towards nothingness. But for Valéry, such a condition is real, not unreal and has a strong positive value, so such terms as negative, nothingness would be inaccurate. A second pattern suggests a somewhat rough, acrid cast to the atmosphere ("gratte", "sécheresse", "brûlé", "sévère", "amertume"). And a third pattern provides what one might superficially term a paradoxical counterpart, a pleasurable tone ("paresse", "la vie est vaste", "ivre", "douce", "clair"). Actually, the three patterns fuse quite naturally in a single, instantaneous immediate absorption by the spirit of the surroundings. Therein lies the meaning.

The midpoint of the whole poem, stanza XIII, resumes the tone of equilibrium and peace hitherto pervasive and it evokes again the midpoint of the day, "Midi là-haut, Midi sans mouvement". In addition, it marks the midpoint of the stanza. Frequently, throughout "Le Cimetière marin", key lines are to be found in this central position. First lines serve to bridge thematically from a preceding stanza, or to set the scene in time and place with adverbial phrases or appositions, or to set the tone. This technique is so intricate and effective that it merits a short digression. Let us take for instance the opening lines.

Ce toit tranquille, où marchent des colombes,
Entre les pins palpite, entre les tombes;
Midi le juste y compose de feux
La mer, la mer, toujours recommencée!

The first two lines have a swinging rhythm. The break comes exactly in the middle after the fifth syllable, clearly marked with commas and they have an internal assonance ("tranquille", "palpite") ending with a mute e which lengthens the pause. The rocking motion is reinforced by the vowel patterns in the rhymes, in both cases moving from i to ɔ̃ and it strongly evokes the rolling of waves and also introduces the notion of peacefulness. The next two lines are less impressive as sound patterns, but they state directly the two principal external elements of the whole poem, actually, "Midi" was not mentioned here in the earliest versions but always kept its position in the center, even though the total number of verses varied greatly, from seven in the first sketch, ten in the second, to twenty-three in the third.

Returning to stanza XIII, one notices that the theme of change reappears in the last line ("Je suis en toi le secret changement") without much emphasis or sense of distress. Nevertheless, it provides the seed for development in the next five stanzas of a progressively gripping intellectual and emotional dilemma. The concern is so powerful that, for this period, all traces of sensation coming from the outside disappear. Gone are the sensations of light, of heat, of the forms of the tombs and the cypress. Instead, the narrator's thoughts are self-enclosed, self-perpetuating, pursuing lucidly and bitterly the implications of human sensitivity and change.

The relationship between the narrator and the sun suggests what one might term a poetic cosmology. The sun, with its self-contained force and creative power, and man, powerful by virtue of his capacity to reflect and reflect upon the merciless source of light, appear as the two protagonists in a brief mythical drama. For the perfection of the sun is challenged and, in the end, modified by man's power of thought which, in contrast to the sun's equilibrium, is beset by doubts, regrets, constraints. But, since man is a part of the sun's domain, these appear subsumed in a seed of weakness within the all-powerful: "Tu n'as que moi pour contenir tes craintes."

"L'Ebauche d'un serpent", another poem by Valéry, very different in tone and structure, treats this same question more directly and more explicitly.*13 Through the brilliant, seditious, wryly ironical, beautifully vicious tongue of the serpent, who is not simply a vehicle for Satan's ruse but a full embodiment of the Evil Spirit, we hear the full story of the Creation and of his subversive role in the world ("Je suis Celui qui modifie"), in addition to a delightful rendition of his encounter with Eve. The Creation is seen itself as a fall - from the purity of Non-Being.

> O Vanité! Cause Première!
> Celui qui règne dans les Cieux,
> D'une voix qui fut la lumière
> Ouvrit l'univers spacieux.
> Comme las de son pur spectacle,
> Dieu lùi-même a rompu l'obstacle
> De sa parfaite éternité;
> Il se fit Celui qui dissipe
> En conséquences, son Principe,
> En étoiles, son Unité.

The Creator's first word, the sun, is the first superb and dazzling mistake: "Soleil, soleil...Faute éclatante!" The role of the serpent (and later by extension men, infected with thought, desire of perfection, revolt) reflects the First Cause. Valéry uses the mirror image here too. "Regardez-vous dans ma ténèbre!" says the Serpent to the Sun,

> Devant votre image funèbre,
> Orgueil de mon sombre miroir,
> Si profond fut votre malaise
> Que votre souffle sur la glaise
> Fut un soupir de désespoir!

The narrator of "Le Cimetière marin", although clearly showing a thirst for perfection, has no such conception of himself as undertaking revolt as a profession. On the contrary, his recognition of personal weakness, doubts and regrets at first has only a slightly regretful tone. And his thoughts about the community of the dead, who slowly have rejoined the material world, have something of a resigned cast. These thoughts continue through stanza XV. To start with, death is even seen poetically transfigured. The exquisite line, "L'argile rouge a bu la blanche espèce" (part of a verse present from the beginning stages of the poem), shows the slow process of refinement. The first words, "L'argile rouge", were set from the start, restating concretely what was introduced abstractly in the first line as "absence épaisse". But "la blanche espèce" (mankind) was for a time "l'antique espèce". The final contrast of colors is all the more striking since colors are rare in Valéry's world.

Then, the question which closes the stanza and its reply introduce the first note of real anxiety. "Où sont des morts les phrases familières, / L'art personnel, les âmes singulières?" The poet names and qualifies very exactly three aspects of an individual, unique human personality. Since all three pertain to general spiritual qualities, the extraordinary stanza which follows describing a very physical act of love reinforces its effect by a certain shock value.

The terms of the description are all very concrete, exact. Only two words modify a nearly clinical style, "feu" and "dons" both common seventeenth century periphrases. Interestingly, "dons" was in early versions "plis" which of course was one more highly accurate element. Gustave Cohen commented that this verse was an example of how the author's excessive penchant for abstraction led to "rêves brûlants".*14 Valéry did, it is true, throughout his life pursue a multitude of problems in many fields (mathematics, philosophy, psychology, literature). And his habits of thought certainly showed a tendency towards abstraction. Yet this did not exclude an interest in and an astute awareness of all emotional and physical phenomena, including, naturally, love. In the early part of his life, his attitude towards love combined fascination and attraction with a marked apprehension and even derision stemming mainly from the fact that love obfuscates and overpowers that lucid self-control which he prized above all other powers of the mind. But, later, around 1920, a change took place. In his later Cahiers there are passages which picture love as a means of attaining the most extreme heights of sensitivity and the limits of knowledge. The character, Lust, in Mon Faust (written in 1940) suggests the force and the positive elements of feminine sensitivity and sensuality. And allusions in his Cahiers to an unwritten fourth act carry further a presentation of love as fulfillment.

Such a tone is far from evident, however, in "Le Cimetière marin" where, in stanza XVI, bitter irony pervades the lines. The two following stanzas carry that tone to a climax. The question in stanza XV, which was rhetorical in nature, now is expanded and highly personal, directed to himself as in self-flagellation. "Et vous, grande âme, espérez-vous un songe/Qui n'aura plus ces couleurs de mensonge...?" "Chanterez-vous quand serez vaporeuse?" The answers, a long series of exclamations, elaborate the vulnerability and the helplessness of man including his impassioned but futile efforts to avoid the bitter truth. "La sainte impatience meurt aussi!" Man's laudable capacity for revolt, his thirst for perfection are also mortal. Immortality, whom he paints grotesquely and personifies as thin, black, a parasite of death, is a fabrication of lies, a pious trick.

"Qui ne les connaît, et qui ne les refuse, /Ce crâne vide et ce rire éternel!" With this desperate cry of horror and of harsh recognition of his ultimate weakness and imperfection, once again he invokes the dead. This time, rather than pitying them, he discovers the real torment - in life, not death. The image which Valéry uses to develop this idea has its source in stanza XV when the narrator observes "La larve file où se formaient des pleurs." That worm, now a symbol of the conscious mind, devours its host. Our slang expression, "what's eating you", has exactly the same metaphorical source. If the truth, now clear, locates the source of all doubts and distress not in death but in life, it contains nonetheless the seeds of delivrance. The last line, "Il vit de vie, il ne me quitte pas!" states the revelation in full force and the repeated, vibrant i sounds and the reciprocal sound and sense of "vit" and "vie" counteract the formerly unrelieved black, bitter mood. It is the first indication of the sound pattern and the theme whose intensity rises in an unbroken curve to the end.

" Amour?...haine?" Although in stanza XX the narrator still indicates the double-edged nature of his symbolic enemy, he not only recognizes him as something close to the core of his very being, but embraces him as a veritable raison d'être. "A ce vivant je vis d'appartenir!" This line restates the content of the last line in stanza XIX and eliminates any remaining negative suggestion. "Il voit, il veut, il songe, il touche!" Human consciousness is thus pictured as active in a multitude of domains: physical perceptions, willing, thinking, and dreaming. And in that particular list, pure intellectual activity is only suggested as a part of "il songe". The other mental functions are more directly related to the outer realm of experience.

The next stanza (XXI) appears to be none other than a decided rejection of pure thought carried to an extreme. This is one of the earliest parts of the poem, appearing in final form even in the first version. Valéry remarked that it was intended to provide the intellectual component necessary to round out a total thematic diversity.*15 If this stanza was easy to write, it is not easy to decipher. The patterns of meaning are indeed complex. There is, for instance, a violent cast ("Cruel", "percé", "tue" plus the succession of z sounds in the first line). However, there is also a counteraction: the thinker rejects the philosophical dilemma and even perhaps the mental torment caused by the problem. The second syllable of the Greek philosopher's name, repeated three times and becoming very emphatic, suggests in itself refusal (Zénon), especially since "Non, non..." is restated as the first words of the next stanza. The following sentence, "M'as-tu percé de cette flèche ailée/Qui vibre, vole et qui ne vole pas!" is in part an accusation. But also, by virtue of its being an exclamation, including an inverted subject and verb which normally is only used in questions, it creates the effect of ironic scepticism. That taken with "Le son m'enfante et la flèche me tue!" suggest too that the speeding arrow, claimed immobile by Zeno, through its sound can awaken the mind and through its impact can kill, thus belying its philosophical inertia and abstraction. The last two lines have a similar effect, though at first glance they appear an impenetrable maze of poetic syntactical distortion. The "ombre de tortue" must be a complex metaphor having a double source. On the one hand, it recalls Zeno's example of Achilles' never-ending race with the tortoise which has such a disturbing effect on the mind trying to resolve the paradox. On the other hand, it reintroduces tacitly the image of the sun. "Ah! le soleil...", I think, is first of all a brusk return to reality. It is the first direct mention of the immediate scene since stanza XV. The narrator suddenly notices the sun again, and immediately integrates it in his final comment concerning the puzzling and sometimes depressing effect of abstract problems ("Quelle ombre...pour l'âme"). It seems likely that three other solar aspects enter into the formation of that metaphor. First, its round shape resembles the shape of a tortoise. Second, the "ombre" may come from a photographic negative: the sun's whiteness contrasts with the dark color of a tortoise and also the shadow of intellectual perplexity. The third element is clear. Just as Zeno pictures Achilles immobile in his swift course, so the noonday sun appears motionless despite the real speed of all heavenly bodies, literally beyond the grasp of human imagination.

That shadow cast by thought fades away in the next stanza (XXII).

"Une fraîcheur, de la mer exhalée, / Me rend mon âme." A rapid-fire succession of exclamations and exhortations punctuate a decisive new frame of mind. The narrator's quick movement towards action coincides with a change in time and in the surroundings. Total absorption in the present, at that immobile moment of noon, is broken by thought of the future, "l'ère successive". The ocean and the air, too, come to life. The wind rises, the waves break. The full force of decision, of will affirms its authority over the body. The narrator rises, breathes deeply and then, envigorated, runs to plunge in the sea.

One of the first decisions is of particular interest. "Brisez, mon corps, cette forme pensive!" It recalls unmistakably the phrase early in the poem, "Edifice dans l'âme", where the sea was perceived as solid and structural. So that the exhortation could have one meaning of breaking into what appeared solid by splashing into the water. But, another sense seems pertinent too. By stretching, standing, and running the narrator in effect breaks his line of thought, his previous reflective activities - the course of the poem up to this point. Valéry, searching for ways to describe the nature and forms of mental life, proposed the term "phases" as fruitful in examining the relation between certain forms of activity. Some kinds of activity, he noted, are incompatible: one can dream only when asleep; one cannot exchange ideas with another person and at the same time maintain a state of full attention; one cannot engage in full physical activity and all the while pursue complex intellectual problems. It is necessary, then, to change from one "phase" to another, to change one's total mental-physical orientation (voluntarily, at times, it would seem) in order to shift from one field of activity to another. One can't "passer de l'idée de l'acte à l'acte sans le montage de la machine de l'acte - L'homme assis, avant de courir, doit se transformer."*16 Just such a voluntary shift of fields is what takes place in "Le Cimetière marin" when the narrator cries "Brisez, mon corps, cette forme pensive!"

As in the opening lines, the visual splendor of the sea rivets all attention. Stanza XXIII paints the metamorphosis caused by the wind in a new series of original images. Dazzling, exotic, wildly aroused, an air of delirium and intoxication ("Grande mer de délires douée", "ivre de ta chair bleue") pervades the atmosphere. The sea's tumult is paired with the narrator's excitement. "Ivre" reappears as an overtone in the rhymes "vivre" and "livre" in the last stanza. The will, the potential energy and the sense of effort in stanza XXII reappear: "il faut tenter de vivre", "La vague en poudre ose jaillir des rocs." And, contrary to the rest of the poem (and to Valéry's style in general) action verbs wildly succeed each other ("se lève", "ouvre", "referme", "jaillir", "Envolez-vous", "Rompez... Rompez"). Similar to "Les Pas", this poem has a circular form. The end rejoins the beginning. We find the narrator again fully absorbed by the sense and the sight of the bright sea. Contemplative ecstasy becomes active ecstasy. Intense pleasure is transformed into pure joy. "La joie est comme une énergie qui rayonne d'un être, une lumière d'or qui lui dore tout ce qu'il voit",*17 as the author himself describes such a powerful sensation. The narrator's joy then fuses with the dazzling noonday sea to achieve the finale.

Since Valéry enjoys a reputation as a poet whose expression is as dense with abstract thought as it is obscure, whose intellectual activities attain such extraordinary breadth and scope, those very characteristics tend to overshadow the other aspects of his personality. A poem which ends with such an energetic burst of action may thus appear puzzling or even artificial. The fact is that Valéry was not only brilliant but a warm human being. The life-long correspondence between Valéry and Gide furnishes ample evidence of humor, friendship, an open and responsive nature. His penchants included not only ascetic introspection and the desire to pursue scientific and philosophical problems but also a love of physical activity. In a letter to Gide, written in his twenties just after he had moved to Paris he says, "Si j'étais riche - aujourd'hui - sais-tu ce que je ferais? Vie physique. Je me mettrais à la discipline de la rame, des altères [sic] et du cheval. Et je ne ferais que ça et nager du matin au soir." And elsewhere he describes his enthusiasm for swimming in the sea, extolling the freedom, the total use and absorption of body and mind, the sense of life and movement of the waves and the sand.*18 So that the final scene of "Le Cimetière marin" should be accepted as a completely natural gesture, neither as a reluctant recognition that one must try to live since pure thought, perfection, and immortality are impossible, nor as a rejection of intellectual endeavors. It is rather the normal counterpart of thought, in this particular case, simply what the narrator does at the end of a morning spent in the cemetery viewing the sea. One can picture him soon picking up his book again and resuming his thoughts.

Valéry notes in his <u>Cahiers</u> that for this poem the themes were "choisis pour satisfaire à une exigence de plénitude", and that "...les parties successives devaient se modifier réciproquement dans une simultanéité résolutoire".*19 This cohesive and progressive modification of sense and feeling is clear in "Le Cimetière marin" as we read it. Surprisingly, this flowing natural line is only marked at the very end of the creative process. The poem appeared with a different balance of theme and a different structure in each of the three versions preceding the final one, although the dominant tone (lyricism of a marine symphony) and the basic scene (cemetery, sea, narrator) were evident from the start. In the first version, for instance, the cemetery with its evocation of death are only touched upon lightly. In the second sketch, the theme of the poet seeking inspiration from the sea is developed, as is the abstract section on death. In the third version, the poet-sea theme remains. The rest of the stanzas are in nearly definitive shape; but, except for the central section, the order of the stanzas is very different. Sometimes there is no link from one stanza to the next. At other times the link is intellectual rather than tonal. From the evolution of the poem and from the evidence of the shifts of wording and the notes in the margin, one concludes that Valéry wrote the individual stanzas quite separately with a clear view of the tone and the theme of each, but they were joined in a continuous tonal line only at the very end. This is all the more striking since the emotional climaxes (heights of ecstasy and disdain at the first; intense revelation at the end) are also something of an ultimate inspiration. The years of creative effort were thus fully justified since those emotional climaxes together with the subtly shifting psychological nuances are what constitute the poem's beauty and originality.

NOTES

*1 In a letter to Gide (August, 1922), with whom he carried on a life-long and intimate correspondence, Valéry remarks that a poem he recently "improvised" resembles the "voice" and "movement" of "Le Cimetière marin" and then concludes " 'Le Cimetière marin' serait donc le type de ma 'poésie' vraie et surtout les parties plus abstraites de ce poème. C'est une espèce de 'lyrisme' (mi capisco) net et abstrait mais d'une abstraction motrice, bien plus que philosophique" (Correspondance d'André Gide et de Paul Valéry, 1890-1942 [Paris, 1955], 489). And in a letter to Jacques Doucet accompanying a handwritten copy of Charmes (1922) he says: " 'Le Cimetière marin' est ma pièce personnelle. Je n'y ai mis que ce que je suis. Ses obscurités sont les miennes. La lumière qu'il peut contenir est celle même que j'ai vue en naissant."

*2 There is an early unpublished poem, "La Mer" (OEuvres I, 1586) in sonnet form, descriptive in nature, where one sees the sun at its zenith, the sea likened when calm to a mirror and when rolling gently to a "serpent sacré", which in "Le Cimetière marin" becomes a "hydre absolue". "Valvins", whose style and site recall Mallarmé, alternates reflection and look from book to water on a summer day. "Eté" captures the humming essence of summer heat, here in seascape; and the ocean is seen as a "maison brûlante", the forerunner of the "Toit tranquille". "Profusion du soir", Valéry's first release into a longer freer form, again has a marine setting, where the narrator immersed in the sea welcomes water and wave. One part especially resembles the spirit of total fusion of "Le Cimetière marin":

Je me sens qui me trempe, et pur qui me dédaigne.
Vivant au sein futur le souvenir marin,
Tout le corps de mon choix dans mes regards se baigne!

*3 Perhaps even the memories created the rhythm. An essay born of his puzzled reaction to Gustave Cohen's exegesis of the poem at the Sorbonne ("Au sujet du 'Cimetière marin' " [1933], OEuvres I, 1496-1507) and conversations with friends provide information about how Valéry conceived the poem. To Frédéric Lefèvre (and at a later date in the afore-mentioned essay) he said that, as was the case with most of his poems, this one was born with the presence of a certain rhythm: "Je me suis étonné, un matin, de trouver dans ma tête des vers décasyllabique" (Frédéric Lefèvre, Entretiens avec Paul Valéry [Paris, 1926], 62-63). To Henri Mondor, he confided that the idea for the poem came to him in Paris probably with nostalgia for his beloved Midi home: "Dans une petite chambre de très petit hôtel de la rive gauche, une insomnie m'amena à ce premier mot ou plutôt amena ce premier mot du 'Cimetière marin' jusqu'à moi" (Henri Mondor, Propos familiers de Valéry [Paris, 1957], 162). Since one can hardly judge in such intimate moments of inspiration which may be cause and which effect, one must simply note the simultaneous presence of emotion, memory, and form.

*4 Stage One would include stanzas I-V; Stage Two, stanzas VI-XIII; Stage Three, stanzas XIV-XVIII; Stage Four, stanzas XIX-XXIV.

*5 The immediacy of this introduction recalls Wittgenstein's insistence on the close connection between language and behavior and the basic role of what he calls ostensive teaching and ostensive definition whereby one shows what one means by pointing out something either concrete (this book) or abstract (this sentence).

*6 "Inspirations méditerranéennes", Variété, OEuvres I, 1094.

*7 This essay was published in 1936 as a preface to a book on Swedenborg (OEuvres I, 867-883). Two other passages show the positive value he attached to a certain sort of mystical state. One is an essay on the painter Berthe Morisot, published in 1926, which contains a series of highly perceptive and stimulating reflections on the nature of art (OEuvres II, 1302); and the other is a note in Cahier VI, page 263: "La mystique va d'une coupure à une organisation. La propriété de cesser de comprendre même ce qui était le plus clair. La possibilité de regarder les choses sous l'aspect d'un incident, de percevoir au premier plan la perception d'une façon subordonnée les choses perçues. L'art de se faire pleurer; celui de s'écouter si bien que les moindres touches internes, les images, les formations de paroles prennent une netteté, une objectivité."

*8 Introduction à la méthode de Léonardo de Vinci, OEuvres I, 1164-1172.

*9 Tel Quel, OEuvres II, 650.

*10 Gide-Valéry Correspondance, 402. Dates are a central image and subject in another poem, "Palme", also from the collection Charmes.

*11 There is an admirable edition of "Le Cimetière marin" published by the Cercle des universitaires bibliophiles (Grenoble, 1954). The first volume presents the final poem with an excellent preface by Henri Mondor which, together with the valuable article by L. J. Austin, "Paul Valéry compose 'Le Cimetière marin' " (Mercure de France, avril et mai 1953), guides the reader through the long genesis of the poem. The second volume contains reproductions of the manuscripts of the successive drafts designated for convenience A, B1 and B2, C. The line I have quoted above comes from version C.

*12 OEuvres II, 1617.

*13 This poem was conceived as a burlesque monologue (see the poet's explanation in a letter to Alain, Jan. 4, 1930, Lettres à quelques-uns, Paris, 1952); it typifies the Voltairian streak in Valéry's temperament. He considered the question of the existence of God to be devoid of sense, a verbal game; and he judged religious faith to engender facile, affective solutions abdicating reason, rejecting objective analysis. But he no doubt found the myth of the creation fascinating because it dramatizes double the revolt of men against the world as it is. First, seeking a system and a perfect one at that, the human mind poses God and the Creation. Second, a proud challenge to that divine tyranny appears immediately in the form of the arch-hero Satan.

*14 Gustave Cohen, "Essai d'explication du 'Cimetière marin' ", Nouvelle revue française, XXXII (février 1929), 216.

*15 OEuvres I, "Au sujet du 'Cimetière marin' ", 1506.

*16 Judith Robinson quotes this passage (from Cahier XXII, 663) in her discussion of the connection between Valéry's thought and thermodynamics, pp. 66-67.

*17 Mauvaises pensées, OEuvres II, 813.

*18 Gide-Valéry Correspondance, 212; Variétés, OEuvres I, 1090-1091; Tel Quel, OEuvres II, 667.

*19 Cahier XXIX, 600 and 91.

UNE SENSATION D'UNIVERS

Throughout his essays and notes concerning artists, art, poetry, Valéry reiterates a basic definition - the artist proceeds from the arbitrary to the necessary, taking his raw material from the incoherent flux of experience and transforming this material into an ordered world. "Univers" is a term he uses frequently, which combines a sense of magnitude with order. A passage from "Propos sur la Poésie" presents these ideas succinctly:

> J'ai dit: sensation d'univers. J'ai voulu dire que l'état ou l'émotion poétique me semble consister dans une perception naissante, dans une tendance à percevoir un monde, ou système complet de rapports, dans lequel les êtres, les choses, les événements et les actes, s'ils ressemblent, chacun à chacun, à ceux qui peuplent et composent le monde sensible, le monde immédiat duquel ils sont empruntés, sont, d'autre part, dans une relation indéfinissable, mais merveilleusement juste, avec les modes et les lois de notre sensibilité générale... Ils se trouvent... musicalés, devenus commensurables, résonants l'un par l'autre. *1

In order to understand as fully as possible Valéry's poetry, I think it should prove fruitful to examine very carefully the components of that world. Before searching for symbols and hidden meanings of an intellectual nature, it would be well to consider carefully the "beings, things, events and acts" which make up his world. For this constitutes the first and basic poetic experience - for both the poet and the reader.

Narcisse, the Jeune Parque, Eve and the Serpent, an angel, a sylph - mythological figures appear whose allegorical functions fade in proportion as their individual personalities blossom. Many of the central figures are feminine. Valéry, quite unaffectedly, imagined the presence in his creative activities of a Muse-like companion whom he called Laure.*2 The pure person of "Les Pas" and the mysterious slave in "Intérieur" are doubtless forms of her alter-ego in the poetic world. They all live, breathe, and carry on impassioned and lively conversations either with themselves or with an unidentified narrator whom we frequently suspect may be a poet (!) but who clearly prefers to remain anonymous. Someone very like Valéry but who must certainly not be equated to the author. As Proust described his narrator in A la Recherche du Temps Perdu, he is simply "un monsieur qui dit 'je'".

Unexpected heroes pursue similar activities. Three poems have inanimate objects not only for subject and title but also as protagonist:

"Colonnes", "Au Platane", and "Palme". The columns, "incorruptibles soeurs", intone a hymn to their existence, radiant, graceful and untouched by time. "Palme" (one of the poems which explicitly deals with poetic creation) symbolizes the patience necessary for a poem to mature but that palm tree becomes in the course of the verse a calm, voluptuous feminine figure. The plane tree, on the other hand, is substantially masculine, a noble impatient and proud being who challenges the forces of nature. Valéry was so taken by the multiple analogies with human life suggested by trees that he expounded upon the subject lengthily in his later Dialogue de l'arbre, imagining a conversation between Tityre and Lucretius.

These are the most pronounced examples of an esthetic urge to conceive of inanimate objects in anthropomorphic terms. A conversation retold by Lucien Fabre shows this tendency in a playful spirit. Valéry and Fabre were returning from a walk, had stopped on a bridge and were watching a stream.

> ...un petit ruisseau qui se cherchait un lit dans le sable, hésitait, refluait, prenait et déposait les silex minuscules...
> - 'Encore un problème, mon vieux, fit-il; c'est le drame de ce ruisseau qui ne s'en tire pas avec ses petits cailloux... Admettons notre ruisseau anthropomorphisé. Comment définir son histoire actuelle?... nous devrions pouvoir condenser cette histoire en un mot, en une épithète ambiguë, qui montrerait à la fois le côté matériel de la chose: le ruisseau, quoi? caillouteux? pétré? (il ajoute en riant, galetteux?) - et le côté, dirai-je! moral? de ce ruisseau qui cherche son chemin, hésite et se le fraie et pour cela place, déplace, palpe, replace ses infimes silex, suivant quelque convenance profonde, en obéissant rigoureusement aux lois... Voilà notre vraie tâche d'évrivains.
> (M. Fabre propose 'scrupuleux'.)
>   Il se redresse, ravi: - 'Bravo', dit-il, 'Scrupulus, petit caillou. Le mot existait donc!... *3*

Light in tone but serious in spirit, this passage shows succinctly the nature of Valéry's creative imagination. First of all, he is fascinated by, highly sensitive to, and warmly sympathetic with natural phenomena of all sorts. The activity of the object, what it is doing, why, its relation with the surroundings (sometimes in conflict sometimes adapting itself) all of this sparks his interest; and the event takes the shape of a drama. So far, the creative gesture is on an unconscious level and very individual. Observing the activity minutely, he then searches for a word, the exact word which will express both the material and the spiritual side of what is happening - remaining faithful to what he sees, to the object itself, but admittedly superimposing human intentions, efforts, thoughtful movements. There is no confusion or mystification about which elements are there in the pebble and which elements are borrowed from human experience. Here Valéry differs basically from a phenomenological poet like Ponge who seeks a direct understanding of the thing itself, but who blurs the edges between the human and the material.

Constantly, self-critical and analytical reflections about and observations of the outside world recur throughout Valéry's prose works. Perhaps the most brilliant is his Introduction à la méthode de Léonard de Vinci which was written in 1894 and then extended by marginal comments, a sort of self-annotation, for the next thirty-five years. The Italian genius was simply the starting point of a somewhat unsystematic but dense and penetrating discussion of human perception. Perhaps the key feature of his analysis is not the search for "continuity" (a word which he uses frequently but which he also seems unsatisfied with as an exact term) but the idea that thought looks for and establishes groups, patterns, periodical functions. For instance, says the author, a curious and unprejudiced observer may see (imagine) the curve traced by a stone thrown into the air, will hear a thousand vibrations as a continuous sound. Objects may appear to act: language permits us to say that "une jetée s'allonge, qu'une montagne s'élève, qu'une statue se dresse" And beyond the satisfaction of seeing such patterns in experience there is also the advantage of understanding the forms of thought through analogies with the natural world. Considering the complex drama of the mental world Valéry poses this possibility:

> Les acteurs d'ici sont des images mentales et il est aisé de comprendre que, si l'on fait s'évanouir la particularité de cés images pour ne lire que leur succession, leur fréquence, leur périodicité, leur facilité diverses d'association, leur durée enfin, on est vite tenté de leur trouver des analogies dans le monde dit matériel, d'en rapprocher les analyses scientifiques, de leur supposer un milieu, une continuité, des propriétés de déplacement, des vitesses, et de suite, des masses, de l'énergie.*5*

Here his hope is to find a way of elaborating descriptions of the mind using the concepts and technical vocabulary of modern mathematics and science. But the implications for artistic precision are equally important. For metaphors from the outside concrete world can then be used to translate roughly the inner psychological world. (He gives as examples "pensée" and "pesèe", "saisir", and "comprendre".) Aside from the philosophical and scientific interest of such a view, an immense range of expression is opened up for a poet. In poetry, the real world can be described in all its concreteness and its movements, rendered vivid by images borrowed from man. And at the same time, the concerns, actions, and transformations of the mental world may be made perceptible, "real" when presented through natural images. And the stream, winding its way amidst pebbles, acquires a "life-like" quality by being termed "scrupulous". The verbs Valéry uses endow it with human habits - it seeks its way, it hesitates. Similarly, a scrupulous person, at odds with a problem, in his efforts to find the solution could be described by means of the tale of the pebbly stream. So, when studying Valéry's imagery, it is often difficult to distinguish which is the thing described and which is the image, in the terminology of I. A. Richards to distinguish between the tenor and the vehicle. Often, the two terms appear to have a reciprocal relationship, mutually resonant. Such anthropomorphism is immensely fruitful - poetically and conceptually.

If the protagonists of these poetic dramas are individualized, the settings in which the actions take place, short or long, are also very carefully arranged. Some of the shorter poems contain little or no stage directions. The bed in "Les Pas" is the only indication other than that of the pure person and the narrator. "Grenades", "L'Abeille", and "La Dormeuse" have little else than a very detailed description of their protagonists. Their import is mainly symbolical. The pomegranates suggest the architecture of the soul. The bee typifies the quick sharp impulse which provokes thought to become language. The sleeping woman shows that strange relationship between body and mind during sleep. The force of these poems comes from the masterful, exact evocation of the one central image – so that the intellectual content is encased in a vivid life-like envelope. The absence of surroundings heightens the symbolic effect.

However, all three of the long poems have very carefully indicated settings. The Jeune Parque finds herself on a rocky island in the sea; the sky is clear, starry, the wind blows and the waves are murmuring. The tragedy of Narcisse, also nocturnal, takes place in the woods by a fountain, a light breeze in the air. "Le Cimetière marin", by contrast brightly lighted, contains however the same elements of water and wind. Always, the scene is presented through the perceptions of the protagonist. The Jeune Parque and Narcisse, because of their self-absorption, transmit to us only vaguely sensations of the sounds of the wind and the water, dim shapes perceived mainly through touch, or sight and sound distorted by dreams and night shadows. But the narrator of "Le Cimetière marin", alert and with a thirst for exploring the world, staggers us with a multitude of visual and conceptual images of the site. All three nevertheless are extremely sensitive to their surroundings, noting minute changes and reacting to them. Smoothly continuous duration, taking shape and direction within the monologue reflecting phases of the protagonist's consciousness is one essential aspect of the structure of these poems. But there is always an awareness, filtering through the thoughts to a varying degree, of time and place. And changes in these conditions are noticed, taken account of by the heroes. The wind, particularly, as it appears or disappears, serves to punctuate everyone's awareness of time passing. Ours too. The Jeune Parque, in the first lines of her recitative, wonders, half-woken from her sleep: "Qui pleure là, sinon le vent simple... Mais qui pleure, Si proche de moi-même au moment de pleurer?" She is aware both of the sighing of the wind and of her own tears but, still numb with sleep, mingles the two sensations. Narcisse, with his melancholy sensitivity, absorbs all movements of the moment: "J'entends l'herbe des nuits croître dans l'ombre sainte, / Et la lune perfide élève son miroir... Rien ne peut échapper au silence du soir... / La nuit vient sur ma chair lui souffler que je l'aime." And the narrator of "Le Cimetière marin" emerges from his bitter contemplation of the human condition just when the wind rises, churning the sea and quickening the pulse. It is almost as if the change of the moment were itself responsible for the decision to act. Similarly, the moment of daybreak, infuses the troubled spirit of the Jeune Parque with the necessary force to greet the new day warmly.

Within the range of physical sensations, the sounds are gentle (wind and water) with no harsh reports which might distract the mind from self-exploration. Touch and taste are suggested in light, delicate gestures. In a shiver of soul, body and water Narcisse gently falls into the fountain. "L'insaisissable amour que tu me vins promettre / Passe, et dans un frisson, brise Narcisse, et fuit... " Taste appears only metaphorically and abstracted into pure pleasure, pure nourishment as we have seen in the verse of "Le Cimetière marin" which begins "Comme le fruit se fond en jouissance... "

Vision is the principal sensation through which the mythical figures and the thinker in Valéry's poetic world seek to orient themselves. A gleam of light introduces, illuminates the dark contours of the Jeune Parque's island and Narcisse's wooded pool. Perplexed by the sound of the wind, the young goddess awakening perceives without confusion the stars, "diamants extrêmes". Narcisse, arriving at the fatal pool, announces in the first line "Que tu brilles enfin, terme pur de ma course!" And thenceforth, he is caught in the spell of his mirror image, the clear but fragile, real but immaterial reflections in the water - his eyes, his entire form, and the surrounding forms of reeds and trees. The most primitive and basic quality of vision, sensitivity to light, thus opens the thought sequence of these two major poems. In "Le Cimetière marin" the very source of light, the sun itself, not only composes the seascape and makes all below - water, rock, trees shimmer by virtue of its intensity but also provides a major challenge to the narrator. With eye and will of heroic caliber, the narrator measures his force against that of the sun. "L'âme exposée aux torches du solstice, Je te soutiens, admirable justice / De la lumière aux armes sans pitié!" Face to face with the fiery orbit, human vision proves its power of reflexion. But in the same breath the narrator takes account of the earthy corollary of pure light, shadow, in this case felt as a corporal anchor, a defect in the free play of spirit and with funereal overtones. "Mais rendre la lumière / Suppose d'ombre une morne moitié." Whatever personal implications the sight of his shadow may have, the initial act is simply perception of that shadow. And the contrast of light and shadow is essential to his picture of the scene. With a minimum of metaphor he describes the cemetery as "Composé d'or, de pierre et d'arbres sombres, / Où tant de marbre est tremblant sur tant d'ombres."

Statistical studies of Valéry's vocabulary and the key words therein show "ombre" figuring high on the scale.*6 Since this is also the case with Mallarmé, one is naturally curious to find what the meaning of this may be in the total context. Considering the particular uses of that word, and in relation to the overall tonal background, what one sees is differences rather than similarities. For Valéry uses "ombre" most frequently in an exact, visual sense. This is so in the line cited above; it is also the case elsewhere, for instance in "La Dormeuse" where the sleeping woman is seen as an "amas doré d'ombres et d'abandons". Mallarmé, on the other hand, uses the same term figuratively. La Nourrice says to Hérodiade: "Tu vis! ou vois-je ici l'ombre d'une princesse?" And in a breath the princess appears as a shadow of herself, "abolie", reduced to near nothingness with the heroine embracing, perversely pleased, the condition of non-being - "J'aime l'horreur d'être vierge" - characteristic of the poem's general atmosphere. Palor, omnipresent shades of white have, interestingly, the exact same function in Mallarmé's poems, painting states drained of life, immobile, withdrawn. Thus one might compare succintly the two poets by posing the absolute of Midnight, the moment at which the tragic action of "Igitur" takes place, as Mallarmé's poetic time-pole and the Midday of "Le Cimetière marin" as Valéry's most typical temporal floodlight. The several poems in Valéry's world which take place at night, are thus arranged not to isolate the protagonist from life forces but rather as withdrawal from distracting, banal, mundane conditions the better to examine the source of existence - to attain the inner regions of the soul.

As one can plainly see in "Le Cimetière marin", the perceptual field of a real scene, a real moment in broad daylight, provides a wealth of impressions which the mind sorts, transforms, and combines in a complex of sensual, esthetic and intellectual modes. The extent and influence of this perceptual field is at the base of all Valéry's preoccupations. So that he poses human activity as deriving from an initial tripartite relationship between "L'Esprit, le Corps et le Monde". The initial product of these three perceptual sources he calls "sensibilité", the continuous unprocessed inflow of impressions. One can see the importance he attached to this psychological phenomenon by the fact that "sensibilité" furnished the starting point and the connecting thread for the series of lectures he gave at the Collège de France on esthetic theory, his "Cours de poétique".*7 And one is then not surprised to discover that the subject, "esthétique" is modified into "esthésique" thus focusing the study of art on the study of perception.

Although he includes in his discussions facets of all types of sense-data, he speaks most frequently of vision and he appears to consider it the most important of all faculties. A short passage from a collection of miscellaneous notes shows this predilection.

L'esprit est à la merci du corps comme sont les aveugles à la merci des voyants qui les assistent. Le corps touche et fait tout; commence et achève tout. De lui émanent nos vraies lumières, et même les seules, qui sont nos besoins et nos appétits, par lesquels nous avons une sorte de perception 'à distance' et 'superficielle', de l'état de notre intime structure. 'A distance' et 'superficielle', ne sont-ce pas là les caractères de la sensation visuelle? C'est pourquoi j'ai employé le mot: lumière.*8*

The main thread of this reflection is that the mind is totally dependent on the body for information even regarding itself, its intimate structure. But concurrently Valéry reveals the incomparable value of sight. Our eyes introduce into the mental system, literally and figuratively, a necessary component of understanding. But perhaps more important, is the fact that sight (and he suggests that other faculties can produce a parallel result) permits us to escape from a totally interior formless subjective world by orienting us in space, at a distance, in a world of apparent surfaces. It involves the inestimable gift of perspective, enabling us to view the world and our bodies from a certain vantage point where the distance achieved includes the sensation of objectivity, or even perhaps domination or power. It is what the protagonist of "Le Cimetière marin" achieves in a brief moment of ecstasy: "A ce point pur je monte et m'accoutume." It is what Valéry calls in "Notes et Digressions" "le moi pur", undistracted conciousness viewing and grasping all within a given existence.*9 This appears similar to Husserl's transcendental subjectivity, the unobserved observer that resides in all our perceptions, feelings, thoughts - with the important difference that Valéry recognized, not without distress, limits to the possibilities of self-observation.*10

At a far more modest and personal level, the visual world is a source of sheer pleasure. The Dormeuse seen as that "amas doré d'ombres et d'abandons", her "forme au ventre pur qu'un bras fluide drape". The cemetery and sea give rise to a myriad of dazzling images. This is the natural poetic world of a man who could note to himself at daybreak, "SALUT... Choses visibles!... A cette heure, sous l'éclairage presque horizontal, Voir se suffit. Ce qui est vu vaut moins que le voir même... "*11

A question remains however of some complexity, namely how to characterize accurately the role of vision in Valéry's creative act as well as in his poetic world. Aside from philosophical fascination and personal pleasure, exactly how does sight enter as a component in the creative schema? The first consideration that comes to mind is that a visual framework is by no means necessary. Many of his poems are remarkable for their absence of visual setting. "Les Pas" is one example of this sort, where, although a few physical elements are indicated (a bed, bare feet), the narrator is not in the least concerned with appearance or form. The atmosphere is rather one of formlessness and misty contemplation. So, one must conclude that the poet did not have as a principal poetic aim the description or even the suggestion or metamorphosis of visible reality. His interest in sight, light, form are instead part of a general concern with all aspects of spiritual activity. Similarly, even the brilliant succession of spontaneous metaphors - the sea seen as a "toit tranquille", "OEil", "peau de panthère", "hydre absolue" - is not so much a multivalent description of the sea itself as it is a display of the mind's magical versatility under the driving force of thirst for continuity and order. The first step of esthetic contemplation is to look ("regarder") free from the bonds of habit and reason. The second is to welcome what the eye proposes as possible even though a rational judgment would make short work of rejecting the suggestion. "Edifice dans l'âme, / Mais comble d'or aux mille tuiles, Toit!" So, the observer realizes full well the measure of actual distortion. Based on something exterior, verifiable, in the full light of day, the image is thus not completely unreal, a dream; but its value (meaning perhaps its subjective impact), says Valéry, is closest to that of a dream.*12 In the Cours de poétique he even elaborates at length the idea that the human mind in its simplest activities ("la sensibilité") is creative. He gives as one example the retina which, when receiving impressions of a certain color, reacts by the emission of the complementary shade. For another, he notes the tendency to fill up empty spaces as when one feels the urge to discover minute cracks in or to draw on an empty wall. All the more, for a poet or any artist, the exterior, visible world provides raw materials in the form of sensations which are then sifted, integrated and intensified, the whole becoming, as he said, harmonized, mutually resonant.

As impressive as this refined visual sensitivity may be, which renders Valéry's poetic world so vivid, one is equally aware of pervasive indications of things intangible. Secrets, mysteries, silence, absence, unspoken words, unspecified actions, all these facets leave the reader as if blinded by a luminous mist. "Les Pas" along with two other poems, "Le Sylphe" and "L'Insinuant", carries the sense of unseen, unnamed, disembodied presence to an unprecedented extreme. But, if one is unable to identify the mysterious source from which the atmosphere emanates, one is nevertheless sure of an individual personality and a psychological direction to the speech or gesture. The pure person of "Les Pas" moves gently, carefully towards the thinker's bed bringing sweetness and spiritual nourishment. The sylph, immaterial as a breeze, teases the writer with the impossible puzzles of his craft.

> ... Ni vu ni connu,
> Hasard ou génie?
> A peine venu
> La tâche est finie!
>
> Ni lu ni compris?
> Aux meilleurs esprits
> Que d'erreurs promises!... *

In order to penetrate such an evasive problem we can examine specific themes where the mystery is somehow stated. Within the course of "Le Cimetière marin" all of these intangible facets, recurrent throughout Valéry's poems, reappear in one form or another as a leit-motif. There is the silence in the third stanza: the narrator exclaims, "O mon silence!" and thus terminates the series of sea-changes ("Stable trésor, temple simple à Minerve..."). There are the "secrets éblouis-sants" of stanza IX, reflections of the sparkling water penetrating closed eyelids. There the "moutons mystérieux", the tombs of the cemetery which prefigure that essential "mystery" - death; and there is the transfiguration of the bodies of the dead into an "absence épaisse" (stanza XV). This particular image shows exactly what the poet is so very conscious of, a haunting all-pervasive train of thought: the idea that all matter is in a sense immaterial. The dead no longer what they were, thus absent, are still present, not dust but thick clay. The narrator, too, partakes of potential immateriality - "je hume ici ma future fumée", "ma présence est poreuse".

Just as important as the silences (the absences indicated by words) are the frequent intervals within the sentence structure, marked by an ellipsis. These are a unique characteristic of Valéry's style and are certainly due neither to inadvertance nor to airy unconstraint. In "Le Cimetière marin" they occur seven times! In each case, I think, they indicate an unnamed mental readjustment after a particular discovery, which is followed by a definite reaction to that discovery. In stanza VII the narrator finds within himself the power to respond to the sun's

challenge and then after a moment of pride in that accomplishment
pursues the inference, recognizing his vulnerability: "Je te rends pure
à ta place première: / Regarde-toi!...Mais rendre la lumière / Suppose
d'ombre une morne moitié." In the last stanza, instead of an intellectual discovery pushed to a logical conclusion it is a physical sensation,
suddenly noticing the wind, to which he responds by affirming his will
to live. "Le vent se lève!...Il faut tenter de vivre!" The ellipses then
mark the moment during which an unverbalized thought process takes
place. In the last lines of "Fragment de Narcisse", the poet uses this
technique, with a perfectly natural and delicate quality, to suggest the
final instant when the hero's consciousness is disappearing in the fatal
plunge. "L'insaisissable amour que tu me vins promettre / Passe et
dans un frisson, brise Narcisse, et fuit..."

The key to the whole question, to the elusive qualities of this poetic
world lies in understanding that far from being the results of a willed
drive towards obscurity they are the results of an effort to show how
apparent absence or silence can be pregnant with sense. From the
thinker's silence in "Les Pas" is born a pure person suggesting a potential of such great value that an effort is made to preserve it as such.
The hollow, sonorous depths of the soul in "Le Cimetière marin" by
virtue of the emptiness contains the possibility of resonant grandeur.
Spiritual secrets, thoughts and feelings unnamed and unspoken, as well
as immaterial physical phenomena, such as the transparent brilliance
of light, all deserve a place in a poetic world which, by definition,
contains the ineffable.*13

Stripped of name, symbol, and scenery, one lone subject remains the
arch-hero on Valéry's stage - the human mind. Inexhaustible, elusive,
it is impossible even to confine within one word: "Amour peut-être ou
de moi-même haine? / Sa dent secrète est de moi si prochaine / Que
tous les noms lui peuvent convenir!" Briefly to present this mystery
of all mysteries, all one can do is point out several of the main characteristics.

Born of the world and rooted in that world, the thinkers and the
thoughts in Valéry's poetry always reflect the sensations of a given
time and a given place. The mind is by nature inclusive. Without using
the vocabulary of phenomenology and more importantly without the desire or the aim of elaborating a metaphysical system, Valéry nonetheless portrays the basic concept of intentionality, showing all thought
as arising from and dealing with something beyond itself. "Le Cimetière marin" is the most vivid example of continuous sensitivity of
thought to nature, of a constant interchange and reaction between the
protagonist and the surroundings, of abstract thought springing from
immediate phenomena - the sun, the sea, the tombs. In "Les Pas" one
single perception of heartbeat, creates therefrom a seemingly real
figure, born of desire and who fills the atmosphere and sustains the
mood of watchfulness and expectancy.

The mind is inclusive in a temporal sense also. In the course of the
night, the Jeune Parque's dreams, half-dreams, and moments of wake-
fulness constantly weave back and forth between what she was and had
done, her memories relived in dream, what she gropingly distinguishes

as herself in the present and what she obscurely projects as future
possibilities. The protagonist of "Le Cimetière marin" also is aware
of the portent of the future and seemingly with intent incorporates it
in the moment ("Je hume ici ma future fumée", "Ici venu l'avenir est
paresse", "Debout dans l'ère successive"). In a fancifully abstruse,
wandering dialogue between two intellectuals, Valéry describes what
he means by "Implexe", one of the key notions in his psychological
system. He says that it is not activity but capacity, our individual
capacity to feel, to react, to do, to understand, to resist. And to explain the various modes of these possibilities he uses the conjugation
of a verb ("Je marche... Je marchais... Je marchai... Je marcherai")
adding that there are really an infinite number of such nuances surrounding the "point" of the present.*14 The "Implexe" then appears
as the sum of the possible as it takes shape from the reservoir of the
past. And it appears as the enduring substratum of his poetic personalities.

Another trait of the mind in Valéry's poetic world is mutability. We
have already noted the striking changes which took place in the sweep
of what one might call mental events in "Le Cimetière marin". Throughout the movement of the poem there is a complex, continuous shift of
emotion, attention, rest, activity, preoccupation with sensation or
with abstraction. Some dispositions are mutually exclusive, others
can occur simultaneously. Just as the calm noonday sea betrays an
inner energy through its quick, sparkling reflections ("le Temps scintille"), so there is a restless quality to the protagonist's spirit, an
undercurrent of energy which constantly modifies, constantly shifts
his attention. On an intellectual plane, the conjunction "mais" indicates
the drive to explore all consequences and at the same time to refuse
rejection of what may seem contradictory or even disagreeable: "Edifice dans l'âme, / Mais comble d'or aux mille tuiles, Toit!"; "Regarde-
toi!... Mais rendre la lumière / Suppose d'ombre une morne moitié."
Interestingly, his thought process does not involve categories of cause
and effect, does not entail a language molded by conjunctions which
explain intentions or results. Propositions in this poetry are generally
either simple statements of fact or impression, or exclamations indicating emotion or impression reinforced by emotion ("Ah! le soleil!...")
or questions like those of the Jeune Parque seeking to know herself
("Qui pleure là?... Mais qui pleure, Si proche de moi-même au moment
de pleurer?"), questions which remain unanswered because they are
bitterly rhetorical ("Chanterez-vous quand serez vaporeuse?") or because they are impossible ("Amour, peut-être, ou de moi-même
haine?"). The long conditional sentence which forms the two final
stanzas of "Les Pas" is no exception to this tendency. The conditional
clause ("Si... tu prépares pour l'apaiser, / A l'habitant de mes pensées /
La nourriture d'un baiser") is more of a hypothetical, self-induced
wishful delusion – of which the esthetic result is suspense. And the
explanation at the end ("Car j'ai vécu de vous attendre, / Et mon coeur
n'était que vos pas.") is not so much a revelation of cause as it is a
return to reality. Even in such a short poem as this one, where there
are no exterior events whatsoever, there is constant progression and
shift of feeling. From fascinated observation, to ecstasy, to intense

desire, finally to a plea for suspension of further change there is nevertheless an innate drive towards lucidity which culminates in the avowal,
"Et mon coeur n'était que vos pas."

Gerard Manley Hopkins and Rilke, both poets who also rendered
poetically structures of consciousness and finely chiseled acts of perception and feeling, approached however their particular scenes and
subjects within a relatively static framework, in poems which explore
the multiple spiritual facets of a given moment. Valéry, on the contrary, traces the curve of a spiritual duration, whether the evolution
of thoughts within a few instants or in the course of a longer interval
such as the Jeune Parque's life within a night.

Throughout the wide gamut of particular manifestations of spirit in
this poetic world, perhaps the most impressive single trait is that of
will. Its modes are varied. In "Sémiramis", in "Ebauche d'un Serpent",
in "Grenades" it takes the form of unmitigated pride, a conscious
pleasure in the sensation of intellectual energy so great it must exceed
the confines of the individual sphere of action. "Grenades" communicates this trait forcefully in a symbolic, entirely impersonal yet vivid
fashion.

Dures grenades entr'ouvertes
Cédant à l'excès de vos grains,
Je crois voir des fronts souverains
Eclatés de leurs découvertes! *

The Jeune Parque, Narcisse, and the protagonist of "Le Cimetière
marin" each exhibit a similar tendency in the course of their mental
peregrinations, the latter when he climbs to the point of supreme vision
(stanza IV). Elsewhere, it takes the form of a momentary resolution,
a decision to act breaking a previous introspective spell. Such is the
case at the end of "Le Cimetière marin" and of "La Jeune Parque",
also, tragically, when Narcisse plunges to oblivion. Yet another fine
poem, "Le Rameur", closes a dream-like sequence of difficult interior
exploration with a movement which ends the train of thought by consciously inducing sleep.

... L'âme baisse sous eux [vaulted bridges]
Ses sensibles soleils et ses promptes paupières,
Quand, par le mouvement qui me revêt de pierres,
Je m'enfonce au mépris de tant d'azur oiseux. *

Although the statistical analysis of Valéry's vocabulary indicates
that verbs having to do with operations of will are relatively infrequent,
the sense of such lines seems to me clearly evocative of resolute decision and action.*15 It is perhaps the case that Valéry preferred to
suggest the forms and the effect of will rather than naming it or its
actions directly. Certainly, the values expressed in his discursive
writing put mental capacities realized in action, very high on the scale.
The following two epigrammatic statements are unambiguous on this
score: "Qui es-tu? Je suis ce que je puis"; "Les esprits valent selon
ce qu'ils exigent. Je vaux ce que je veux."*16 If words of volition do
not appear in his poetic expression it is perhaps that here he is following the counsel of Mallarmé, "peindre non la chose mais l'effet qu'elle
produit".

Less dramatic but just as incontrovertible evidence of the thin and invisible but tough fiber of will, two other themes in Valéry's poetic world deserve comment. First, the theme of plan or design which is treated as such in "Ebauche d'un Serpent" and in "L'Insinuant". In both cases, Valéry plays on the graphic image of design and in both cases also the intent is mischievous as well as clever. The Serpent elaborates and carries out his plan of seduction which has the doubly seditious effect of tricking mortals and of challenging the perfection of the divine scheme. L'Insinuant, nameless and disembodied, unrolls the thread of her undivulged intentions, tantalizing and provoking to the end. The graphic image which Valéry reiterates is interesting: "ébauche", "dessein", "courbes", "l'insinuant". Contained therein is a suggestion of direction and cohesion and continuity together with the abstract, unnamed character open to different possibilities which are characteristics of art and of mathematics, fields which he admired for just such traits which do not come so naturally in verbal creations.

The second theme implying a persistent, invisible undercurrent of will is that of expectancy and attention which we have already analyzed in "Les Pas". Despite the apparently passive nature of this sort of mental activity, it requires nonetheless a perseverance and complete receptivity impossible without a strong measure of desire and resolution. Such, at any rate, is a basic disposition of the mind in Valéry's poetic world as it appears to the reader. The long, sustained period of reflections in "La Jeune Parque", "Narcisse", and "Le Cimetière marin" presuppose similarly an undercurrent of energy which is directed, focused, and maintained at the highest level of concentration and activity. The level of concentration reminds one of the rarified and restricted field of personal crisis in seventeenth century classical tragedy, the theater of Corneille and Racine, with the important difference that Valéry portrays the spirit not so much at a moment of exceptional crisis but in the course of ordinary but lucid introspection.

NOTES

*1 OEuvres I, 363.

*2 Mauvaises pensées, OEuvres II, 857-858.

*3 Paul Valéry vivant (Marseille, 1946), 161-162.

*4 OEuvres I, 1169.

*5 OEuvres I, 1159.

*6 Pierre Guiraud, Chapter VI, "Le Vocabulaire", Langage et versification d'après l'oeuvre de Paul Valéry.

*7 For his basic definition of mental activity as a complex of mind, body, and world see the short note in Tel Quel (OEuvres II, 712), the important essay, "Poésie et pensée abstraite" (OEuvres I, 1314-1339) and the notes from the seventeenth lecture of his "Cours de poétique" (Yggdrasil, 25 déc. 1938, 139-140). A word about the sources on that famous series of lectures given at the Collège de France might be useful. The first lecture, entitled "Première leçon de poétique", appeared in printed form in a number of publications and is included in Variété (OEuvres I, 1340-1358). The subsequent lectures were never transcribed and published by Valéry but two sets of documents are available which indicate their contents. Extensive notes on the first seventeen lectures (1937-1938) taken by Georges Le Breton were published in the periodical Yggdrasil from Dec. 1937 to Dec. 1938. When using these résumés as sources it is important to remember that the phrasing is probably not in most cases that of Valéry and that some measure of distortion of his thought is not impossible. Still, they are useful indications of his position on certain key subjects. As a record of the sixteen lectures given early in 1945 there is a typescript in the Valéry collection of the Bibliothèque Doucet. The content of these is repetitive and less interesting as a whole.

*8 Tel Quel, OEuvres II, 780.

*9 This concept of a central and invariable "self" (which he contrasts with "personality", limited, limiting and subject to change) is an essential feature of his own intellectual makeup as well as his philosophical and psychological schema. For more information on this interesting subject, I would recommend a short passage from a letter (written in 1943 and reproduced in the notes of OEuvres II, 1503-1505) and an essay which Valéry himself considered a good exposition of these ideas, "Note et digression" (1919), OEuvres I, 1199-1233 and particularly pages 1228-1230. Further quotations and synthesis of relevant notes from the Cahiers are to be found in an article by James R. Lawler, "Huit volumes des Cahiers de Valéry", Revue d'histoire littéraire de la France, janvier-mars 1963, 62-89, and in Chapter VI of Judith Robinson's book, particularly pages 149-154.

*10 For instance, in the sixteenth lecture of the "Cours de poétique" (Yggdrasil, 25 oct. 1938, 102-103) he points out how our thought loses a measure of its freedom when examining itself, just as in modern physics when observation modifies the phenomenon under examination.

*11 Mauvaises pensées, OEuvres, 859.

*12 Mauvaises pensées, OEuvres, 860.

*13 As such, this poetic world reflects the same ambiguities as the real world. Briefly, in Tel Quel (OEuvres II, 712) he remarks: " Le vague, l'hiatus, le contradictoire, le cercle - véritables constituants de tout et de chacun, substance la plus fréquente de chaque esprit."

*14 L'Idée fixe, OEuvres II, 234-235.

*15 This is one example of a limiting factor inherent in statistical studies of literature. They depend for the raw material of their investigations on what is stated directly, particular words and phrases, without being able to take into account what may be implicit in a writer's verbal expression. The value of statistical analysis is that it points out clearly and certainly words (or word structures) which recur with significant frequency, for instance the prominence in Valéry's poetry of the word "ombre"; but only textual analysis weighing shades of meaning can place those words in the proper perspective within the work as a whole.

*16 OEuvres I, 396; OEuvres II, 866.

IV

LE SON ET LE SENS

The charm of Valéry's poetry is undeniable. And charms he wished them to be, entitling the main group as such <u>Charmes</u> whose Latin form, <u>carmina</u>, signifies both "poem" and "incantation". But the curious reader cannot help but wish to know what measure of abstract meaning may be contained therein, especially since the preoccupations of the heroes reflect a philosophical cast of mind. Many interpretations of his work are highly abstract. No doubt, a common and oversimplified view of the French symbolist movement, which considers images as devoid of intrinsic meaning and as simple references to some abstract concept, has contributed greatly to this critical current. Valéry, in a preface to the edition of <u>Charmes</u> presented by Alain, saying graciously "Mes vers ont le sens qu'on leur prête",*1 apparently opens the field for further criticism of the same sort. However, numerous other remarks concerning the aim of particular poems, the way in which he wrote and general view on poetry, give quite a different impression.

Particularly striking is his insistence that the sound of a verse is as important as its meaning. Both when describing his own way of writing and when speaking of what he finds significant in other poets' works, he uses the analogy of a pendulum. The continuous swing of a pendulum balances from one pole of sense to the other pole of sound. Sound and sense thus appear as two equal components of the act of creation and of the act of esthetic comprehension. Valéry even exhibits a tendency to value more highly verse which is non-intellectual or even non-sensical. For instance, in a letter to Pierre Louÿs, an intimate friend, he quotes these lines of a nineteenth century poet, Marceline Desbordes-Valmore, "...Allez, navire! / La danse vous salue au fond de vos couleurs.", and comments thereupon: "Vers qui n'a aucun sens, mais qui l'emporte sur tous les vers." And in one of his many essays on Mallarmé he speaks of lines which may seem obscure, hard to decipher, but which are unequivocally clear as pure poetry, whose quality shines through and dominates, luminously musical.*2 From this one would conclude that his test of great poetry and the way to appreciate it excludes active search for clear discursive sense. For an initial reading of a poem and for further readings, when one seeks the total esthetic experience, no doubt Valéry would recommend this suspension of reason.*3

In connection with his own poetry, other remarks clarify his conception of the equilibrium of elements. In reply to a query from a literary critic concerning the composition of "Le Cimetière marin", Valéry says simply:

Vous m'embarrassez de vos questions... Ce dont je me souviens, c'est d'avoir tenté de maintenir des conditions musicales constantes, c'est-à-dire que je me suis efforcé de soumettre à chaque instant le contenu significatif à la volonté ou à l'intention de satisfaire le sens auditif.
   Le rythme, les accents, les timbres doivent, à mon avis, être des facteurs au moins aussi importants que l'élément abstrait du langage poétique...*4 *

This insistence on the importance of non-rational or non-discursive components of poetry has several important consequences. One is that the total significance of a poem will then include the impressions deriving from the rhythm, the sound and the form. Valéry himself suggests that all these ostensibly formal elements themselves have more than some vague emotional value when he speaks of form as giving birth to ideas ("une forme est féconde en idées"), using mathematical analysis as an analogy.*5 This consequence is not only an important one but also very helpful, enlarging the field of potential meaning for the reader. It is what I have undertaken in considering the form as movement of consciousness and in analyzing tonal patterns. The second consequence, on the other hand, makes things rather more difficult. Since the poet admittedly in case of indecision or conflict, opts for a word or phrase which satisfies the ear even if the literal sense may have no strong relevance, how is the reader to judge which expressions may be interpreted as having legitimate literal weight? When should one abandon a search for distinct rational meaning? There is obviously no practical answer except to be aware of the possibility that a given word may not be fair game for metaphorical extension. To take a rather minor example, in a line from "Le Cimetière marin" (stanza XII), "L'insecte net gratte la sécheresse", I think the adjective "net" was used not for a particular precision of meaning, a real quality pertaining to the insect, but for its sound. It repeats two sounds from "insecte" ($ɛ$ and t), leads into a modulation of the vowel to a in the next word and it reiterates the t - all of this adds up to an important, purely phonological function.
   Yet Valéry was highly sensitive to shades of meaning contained within words, witness the very title of his collection - Charmes - and he was equally possessed of an urge to avoid imprecision - Charmes - and he was aware that many commonplace terms such as "time" and "life" appear more enigmatic than clear under close scrutiny.*6 He therefore avoided such terms as much as possible. His search for the right word to describe the brook's activities is typical of his ideal of rigorously exact expression. In addition, he shared the interest of his contemporaries in the esthetic function of symbols. A speech of Socrates in L'Ame et la danse analyzes the qualities of the bee, a recurrent metaphor in Valéry's poetry. This analysis first evokes the bee as "cette puissance légère" and continues by indicating its force, its concentrated movement, its vibration, its suspended flight, hesitating to choose between a multitude of flowers, here brushing lightly, there

penetrating or stinging, departing suddenly. All are qualities which contribute to a composite picture.*7 So, one would conclude that a given image such as that of the bee or, to take another example, that of the tree which recurs throughout his poetry is by nature multivalent. It would be inexact to say simply that for him the bee is a symbol of a word. That may be the reference at one point such as in the "Ebauche d'un Serpent" when the villain says "si ma parole / De l'âme obsédant le trésor, comme une abeille une corolle / Ne quitte plus l'oreille d'or!" But in "L'Abeille" the bee signifies not only a word sought but also concentrated force, movement, possibility, stimulation. Furthermore, one should bear in mind that in Valéry's imagery the relationship between a natural object and a spiritual tenor (the thing symbolized) is usually reciprocal. Thus the description of the tree in "Au Platane" may suggest and symbolize certain human characteristics but it also is a detailed, imaginative portrait of a tree. Certainly, in "Le Cimetière marin" the sun and the sea are basically very much themselves, natural phenomena, brilliantly viewed. One might conceive of that sun as suggestive of omnipotent knowledge and the sea as a source of life and change, but such conceptions are surely secondary to their vivid presence as real sun and real sea.

The most valid extension of the significance of Valéry's poetry on an abstract level is possible, I think, in quite a different way. In the course of my search for intrinsic sense, I was struck by a number of references and structures having to do with time, not appearing as central themes but persistant and suggestive of an undercurrent of philosophical preoccupation. His essays, books, and other writings show distinctly a life-long concern for this phenomenon basic to philosophy, science, and all human experience but so difficult to define and apprehend clearly. What, then, was the nature of the question for Valéry? And how did he go about finding a satisfactory answer?

The simple, quasi+instinctive force behind his reflections on this subject is a human distress to discover that man and his surroundings are doomed to destruction and that experience in its most raw state suggests that disorder and discontinuity reign in the natural world. In remedy to the insufficiencies of nature, man, fortunately, actively seeks to satisfy his own desires by creating what is lacking. Through the words of Socrates in Eupalinos ou l'architecte Valéry proposes that, to satisfy his body, man constructs things which are useful, ranging from a humble object, such as a table, to the ambitious, complex construction of a port. To satisfy his soul, seeking beauty, he creates works of art. And to counteract the destructive movement of nature, he tries to endow all of his works with resistance, he thus seeks solidity or duration.*8 As one might expect of a dialogue written to appear in the review Architectures the protagonist emphasizes that of all the arts, architecture alone unites all three aims - utility, beauty, and solidity - and carries them to an ultimate perfection. That Valéry really did admire greatly architecture for these reasons, one can see in the proud, self-entoned praise of the Greek columns, "Cantique des Colonnes". Venerably young, embellished by the sun, with an unsatiable thirst for centuries they glide smoothly through time.

Nous marchons dans le temps
Et nos corps éclatants
Ont des pas ineffables
Qui marquent dans les fables... *

On a more personal level and with a more original statement of the
problem, the author considers at length in his Cours de poétique the
radical disorder and discontinuity of experience in its most immediate
and simple form, in what he terms sensibility. The sensibility as
Valéry conceives it, is comprehensive: the totality of images, impressions, impulsions, words, schemas - all that is given, present
in the mind at any given moment. It is completely receptive, omnivor-
ous, aimless and undirected. Interestingly, its functioning includes
both sensations and the intelligence.*9 By virtue of this comprehensiveness it is utterly chaotic. Yet it permits us to relate ourselves in
the temporal world. Although devoid of order, it represents for us
this much: an event, a duration, and the place in which the event is
situated. Considered altogether it gives, in a sense, a definition of
the instant. "Ce corps, ce monde, cet esprit envisagés du point de vue
de la sensibilité sont des variables, des dimensions de l'instant
même."*10 Although rich in potential, it is distressing to realize how
it is bound to the instant. It is almost tragic, suggests Valéry, to think
of the immense potential contained in the instant together with the fact
that man, in a given short instant, is nothing.*11
    The word "tragic" is exceptional in his expression. Still, implicit
in his judgment of the sensibility, thus conceived, is a deep and restless dissatisfaction with its ephemeral and disorderly qualities. Fortunately certain of its characteristics offer the means to overcome
these insufficiencies. For, although chaotic, the sensibility is rich,
bursting with potential, although reflecting the disorder of nature, it
is expectant, intrinsically creative. The sound of one note leads one
to await another, arouses an urge to fill the emptiness, the sight of a
bare wall arouses the desire to trace a design. The author calls this
its "caractère récepto-émetteur".*12 Perhaps most important is the
sensibility's talent for raising questions. This is at the bottom of its
creative activities. Due to this "sensibilité de l'étonnement", the capacity to be surprised, to doubt and to inquire, mankind has produced
scientific discoveries, metaphysical systems, and works of art.*13
The composer turning his attention towards sounds, the painter envis-
aging colors, the poet working with words will establish a network of
connections and relations - a "univers" - thereby counteracting the
arbitrary nature of immediate experience. A well-made poem, says
Valéry, is one way of battling the sensibility.*14
    This artistic universe satisfies principally man's desire for order
by proposing continuity. Here, the ambition is more realistic than in
his discussion of architecture. For a temple, although solid and long-
lived, will at some point crumble and decay. Its permanence is still
relative. A goal which is more accessible to the human spirit and just
as gratifying is that of connecting isolated points in space and time,
elaborating a network of relations. In the esthetic domain this can be
done best in art and in music. Valéry admired greatly this potential.
In his essay on Leonardo da Vinci he analyzed the way in which graphic

art can constitute a sort of "idéographie" of figurative relations between qualities and quantities and the way in which music can offer auditory formulas for changes in our affective life. In his own poetry, he incorporated both these possibilities of expression suggesting graphic visual forms and heightening the patterns and the modulations of verbal sounds, developing them to extraordinary complexity.*15

Concerned with the basic problems of defining continuity and time, Valéry on the one hand scrutinizes the most minute and immediate apprehension of time, the instant. As we have seen, he proposed in the Cours de poétique that the sensibility contains the "dimensions of the instant". In a series of related but disjointed remarks, entitled "Brièvetés", he circumscribes the value - immediate and potential - of the shortest interval.

> L'action est une brève folie.
> Ce que l'homme a de plus précieux est une brève épilepsie.
> Le génie tient dans un instant.
> L'amour naît d'un regard, et un regard suffit pour engendrer une éternelle haine.
> Et nous ne valons quelque chose que pour avoir été et pouvoir être un moment hors de nous.
> Ce petit moment hors de moi est un germe, ou se projette comme un germe. Tout le reste de la durée le développe ou le laisse périr.*16 *

Presenting the gestures of such moments as instinctive, irrational, and uncontrolled, he gages their value by the force of the insight or emotion and by their subsequent development. The latter, of course, is a very significant factor, and one which he really prized above all else. Only slow maturation, continuous effort and care can produce succulent dates, a fine wine or a really good work of art.

Most of his poems are carefully delimited temporally within a considerable range. "La Jeune Parque" is perhaps the most ambitious, filling a long span of night. "Le Cimetière marin" would then represent a moderate interval, albeit packed with events. A short poem, "La Ceinture", concentrates on an instant, the brief moment when the horizon at sunset is suffused with color yet perceptibly outlined with a narrow band of shadow, the augure of night. The first verse indicates that exact instant.

> Quand le ciel couleur d'une joue
> Laisse enfin les yeux le chérir
> Et qu'au point doré de périr
> Dans les roses le temps se joue. *

The verses which follow sustain the moment, a thin, silent tie between the eye and world, immaterial yet full of portent. It comes directly after "Les Pas" in the collection and has the same quality of delicate briefly sustained concentration.

With an eye resembling astonishingly that of a scientist or a philosopher, the poet relates other brief perceptions, impressive mainly in that they serve to pinpoint the instant. We have already seen in "Le Cimetière marin" how the protagonist absorbs the peaceful splendor

of the midday sea remarking, "Le Temps scintille et le Songe est savoir." In "Narcisse" there is a parallel passage where the hero is en-
tranced by his reflection in the water, perhaps lightly distorted by a
breath or a breeze playing on the surface.

Voir, ô merveille, voir! ma bouche nuancée
Trahir...peindre sur l'onde une fleur de pensée
Et quels événements étinceler dans l'oeil! *

Whether the sparkling has its source on the water or in the eye, the
abstract sense remains unchanged: the rapid succession of sparkles
defines the moment; and, in addition, they are conceived of each as a
distinct event, so minute that the human mind can almost only grasp
them as distinct through their occurence in groups. Might one consider
each sparkle as the limit of human temporal perception?

While sparkles offer the possibility of actually seeing units which
define a brief time span, pure vibrations are yet one step further down
the scale of perceptible instants of energy. In "Palme", describing the
fruitful tree, the poet uses that very image with a tone of wonder.

Admire comme elle vibre,
Et comme une lente fibre
Qui divise le moment,
Départage sans mystère
L'attirance de la terre
Et le poids du firmament! *

Using the precise metaphor of a vibrating fibre to portray the long,
thin, sensitive trunk of the palm tree, he unexpectedly mentions in
the midst of the description that it "divides the moment". The main
theme of the poem is, in a sense, temporal, since it follows the slow,
steady maturation necessary for the fruit of a tree, as for the creation
of a poem. But to indicate that the vibrating fibre divides the moment
seems an interesting gratuitous remark of someone with a scientific
curiosity.

Through Valéry's poems, there are a number of other phrases and
favorite words which bely an awareness of basic forms of energy. "La
Dormeuse" contains the suggestive expression "ce rayonnement d'une
femme endormie" which evokes emanation of nearly radiant contained
force. Two other words which appear very frequently as verbs or nouns
are "trembler" and "frémir". The description of the cemetery includes
this remark, "Où tant de marbre est tremblant sur tant d'ombres",
a visual, physical picture of the shimmering glare of the white tomb-
stones in the intense sun. "Aurore", which relates the creative spirit,
fresh after sleep, fairly bursting with activity and poetic potential,
contains a great number of such terms among which the following two:
"...fils primitifs...dans une trame ténue / De tremblants préparatifs...";
"elle [l'âme] s'écoute qui tremble / Et parfois ma lèvre semble / Son
frémissement saisir." Whether such images have to do with defining
an instant of time or whether they describe a physical state, exterior
or interior, the common denominator is constant awareness of an
undercurrent of energy disclosing extreme sensitivity to the perceptive
field and immensely valuable for what it may produce.

Such awareness no doubt has considerable satisfaction for a mind concerned with grasping the dimensions of the world and penetrating the basic mechanisms of nature. But far more satisfying is the creation of some sort of system which relates events and discloses patterns. Early in his career, in the essay on Leonardo da Vinci, Valéry proposed as the aim of scientists and artists the search not only for continuity but for symmetry and periodic patterns. Speaking of such vastly different phenomena as traces of the wind on sand or water or statistics concerning crime, accidents, births, he states: "Les événements les plus surprenants et les plus asymétriques par rapport au cours des instants voisins, rentrent dans un semblant d'ordre par rapport à de plus vastes périodes.*17 In order to construct these orderly cycles at least two mental processes are involved: one being a disposition which consists of looking for relations, connections, temporarily abstracting what may be individual in a given object or event and the other being to consider the whole in terms not of a given moment but in terms of a time span, depending on the function of memory to obtain recurrent features from which to derive the pattern of the whole.

The first process, that of looking for connections and relationships, reflects the influence of Henri Poincaré whose work Valéry followed even before the turn of the century. The second frame of reference, viewing the definition of a phenomenon in terms of successive and discontinuous events taken as a group with regular periodic characteristics, reflects and probably prefigures the methods of scientists in the domain of quantum theory and of relativity. Whitehead, in his presentation of contemporary scientific theories, uses on occasion esthetic terminology to characterize certain patterns. "The problem of evolution", he says, "is the development of enduring harmonies of enduring shapes of value..." and, in explaining the quantum theory he describes the sort of temporal pattern as one of the esthetic contrasts requiring a lapse of time for its unfolding and gives as an example - a tune.*18 As I understand it, his use of such terms is not mere ornament but a serious comparison of the patterns and values of art and science. It is interesting to note that in his discussion of nineteenth century poetry, he points out that the poets sensed and spoke of what was lacking in the science of that period - permanence, one form of which he calls endurance and another form he calls eternality (what remains after a thing has worn away, for instance, color). Valéry does not appear concerned with permanence of this sort, perhaps because of his hesitation to enter the realm of metaphysics. But his search for some sort of endurance leads him to equate his esthetic forms with those of twentieth century science.

In connection with his own poetry, and on a theoretical, abstract level, Valéry considered the process of composition as involving a modification of the chaotic flux of sensibility into an ordered sequence. The creative gesture becomes willed and decisive in his thought as he frequently speaks of this gesture as an "act". In the first lecture of the Cours de poétique he defines such an act as the cessation of the basic indeterminate state, an escape from the closed world of possibility into the world of deeds.*19 And in Cahier VI he broaches the

question of the nature of rhythm, for him often the starting point for a
whole poem, as in the case of "Le Cimetière marin", and in any case
a condition absolutely necessary to the essence of poetry. On one page
of his notebook we find the following thought: "rythme. Si je perçois
des événements successifs - et si cette perception crée en moi in-
stantanément le pouvoir de reproduire cette suite comme si ces événements étaient un seul, il y a quelque rythme." And on another: "Un
rythme est comme une couleur. (couleur pure). Sensation d'une plura-
lité reconnaissable. Cf. polygones."*20 So, rhythm at birth is disembodied, uncomplicated by words, perhaps even by sound. Valéry
names its components, which follow one from another, events. And
the rhythm comes into being instantaneously when the successive, formerly isolated events are perceived as a whole, or seen in retrospect,
as a recognizable series. The description recalls the vision of Narcisse, "...quels événements étinceler dans l'oeil", with the addition
of a further perception of a finite group embracing the individual events.
In a further thought on the subject the notion of action reappears: "rythme - c'est-à-dire division du tout, en actes - ou plutôt la constitution
par des actes d'un tout, Acte ou événement."*21 Thus, what elsewhere
would be a simple event, within the fertile domain of consciousness,
while still remaining event, becomes in addition willed, ordered gesture worthy of being named and capitalized, Act.

The gestures which terminate "Le Rameur", "Le Cimetière marin",
"Narcisse" and "La Jeune Parque" have the same definitive, willed
quality. And, in a more complex fashion, they illustrate the urge Valéry felt to establish cyclical forms. Here, there is a distinct set of
phenomena which he wished to delineate and circumscribe, as we have
seen, the activity of the mind. The events are multifarious, subtly
formed and perceived, inextricably connected, the constant play of
internal and external sensations - memory, physical and emotional
reactions, abstract preoccupations - which all strike the core of being.
While each protagonist appears as real, with an aura of individual
character and personality, the content of the thoughts and feelings is
far removed from petty problems, narrowly egotistical pursuits. They
become of pressing importance not only to the protagonist but to the
reader as well. And while bearing unresolved the weight of the imponderable, the unattainable, the deep imperfection of life, the poet and
the reader participate in the compensating pleasure of seeing existence
transformed into a poetic universe where the modes of human sensibility are harmonized, resolved in a musical sense, and endowed with
temporal form and meaning. Here, language is the key to order. "A
chaque instant, un événement verbal veut répondre à l'événement physique et visuel, et faire passer quelque chose du temps quelconque
dans le temps organisé - celui des actes."*22

Perceiving the order of Valéry's universe, unravelling the threads of
consciousness of his heroes is admittedly no easy task. Sensitive to
the charge of obscurity, he explained that, far from seeking to mys-
tify and complicate understanding, the difficulty of his verse resulted
directly from the difficulty of the task he set for himself, attempting
to project the objects of thought and the complex states of a living be-

ing all the while satisfying demands of plastic and musical continuity. This explanation seems genuine; yet there remains an element of oblique statements, of withdrawal in his poetry which one feels is deliberate. The range stretches from the teasing, needling playfulness of "L'Insinuant" to the sudden changes of unidentified fields of attention in "La Jeune Parque". The aim, I think, is to challenge the reader, to call upon <u>his</u> "sensibilité de l'étonnement". For Valéry, that which appears puzzling, unexpected or startling is exactly that which provides the pleasure and the force of any sort of experience.*23 Even that which is painful is valuable in that it excites, awakens, calls forth a response. In "L'Abeille", the bee performs this symbolic function: "...sois donc mon sens illuminé." The Jeune Parque, awakening, is spurred to thought by her sorrow: "...sur l'écueil mordu par la merveille, / J'interroge mon coeur quelle douleur l'éveille." Valéry displaying as much faith in the spiritual fiber of his readers as he has for himself or for his heroes, presents them with a comparable challenge. Artists and poets, he says, use (and abuse) surprise effects in order to heighten perception and awareness, in order to charm and shock ("séduire et foudroyer").*24 One should thus be reassured that Valéry's challenge is honorable.

In a short essay, replying to objections of the difficulty of "La Jeune Parque", he speaks, a bit playfully, through the mouth of the heroine herself: "Mais je ne suis en moi pas plus mystérieuse / Que le plus simple d'entre vous... C'est de vous que j'ai pris l'ombre qui vous éprouve. / Qui s'égare en soi-même aussitôt se retrouve."*25 If an elliptic image resists simple explanation, if the subject of a given passage is hard to grasp, the first recourse should be to one's own experience, to place oneself in a similar circumstance where a spontaneous image or subject will suggest itself naturally. On the broadest level, most of the preoccupations of Valéry's heroes have an intimately familiar ring: Where am I? What am I doing? Where am I going? Who am I?

NOTES

*1 "Commentaire de <u>Charmes</u>" (1929), <u>OEuvres</u> I, 1509.

*2 "Stéphane Mallarmé", <u>OEvres</u> I, 667-668. The letter to Pierre Louÿs speaking of the poetry of Marceline Desbordes-Valmore is in the notes of <u>OEuvres</u> I, 1616, a brief passage in <u>Tel Quel</u>, <u>OEuvres</u> II, 556-557 comments similarly on a line from Hugo.

*3 In <u>Introduction à la méthode de Léonard de Vinci</u> (1894) he proposes that painting should be approached in the following manner: "...la méthode la plus sûre pour juger une peinture, c'est de n'y rien reconnaître d'abord et de faire pas à pas la série d'inductions que nécessite une présence simultanée de taches colorées sur un champ limité, pour s'élever de métaphores en métaphores, de suppositions en suppositions à l'intelligence du sujet, parfois à la simple conscience du plaisir, qu'on n'a pas toujours eu d'avance" (<u>OEuvres</u> I, 1186). And a marginal note counsels reading poetry first to grasp the sound patterns.

*4 Fernand Lot, "Regard sur la prosodie de Paul Valéry", La Grande Revue, CXXXII (mars 1930), 93. See also Henri Mondor, Propos familiers de Valéry (Paris, 1957), 185.

*5 "Degas et le sonnet", OEuvres II, 1207.

*6 He speaks of this in a note in Tel Quel, OEuvres II, 745-746 and also in his essay "Poésie et pensée abstraite", OEuvres I, 1317-1318.

*7 L'Ame et la danse, OEuvres II, 165-166.

*8 OEuvres II, 129-130.

*9 According to the notes of the fifteenth lecture (Yggdrasil, 25 août-25 sept. 1938, 72) Valéry said "la distinction entre intellect et sensibilité me paraît illusoire quand elle est présentée sans précision".

*10 Notes on the seventeenth lecture (Yggdrasil, 25 déc. 1938, 139).

*11 Note from the sixth lecture (Yggdrasil, 25 fév. 1938, 171): "C'est un fait presque tragique de songer, en regardant un être humain, à ce qu'il peut contenir de possibilités sensorielles: toutes les douleurs, tous les plaisirs et toutes les pensées qui sont possibles en lui. L'instantané n'est rien. L'être humain, dans un instant bien court n'est rien. Tout être humain doit être regardé comme une immense virtualité."

*12 Third lecture (Yggdrasil, 25 jan. 1938, 154).

*13 Lectures five-seven (Yggdrasil, 25 fév. 1938, 170-172).

*14 Eighth lecture (Yggdrasil, 25 mars 1938, 185).

*15 The concept of "idéographie" is developed on pages 1266-1267 of the essay on Leonardo da Vinci (OEuvres I). Geoffrey Hartman's book, The Unmediated Vision (New Haven, 1954) contains a highly interesting chapter on Valéry where he traces just such patterns of syllabic and graphic continuity in two poems, "La Dormeuse" and "Eté". He describes the poet's dominant esthetic drive as an inexhaustible thirst for visual immediacy, "sheer visibility".

*16 Tel Quel, OEuvres II, 612-613.

*17 OEuvres I, 1172.

*18 A. N. Whitehead, Science and the Modern World (Cambridge, 1953), 117 and 166.

*19 OEuvres I, 1357.

*20 Cahier VI, page 12 and page 16.

*21 Cahier VI, 202.

*22 Mauvaises pensées, OEuvres II, 806.

*23 Tel Quel, OEuvres II, 734.

*24 In Cahier VI (179) he states this idea succinctly: "Pour me plaire...
il faut que l'idée, la pensée, l'expression, le motif me vienne - me
surprenne... Le génie serait-il la possibilité de se surprendre."

*25 "Le philosophe et la Jeune Parque", OEuvres I, 164-165.

PART   TWO

SAINT-JOHN PERSE: LES GRANDS LÉS TISSÉS DU SONGE
ET DU RÉEL

Saint-John Perse, trenchantly defining the nature of his work within the larger sphere of modern French poetry and mincing no words, starts by describing the Anglo-Saxon creative process in the following manner. Says he:

> ... L'esprit anglo-saxon est, de longue date, habitué au processus discursif de la poésie anglaise - poésie d'idée, donc de définition et d'élucidation, toujours explicite et logique, parce que de source rationelle, et par là portée aux enchaînements formels d'une dialectique intellectuelle et morale.*1 *

Thus it consists of themes, expressed sequentially, it avoids ellipsis, seems less a revelation than a confirmation. Although concise, this sort of poetry remains commentary and paraphrase.

In contrast, modern French poetry according to his views manifests a total, indissoluble cohesion of all its components. Its ultimate goal he describes thus:

> ... de s'intégrer elle-même vivante, à son objet, entre le poète et le poème. Faisant plus que témoigner ou figurer, elle devient la chose même qu'elle 'appréhende', qu'elle évoque ou suscite... elle est, finalement, cette chose elle-même, dans son mouvement et sa durée... *

Rich in implications which we will pursue later, some perhaps debatable, this dyptich of esthetic principles provides two crucial guidelines for determing the sense and structure of his work.

The poetic substance is formed of dream and reality - what he calls "grands lés tissés du songe et du réel",*2 an almost tangible breadth of cloth and web of song. ("Lés", breadth of cloth, is the phonetic equivalent of "lais", the medieval verse form.) And that substance is infused from the start with its own vitality which includes most importantly, the author says, a temporal dimension. Poetry is the thing itself, in its movement and in its duration.*3 The key word for him is movement, as in the case of Valéry but certainly individually conceived.

NOTES

*1 These important, detailed reflections on poetic theory (including this quotation and the one following) appear in a letter to George Huppert, editor of the Berkeley Review proposing a special issue devoted to the works of Perse. The letter was written August 10, 1956. The full text is reproduced in the collection, Honneur à Saint-John Perse (Paris, 1965), 655-658.

*2 Perse, Neiges, OEuvre poétique , Vol. 1 (Paris, 1960), 213.

*3 For Perse, the emphasis on movement is crucial and is expounded at length also in a letter to Roger Caillois, published first in the book by Caillois, Poétique de Saint-John Perse (Paris, 1954) and then an extract therefrom in Honneur à Saint-John Perse, 654-655.

V

ANABASE, STROPHE VII

Anabase, Strophe VII

Nous n'habiterons pas toujours ces terres jaunes, notre délice...

1 L'Eté plus vaste que l'Empire suspend aux tables de l'espace plusieurs étages de climats. La terre vaste sur son aire roule à
pleins bords sa braise pâle sous les cendres. - Couleur de soufre,
de miel, couleur de choses immortelles, toute la terre aux herbes
s'allumant aux pailles de l'autre hiver - et de l'éponge verte d'un
seul arbre le ciel tire son suc violet.

2 Un lieu de pierres à mica! Pas une graine pure dans les barbes du
vent. Et la lumière comme une huile. - De la fissure des paupières
au fil des cimes m'unissant, je sais la pierre tachée d'ouïes, les
essaims du silence aux ruches de lumière; et mon coeur prend
souci d'une famille d'acridiens...

3 Chamelles douces sous la tonte, cousues de mauves cicatrices,
que les collines s'acheminent sous les données du ciel agraire -
qu'elles cheminent en silence sur les incandescences pâles de la
plaine; et s'agenouillent à la fin, dans la fumée des songes, là où
les peuples s'abolissent aux poudres mortes de la terre.

4 Ce sont de grandes lignes calmes qui s'en vont à des bleuissements
de vignes improbables. La terre en plus d'un point mûrit les vio-
lettes de l'orage; et ces fumées de sable qui s'élèvent au lieu des
fleuves morts, comme des pans de siècles en voyage...

5 A voix plus basse pour les morts, à voix plus basse dans le jour.
Tant de douceur au coeur de l'homme, se peut-il qu'elle faille à
trouver sa mesure?... "Je vous parle, mon âme! - mon âme tout
enténébrée d'un parfum de cheval!" Et quelques grands oiseaux de
terre, naviguant en Ouest, sont de bons mimes de nos oiseaux de
mer.

6 A l'orient du ciel si pâle, comme un lieu saint scellé des linges de
l'aveugle, des nuées calmes se disposent, où tournent les cancers
du camphre et de la corne... Fumées qu'un souffle nous dispute! la
terre tout attente en ses barbes d'insectes, la terre enfante des
merveilles!...

Et à midi, quand l'arbre jujubier fait éclater l'assise des tombeaux,
7 l'homme clôt ses paupières et rafraîchit sa nuque dans les âges...
Cavaleries du songe au lieu des poudres mortes, ô routes vaines
qu'échevèle un souffle jusqu'à nous! où trouver, où trouver les
guerriers qui garderont les fleuves dans leurs noces?

Au bruit des grandes eaux en marche sur la terre, tout le sel de la
8 terre tressaille dans les songes. Et soudain, ah! soudain que nous
veulent ces voix? Levez un peuple de miroirs sur l'ossuaire des
fleuves, qu'ils interjettent appel dans la suite des siècles! Levez
les pierres à ma gloire, levez des pierres au silence, et à la garde
de ces lieux les cavaleries de bronze vert sur de vastes chaussées!...

(L'ombre d'un grand oiseau me passe sur la face.)*

Anabase, a relatively early poem of concisely epic proportions, has
enjoyed just renown and been singled out (and paired with Valéry's
"Cimetière marin") as one of the greatest poems in the whole French
literary tradition. This fame includes recognition of its difficulty even
by such a sensitive poetic mind as T. S. Eliot who effected an English
translation.*1 Hopefully some of these difficulties will be reduced with
a close look at particular passages. But the works of Perse are so immense - in length and in scope - that at best our discoveries will be
partial. However, better a glimpse of the whole than a proliferation of
generalities or reliance on intuition alone.

Before examining Canto VII, one should at least trace the course of
that whole adventure of conquest and exploration by the human spirit.
The title itself, Anabase, indicates upward movement, ascension, an
expedition into the interior of a country and also a more particular
meaning, yet essential too in the inner thematic web of Perse's poem,
the action of mounting a horse.*2 The setting evokes the vast, desert
expanses of the Far East, punctuated by cities whose intricate and rich
economic (premodern), political, and social life forms the background
of the narrative, and whose peaceful, regulated activities are interrupted by the restless movements of nomads and military conquerors.
Except for the short opening and closing passages, all is seen, felt,
planned, dominated by the mind of one extraordinary, unnamed, highly
sensitive and thoughtful leader. More than a narrator, he and his experiences are the rich, radiating central substance of the entire poem.

The successive Cantos recount diverse episodes in the expedition,
alternating repose and construction with restlessness and continued
marches. A short opening Chanson introduces a new-born colt, a
Stranger, a spirit of novelty and open horizons. The leader, whose
voice is immediately and forcefully heard in Canto I, generating a
sense of power and of glory, of morning freshness, evokes a sojourn
of a year or so in a port city and its multitude of people. In Canto II he
is unconfined, but not alone, exploring a country of high hills, encountering Royalty, a Queen and Princess. The passage is suffused with a
spell of sensuality which is finally broken by a sudden sea wind. Canto
III takes place at harvest season, where strange, contradictory, and
often disturbing sensations traverse the atmosphere. In contrast, in
Canto IV he views with satisfaction the foundation of a city, construction,

varied activities, rejoicing in the sight. Once again in Canto V he is alone, again his solitude assuaged by nocturnal Royalty; his thoughts turn to future exploration. For a year, in Canto VI, we witness the ardent enthusiasms of military preparations - by day a sense of powerful destiny, by night the sweet, earthy aura of women. And then, Canto VII (which we will read in detail) together with the preceding Canto form the fused physical, emotional, and spiritual climax of the whole poem; here, achieving the innermost concentration and sensitivity the hero absorbs the limitless desert expanse, and from within that total absorption suddenly wells forth a renewed sombre call to action. Canto VIII follows the long march swept by rain and wind and deep thought until in Cantos IX and X the new country comes into sight, excellent augury for the future, limitless things to forge and to accomplish. At the very end, yet, the leader reaffirms his insatiable thirst for exploration, inseparable from the urge to build: "Terre arable du songe! Qui parle de bâtir? - J'ai vu la terre distribuée en de vastes espaces et ma pensée n'est pas distraite du navigateur." The terminal Chanson, resuming the unimpassioned yet sensitive tone of the first, brings the adventure to rest and to a peacefully reflective halt.*3

The opening line of Canto VII proclaims the central theme and tone of the soliloquy to follow. "Nous n'habiterons pas toujours ces terres jaunes, notre délice..." Except to inform the reader of his intentions, the decisive announcement of departure appears a bit premature, for the heights of sensation, reflexion, and fantasy of seven out of eight of the stanzas reveal unmitigated interest and delight in the present with a substratum of past rather than future.

The first four stanzas are pure embodiment of that delight. They are born of intense, absorptive sense impressions which at times are foreshadowed by and at times overlaid with metaphorical extensions, which, similarly to the "Cimetière marin", are authentically generated in immediate mental gestures. For those who have read the whole poem, the character of the narrator is well-known; but for those whose introduction is this particular passage it might be helpful to point out signs of the man of action, which are here mainly subordinated to the dreamer, signs which are reinforced as the passage progresses. First, using the word "Empire" immediately paired with "Eté", the leader imposes a human dimension of power. In the fifth stanza he addresses his soul, "tout enténébrée d'un parfum de cheval": the horse symbol, whose masculine, adventurous, earthy attributes penetrate the core of his being. Later, in stanza seven, he is concerned with finding warriors to guard the riverbeds; thus we see the leader with practical logistic concerns. And in the last stanza, his great pride bursts forth in the exclamation: "Levez les pierres à ma gloire."

Vast expanses, suspended and extended in time and space by the summer heat, "Eté plus vaste que l'Empire" - this is our opening vista seen through the eye of the narrator. The first two sentences multiply spacial references: "vaste", "Empire", "tables", "plusieurs étages", and again "la terre vaste", "aire", "à plein bords". Once the images of season and expanse are clearly imbedded, details of the landscape painted in color reinforce the sensation of heat. Yellow tones - pale embers, sulfur, honey, dry grass - include the suggestion

of kindling heat, explicitly in the embers, of course, and implicitly
also in the illusion of conflagration of pale grasses. Beyond the image
of fire there is another touch of liquid transformation - a solitary tree
against the sky seen as a green sponge from which emanates the
heaven's purple sap, sharply striking, realistic in color, and metaphorically close to the immediate visual perception. In such intense
heat, colors and forms do have an incandescent dissolving quality. The
blinding light, the fuzzy, shimmering sensations continue in the next
stanza: "Pierres à mica" which later appear as "la pierre tachée
d'ouïes", "pas une graine pure dans les barbes du vent",*4 sensations
which are then translated into sound "les essaims du silence aux ruches
de lumière" - incandescently likened to buzzing sounds. The last remark, suggested implicitly perhaps by the bee analogy, shows the narrator's personal fancies: "mon coeur prend souci d'une famille d'acridiens... "*5 One recalls Valéry's "insecte net", yet another small
creature figuring in a similar hot scene.

The next two stanzas engage in more extended visual impressions,
now tracing the forms perceived. First, the hills receding into the
distance that tenderly evoke the shapes, body markings and movements
of camels. Such is the warmth of the comparison that they appear primarily as camels, gentle camels, and secondarily as hills. To the incandescent yellow tones are now added bluish and violet colors perhaps
prefiguring the dark final shadow of the last line. But the most important note of all is the clear statement and precision of limitless extension in time: "ces fumées de sable qui s'élèvent au lieu des fleuves
morts, comme des pans de siècles en voyage... " Before, we have had
hints of this: "miel" (honey-divine nectar), "couleur de choses immortelles", "l'autre hiver", "là où les peuples s'abolissent aux poudres
mortes de la terre". What is fascinating is the natural process whereby this takes place, simply, in the day-dreams of the narrator passing
from the real visual and aural impression of incandescence to sand,
then smoke, then limitless temporal evaporation.

The fifth stanza breaks the external concentration and here the narrator speaks to himself, resuming his feelings - reverence for the
past, reverence for the present, extreme sensation of delight: "Tant
de douceur au coeur de l'homme se peut-il qu'elle faille à trouver sa
mesure?... " Can such human bliss fail to have some external natural
counterpart? Passing overhead, a flight of birds appear to confirm
his inner sense of well-being.

Up to this point, complete contentment in the present with its overtones of the past dominate. The opening of stanza six retains that
sense of calm stability, with a touch of something exotic sensed beyond
the horizon. Within this, one line, "où tournent les cancers du camphre
et de la corne... " a particularly hard poetic nut to crack, deserves
some close attention. First of all, one should be reassured to know
that Perse, as Valéry, uses all words and images advisedly; and with
Perse it seems even more that the sense is the primary concern.*6
But the problem, here as throughout his works is that the poet combines wide wordly experience, with a vast knowledge of technical scientific vocabulary, with an equally extraordinary ability to synthesize
with precision apparently incongruous or far removed sensations or

ideas. So that readers and critics alike are often left with the feeling
that it is impossible to arrive at a complete understanding. But - one
does one's best! The most immediate impression is that of alliteration,
phonetic resonance (where k sounds, r sounds and two muted ã vowel
sounds resolve to a final ɔ:) and that of a rhythmical sweep which has
the restful majesty of the alexandrin (twelve syllable count) combined
with an iambic thrust. As for the meaning, one should bear in mind
that the visual starting point is the shifting cloud formations on the
horizon. "Cancer" here certainly has a geographical, climatic meaning at its center, perhaps with an initial impetus of shape. The constellation of cancer, the crab-like form having its location in the sky,
and at the horizon, heralds the summer solstice (precisely the season
of this passage). Since the narrator is in fact looking at the horizon,
cloud formations may thus suggest a crab-like figure and then the constellation. "Camphre" is a sensually delightful product of the Far East.
"Corne" is also exotic: the port of Constantinople was thus called as
the center of commerce for products from many lands; its principal
poetic connotation is that of the cornucopia, the horn of plenty. So the
triple image "cancers du camphre et de la corne" combines climatic
geographical, exotic, and sensually full suggestions. These are a part
of the general tonal pattern of that passage. Together with "lieu saint",
"nuées calmes", "la terre tout attente", "la terre enfante des merveilles!", the whole expressed as an exclamation combines an attitude
of wonder, calm, reverence and potential pleasurable abundance.

So far, the level of attention is dreamy, absorbed in the present,
but the last two remarks ("la terre tout attente...", "la terre enfante
des merveilles") introduce the theme of change, expectancy, which in
the final stanzas rises to a crescendo. The initial sentence of stanza
seven gives the first mention of a precise moment, "midi", the point
of noon. Then something happens - a tree root cracks the tomblike
rock, although the narrator's mind is yet somnolent ("l'homme clôt
ses paupières et rafraîchit sa nuque dans les âges"). But his subsequent
thoughts open up perspectives of activity - cavalry, roads, rising rivers - with the first practical concern, where to find the warriors as
guards.

Finally, the rivers rise full flood and the earth trembles. A call to
action penetrates the narrator's consciousness. "Et soudain, ah!
soudain que nous veulent ces voix?" The challenge appears to come
from that multitude of the dead heretofore silent, its presence immobile. The narrator then proclaims his orders: "Levez...!" a threefold
call to action and to glory.

The final parenthetical statement is an extraordinarily effective,
concise poetic gesture. Foreshadowed by the migrant birds evoked in
the fifth stanza, it intones the final note of the passage, one of deep
introspective, instantaneous awareness. Combining the theme of thought
and action, a real event (leaving a trace of uneasiness)*7 is interpreted as an augury and points toward the departure.

Turning to questions of origin and intent concerning the poem as a
whole, we find the poet himself thoroughly familiar with the activities
and the regions described. Anabase was written during the period
Perse was a member of the French diplomatic corps in Peking (1916-

1921). A horseman himself, from childhood, he enjoyed frequent excursions into the Chinese provinces. In an abandoned Taoist temple, a day's journey on horseback from Peking, on a high point overlooking caravan trails towards the Northwest, Perse composed <u>Anabase</u>.*8 Expressing the nature of his interest in the desert in an interview, he places his archeological interests on a secondary plane to emphasize that what he liked most "c'était seulement un mode de vie animale et de nature, qui touche aux choses éternelles, comme toujours le désert".*9 More explicitly an explanation of the aim of this poem, Perse said then also that "<u>Anabase</u> a pour objet le poème de la solitude dans l'action. Aussi bien l'action parmi les hommes que l'action de l'esprit, envers autrui comme envers soi-même. J'ai voulu rassembler la synthèse, non pas passive mais active, de la ressource humaine."*10 <u>Anabase</u> is indeed a poem of action in the epic sense. The passage I have analyzed, one of the reflective episodes, manifests physical action only implicitly - in the plan to fare forth. Yet it certainly fulfills the goal of portraying solitude and, indeed, spiritual action of a most subtle and heroic sort.

The basis for this spiritual activity is wholly visual, immediate, imaginatively free (unshackled), with analogies and speculative developments highly introspective in nature - exactly the same framework of esthetic apprehension as in the "Cimetière marin". "De la fissure des paupières au fil des cimes m'unissant... ": the narrator consciously traces the bond between eye and land. As we discovered before, stanzas one through four and also stanza six are essentially scenes perceived by a painter but with one aural touch - "les essaims du silence" - corresponding to incandescence. Within these absorptive states, two tonal patterns dominate. One is the pure delight announced initially. It suffuses the vocabulary. It is elaborated in the soft lyrical series of descriptions of which one example will suffice to elicit the whole: "Couleur de soufre, de miel, couleur de choses immortelles... " And it is forcefully implicit in the exclamations such as "Je vous parle, mon âme! - mon âme tout enténébrée d'un parfum de cheval!" The other main pattern, both tonal and thematic, is of particular interest - it consists of expansion in space and also in time, again including a plethora of manifestations initiated by the first words "L'Eté plus vaste que l'Empire... " Space: the horizon, the long sweep of the line of hills, shifting cloud patterns in the sky, abstract geographical extensions ("plusieurs étages de climats", "les cancers du camphre et de la corne"). Time: the vast summer, with straw as remnants of the preceding winter, the repeated shades of the dead ("les peuples s'abolissent aux poudres mortes... ", "les fleuves morts", "la suite des siècles").

The most unique feature is that this expansion is not only physical, real but imperceptibly opens out into the domain of dream. There is a blurred quality between what is actually seen and what is imagined. Not just in the traditional poetic passage from subject perceived to metaphor, but in a more individual fashion, particular to the atmosphere of this passage. For the incandescence of the desert air, burnt by the sun, the equally shimmering appearance of the sands and powdery earthen shapes, the vaporous shifting clouds on the horizon all quite naturally dissolve and blend into pipe-dreams: "la fumée des songes", "les fumées de sable", "Fumées qu'un souffle nous dispute!" "Cavaleries du songe... ô routes vaines qu'échevèle un souffle jusqu'à nous!" And it is when the visually vague, but still visual, outlines are finally cut off, when one closes one's eyes ("l'homme clôt ses paupières") that the dream world - of past and future - reigns supreme (in stanzas seven and eight).

Here the spiritual activity is powerful in its freedom, but with its creative direction determined by complete receptivity. The narrator does not search, but finds, absorbing and relishing in both external and internal sensations. Indeed, he manifests in one way that "perfect identity and unity between the subject and the object" proposed by Perse as the nature of French poetry. And, more pertinent to the core of Anabase, this passage exactly relates (in reverse order) what the leader announces as his goal elsewhere in the poem: "beaucoup de choses entreprises sur les ténèbres de l'esprit - beaucoup de choses à loisir sur les frontières de l'esprit..."*11 A leisurely sensitive dream exploration precedes a descent to the depths of the soul and a call to action.

NOTES

*1 Eliot's interest in Anabase was immediate and resulted in a first translation in 1930 (London: Faber and Faber) which was revised considerably for two subsequent editions in 1938 and 1949 (New York: Harcourt Brace) which improve on the original by adhering more closely to literal English equivalents but which still are not entirely satisfactory as there is a considerable divergence of tone and a certain tendency to employ more affected turns of speech. In his preface to the 1930 edition Eliot expresses his admiration of the poem and discusses the difficulties of understanding the sequence of images.

*2 The critical commentaries on Anabase are numerous. Besides Eliot's preface, which draws heavily for its interpretation on an article by Lucien Fabre, "Publication d'Anabase" (Les Nouvelles littéraires, août 1924), the most important analyses are those of Maurice Saillet (Saint-John Perse; poète de gloire [Paris, 1952]), Alain Bosquet (Saint-John Perse [Paris, 1961]), and Arthur Knodel (Saint-John Perse [Edinburgh, 1966]). An emphasis on etymological and spiritual connotations seems to me more pertinent than literary and historical details although those should not be neglected within the broad poetic frame of reference. The study of Monique Parent, Saint-John Perse et quelques devanciers (Paris, 1960), is particularly interesting for its flexible stylistic and thematic analysis and also because the method which she employs, devised by Prof. Imbs of the Université de Nancy, is similar to the technique I have found fruitful of isolating and regrouping tonal and thematic patterns. Prof. Imbs' method consists of considering key words not only according to their syntactic arrangement but independently according to their semantic relationship which often is constructed outside of the grammatical sequence.

*3 The Canto headings proposed by Lucien Fabre (and adopted by Eliot) as well as the list worked out by Arthur Knodel are helpful in a concrete sense. They emphasize physical activity more particularly than mental states.

Fabre

I.   Arrivée du conquérant sur l'emplacement de la ville qu'il va fonder.
II.   Tracé de l'enceinte.
III. Consultation des devins.
IV. Fondation de la ville.
V.   Nostalgie de nouveaux espaces.
VI. Projets d'établissement et de fortune.
VII. Décision d'un nouveau départ.
VIII. Marche dans les déserts.
IX. Arrivée au seuil d'un grand pays.
X.   Accueil, fêtes, repos. Mais la soif de partir de nouveau; et cette fois avec le navigateur.

Knodel

I.   Establishment of a new order in a coastal region.
II.   Chthonic ritual.
III. Reaffirmation of the principle of action.
IV. Founding of the city.
V.   Nocturne: solitude of the Leader.
VI. Propaganda and recruiting.
VII. The eve of departure.
VIII. Migration to the Western Lands.
IX. Reception by the women of the new country.
X.   Celebration, census, and the pursuits of leisure.

*4 "Barbes" is a hard word to translate well. Eliot used "barbs" as the English equivalent in the 1930 translation and changed it to "beard" in 1938. The meanings in French are multiple. Beyond the most common beard, it signifies burr, rough edge on an engraved metal plate, the feathers of a quill, the beard or tip of wheat, the tail of a comet. I think that "burr" might be better to use here since it has the sense of roughness without length and phonetically blends with sounds suggested by wind.

*5 Entomology was a major scientific interest of Perse and in addition there is a warm human attraction as is illustrated by a passage from Eloges, a poem written in 1908 where he evokes the feelings and surroundings of his childhood in Guadeloupe:

"A présent laissez-moi, je vais seul.
Je sortirai, car j'ai affaire: un insecte m'attend pour traiter. Je me fais joie du gros oeil à facettes: anguleux, imprévu..." (OEuvre poétique I, 59).

*6 Perse, when speaking of his poetry does not emphasize musicality as an esthetic principle (as did Valéry), although sound values and modulations are certainly part of the final product. On the contrary he insists on exact expressions, often technical or scientific in nature. In his interview with Mazars he states: "Le poète a parfaitement le droit, et même le devoir, d'aller explorer les domaines les plus obscurs; mais plus il va loin dans cette direction, plus il doit user de moyens d'expression concrets...Je prétends que ma langue est précise et claire..." (Le Figaro littéraire, 5 novembre 1960; Honneur à Saint-John Perse, 618).

*7 Roger Caillois in his excellent book, Poétique de Saint-John Perse (Paris, 1954) suggests that his statement reveals a sudden anguish, a disturbing sense of mortality (p. 201).

*8 This biographical information comes from the presentation by Jacques Charpier, Saint-John Perse (Paris, 1962). His book is excellent also as a general introduction to Perse, the man and the poet.

*9 Interview with Mazars, Honneur à Saint-John Perse, 620. Perse also speaks here of his preference for an active life, telling of an occasion when Briand asked him what sort of diplomatic post he would prefer and when he replied "Monsieur le Président, nommez-moi en Afghanistan, un endroit où je pourrai arriver à mon bureau en bottes de cheval!..."

*10 Mazars, 621.

*11 Anabase, OEuvre poétique I, 149.

VI

EXIL IV

Exil IV

Etrange fut la nuit où tant de souffles s'égarèrent au carrefour des chambres...

Et qui donc avant l'aube erre aux confins du monde avec ce cri pour moi? Quelle grande fille répudiée s'en fut au sifflement de l'aile visiter d'autres seuils, quelle grande fille malaimée.

A l'heure où les constellations labiles qui changent de vocable pour les hommes d'exil déclinent dans les sables à la recherche d'un lieu pur?

Partout-errante fut son nom de courtisane chez les prêtres, aux grottes vertes des Sibylles, et le matin sur notre seuil sut effacer les traces de pieds nus, parmi de saintes écritures...

Servantes, vous serviez, et vaines, vous tendiez vos toiles fraîches pour l'échéance d'un mot pur.

Sur des plaintes de pluviers s'en fut l'aube plaintive, s'en fut l'hyade pluvieuse à la recherche du mot pur,

Et sur les rives très anciennes fut appelé mon nom... L'esprit du dieu fumait parmi les cendres de l'inceste.

Et quand se fut parmi les sables essorée la substance pâle de ce jour,

De beaux fragments d'histoires en dérive, sur des pales d'hélices, dans le ciel plein d'erreurs et d'errantes prémisses, se mirent à virer pour le délice du scoliaste.

Et qui donc était là qui s'en fut sur son aile? Et qui donc, cette nuit, a sur ma lèvre d'étranger pris encore malgré moi l'usage de ce chant?

Renverse, ô scribe, sur la table des grèves, du revers de ton style la cire empreinte du mot vain.

Les eaux du large laveront, les eaux du large sur nos tables, les plus beaux chiffres de l'année.

Et c'est l'heure, ô Mendiante, où sur la face close des grands miroirs de pierre exposés dans les antres.

L'officiant chaussé de feutre et ganté de soie grège efface, à grand renfort de manches, l'affleurement des signes illicites de la nuit.

Ainsi va toute chair au cilice du sel, le fruit de cendre de nos veilles, la rose naine de vos sables, et l'épouse nocturne avant l'aurore reconduite...

Ah! toute chose vaine au van de la mémoire, ah! toute chose insane aux fifres de l'exil: le pur nautile des eaux libres, le pur mobile de nos songes,

Et les poèmes de la nuit avant l'aurore répudiés, l'aile fossile
prise au piège des grandes vêpres d'ambre jaune...
  Ah! qu'on brûle, ah! qu'on brûle, à la pointe des sables, tout ce
débris de plume, d'ongle, de chevelures peintes et de toiles impures,
  Et les poèmes nés d'hier, ah! les poèmes nés un soir à la fourche
de l'éclair, il en est comme de la cendre au lait des femmes, trace
infime...
  Et de toute chose ailée dont vous n'avez usage, me composant un
pur langage sans office,
  Voici que j'ai dessein encore d'un grand poème délébile... *

In 1940, after twenty-five years of a meteoric and brilliant diplomatic
career, Perse found himself severed politically and professionally,
exiled from France, on the Atlantic coast of the United States. This
poem, written on the strands of Long Island, sprung from the well of
spiritual crisis, reflects a deep need to define poetic and human goals.
Although personal in origin and even in details of the setting, the voice
which speaks from within the whirlwind of turmoil is depersonalized,
issuing from a timeless poetic sphere.
  From a fixed setting, "Portes ouvertes sur les sables, portes ouvertes sur l'exil...", a sandy shore swept by wave, wind, and lightning flash, the succession of cataclysmic events, the passage of mythi-
cally elevated characters in the course of the seven Cantos are reached
and viewed not on foot or on horseback as in Anabase but by the imagination cosmically transformed. The scenes, interrogations, pronouncements which appear in the succession of Cantos do not, I believe,
have a clear temporal development but rather represent multiple facets
of a search for word, design, a sense of message and rhythm within
the free wild play of natural elements, with the poetic imagination bared
of preconceptions and of limiting subjects or goals. Thus he announces
"...ce n'est point errer...Que de convoiter l'aire la plus nue pour as-
sembler aux syrtes de l'exil un grand poème né de rien, un grand
poème fait de rien..."*1 Although Perse, faced by World War II, was
moved to seek a valid human tongue, he disassociates himself from
the polemic poetry of the Resistance.*2 Canto IV, which I have chosen
to analyze, most originally traces the search for signs in a wave-washed
nocturnal setting, their apparition, disappearance, and pervasive, uncommitted availability.
  "Etrange fut la nuit où tant de souffles s'égarèrent au carrefour des
chambres..." As in Canto VII of Anabase, the opening line succinctly
orients the reader as to the time, place and esthetic air of the lines to
follow. The extraordinary tonal intricacy of the whole passage as well
as within each stanza is only barely suggested by the initial word,
"Etrange". Perhaps the first theme to take note of, since it derives
from the total poem, Exil, is that of the wanderer. Here, this theme
is meshed in the dream-like queries. It is introduced by "tant de
souffles s'égarèrent"; and other phrases multiply the sense of movement, of being physically restless, uprooted and of the resulting sense
of rejection: "qui...erre aux confins du monde", "quelle grande fille
répudiée...malaimée", "vaines", "Sur des plaintes de pluviers s'en
fut l'aube plaintive, s'en fut l'hyade pluvieuse à la recherche du mot

pur". Two long questions launch the first stanza, questions of the night
dreamer, contemplating broad marine horizons, finding life-like God-
desses performing rituals to disclose for him a vital tongue. "Qui
donc erre aux confins du monde avec ce cri pour moi?...quelle grande
fille répudiée...?" Her name is divulged, "Partout-errante" in the
service of the Sibyls. She is aided by other heavenly maidens ("Servantes") who come to life in the dim coves and recesses of the shores.
Green grottoes, traces left by bare feet, the clean cloths extended
hopefully - all are concrete details which make the presence of these
women vivid and immediate. As near to us as Valéry's "Personne pure",
these figures and many other similar ones are created in Perse's poetic world with no attempt to render their real existence questionable
or to reduce them to a function of Muse-like fantasy figures, which a
down-to-earth, overly sensible reader might suppose. A suspension
of disbelief, a whole-hearted, imaginative embrace of a world not unlike that of Odilon Redon, peopled by classical figures, or the weightless magical beings of Marc Chagall, is necessary to relish the full
flavor of Perse's poetry.

The search for signs, language is pressing. "cris", "vocable",
"saintes écritures", "mot pur", these are simultaneously sensed in
the firmament and actively sought. A curiously beautiful secondary
tonal pattern suggests that message may fall from the heavens. In this
first passage, the horizon and field of action is broad and the sky is
full of stars. There is direct mention of constellations; and another
interesting obscure reference, "l'hyade pluvieuse", echoes that. The
Hyades are, in astronomy, a cluster of stars in the constellation
Taurus, considered by the Greeks to be a sign of rain when they rise
with the sun. In Greek mythology, the Hyades were daughters of Atlas,
so grieved by the loss of their brother that Zeus bore them to the sky
transformed into stars. So that the connotation of grief ("plainte" and
"plaintive" are also in that same sentence) blends with the loneliness
of exil. And the explicit statement of rain combines with other expressions to create an expectation that things may fall from the sky: "les
constellations labiles (unstable, tending to fall)...déclinent"; and then
we see the Servants who are holding out their clean cloths "pour l'é-
chéance d'un mot pur". But one should not try, I think, to reduce these
patterns to a distinct rational message or wish - poetic inspiration
conceived as heaven-sent or present in natural phenomena, for instance.*3 For the evidence is rather that the main elements of the
stanza are mixed, intertwined. "Les constellations déclinent dans les
sables à la recherche d'un lieu pur"; "s'en fut l'hyade...à la recherche
du mot pur": the place, the stars, the search for language seen intentionally mingled and not to be reduced to a single syntactical logical
order or even to be set up as metaphorical equivalents.

At dawn, in the second stanza, the voice of the narrator, enveloped
in the pleasant, dizzying nocturnal cosmic kaleidoscope, still wonders
who accompanied him in his venture and perhaps even carried him
away, appropriated his song: "Et qui donc, cette nuit, a...pris encore
malgré moi l'usage de ce chant?" The first sensation is strong, a residual happy whirl which is reminiscent of the opening pages of Proust's
A la recherche du temps perdu where one is caught up in the fruitful

confusion of the dreamer.*4 Phrases suggesting this whirl are "Fragments d'histoire en dérive... se mirent à virer" and "pales d'hélices". "Hélice" is a most interesting word. It is the spiral of a screw or propeller. It is also a name given to the Big Dipper which always rotates around the North Pole. Etymologically it comes from a Greek word signifying to turn, to roll around. These images all combine nocturnal sky phenomena with a suggestion of an ocean voyage and convey a sense of rotation. Also, the tone of pleasure is explicit in "beaux", implicit as a homonym in "pales d'hélices", that word recurring openly in "le délice du scoliaste".

Then we see the theme of dissolution. Three long sentences, the first an intimate command, describes an inevitable process whereby the words which have been recorded during the night are washed away. "Renverse, ô scribe, sur la table des grèves... la cire empreinte du mot vain." The message appears under diverse names - "histoires", "chant", "mot", "chiffres" - all in the respectful care of classical truth-bearers - "scoliaste", "scribe", "l'officiant" - and this message disappears at the moment when the tide sweeps away all traces from the sands. The second sentence (beginning "Les eaux du large laveront... ") states this most unambiguously. The final long imaginatively transfigured repetition of the same idea is to my mind one of the most beautiful of the whole passage.

> Et c'est l'heure, ô Mendiante, où sur la face close des grands miroirs de pierre exposés dans les antres.
> L'officiant chaussé de feutre et ganté de soie grège efface, à grand renfort de manches, l'affleurement des signes illicites de la nuit.

These lines represent a perfect poetic amalgam of the setting. The tide-washed, rocky, and sandy shore whose sands and green grottoes (introduced in the first stanza) reappear as mirrors of stone, caves. The French word "antres" has a very mysterious, solemn echo. Gray, silent tones of the sand are suggested exquisitely by the costume of the officiating priest, "chaussé de feutre et ganté de soie grège", while the gentle sweep of waves erasing patterns on the sand formed in the past hours is embodied by his gesture "à grand renfort de manches", a phrase interspersed which breaks the otherwise unbroken rhythm of the sentence as does a wave disturbing the smooth surface of a pool.

The last stanza resumes and reinforces necessary destruction of these traces and of the language of the night. First, this obliteration is seen as inevitable. Then it is actively ordered ("Ah! qu'on brûle, ah! qu'on brûle... tout ce débris... "), obliteration of all which is beautiful but vain. The word vain carries many meanings: hollow, futile, empty pride; but perhaps most centrally here that which is perishable or unstable because of those very qualities. All of these tonal elements are prominent in the following lengthy pattern: "Ainsi va toute chair", "cendre" (used twice), "sables", "l'épouse nocturne avant l'aurore reconduite... ", "toute chose vaine au van de la mémoire", "toute chose insane au fifres de l'exil", "débris de plume, d'ongle, chevelures peintres", "trace infime". Hardly a phrase within that sequence does

not contain some variation of these attributes – a tribute to the con-
cision and subtlety of the poet. These are destined to disappear but
nonetheless contain a real though temporary beauty. "Fruit", "rose
naine", "l'épouse nocturne" are all in themselves lovely. One other
word which was changed from the 1945 edition can be added to that pattern, "calice" (flower-cup; also chalice). Its counterpart in the 1960
text, "cilice", retains all but one of the phonetic elements but drops
the connotation of beauty to emphasize a religious theme, repeated by
"cendre" and later "vêpres".

However, the main tone of this final stanza contrasts with the dream-
like quality of the other two by virtue of its firmness. On the one hand,
there is partially bitter recognition of impermanence – "Ainsi va..."
On the other hand, there is the series of exclamations introduced by
"Ah!" which reduce the pain of that recognition by controlling and even
ordering the destruction of things impure. But there is also, at the end,
an equally determined but calm intent to resume the search, fully aware,
even perhaps desiring, the inherently free and unstable quality of such
poetic language.

> Et de toute chose ailée dont vous n'avez usage, me composant un
> pur langage sans office,
> Voici que j'ai dessein encore d'un grand poème délébile...

All winged things ("souffle", "aile" repeated throughout the poem are
metaphorically akin to the shifting sands), free and unfettered by practical functions ("usage"), therein lies the source of language equally
outside the realm of institutional goals or arguments.*5 "Un pur langage sans office": a language whose source and movement is autonomous.
That such speech should be as evanescent as signs on the night sands
is not disturbing but rather quite natural. Earlier in Exil the poet says
quite simply, "...à nulles pages confiées, la pure amorce de ce chant".
This attitude is quite in keeping with Perse's life-long preference for
immediate experience, for knowledge of a precise and concrete nature
(geology, entomology, archeology etc.), for consciously distant relations with the literary world and literary productions. He once said in
a manner more serious than flippant, "un livre, c'est la mort d'un
arbre!"*6

Far from being, like Anabase, a poem of action at one pole and of
receptivity at the other, Exil is rather a poetic search. "J'interroge",
says The Poet in Vents. But, if questions are posed, the answers do
not emerge clearly. Instead, intellectually the poem partakes of the
same quality of evanescence as the traces on the sand and the illicit
signs of the night wiped out at dawn. Another interesting characteristic
is that the web of dream and reality is constructed differently. Here,
the point of departure in time and in space is carefully indicated but
instead of progressing from direct perception of a real scene to an imaginative extension, with the text laden heavily with direct sense data
(color, line, sound), the physical setting is visible and clear under-
neath the concerns and activities of an immediately established poetic
world. One feels that the narrator may well be there, at night, by the
sea. Yet his voice is mainly speaking from within the sphere of winged

maidens wandering free as the wind, the sphere of scribes, priests, acolytes performing rites on the sands and in sea-grottoes. Thus, the unity between poet and poem, subject and object is immediate and inseparable. The priest, shod in felt and gloved in raw silk, has, as if from time immemorial, taken shape and substance from the neutral, soft textures of the sand. He fulfills the goal, "s'y confondre même substantiellement". The poetic sense and pleasure of this passage seem to me inextricably bound in the mythical figures and actions whose existence and relation to any "thought" or sense perception far transcend a possible breakdown into metaphorical components.

NOTES

*1 Exil, OEuvre poétique I, 168.

*2 Although Perse stated that Exil was not a poem about the French Resistance, he favored the Resistance. Throughout the thirties in his influential role as political advisor in the French Government he opposed appeasement of Germany for which reason he was summarily relieved of his function as Secrétaire général by Paul Reynaud in 1940. In an interview in Arts ("Quatre heures avec Saint-John Perse", 8 novembre 1960), Perse expresses his opinion that because of the Resistance the vitality of the country was renewed and strengthened ethically, intellectually, and physically. Concerning the distance between him and de Gaulle, François Mauriac (who had known Perse for years) said that if Perse was opposed to thè Allied recognition of de Gaulle as the official head of the French government during the occupation, it was a question of political propriety. "Bloc-notes", Express, 8 décembre 1960).

*3 Charpier, for instance, interprets such passages quite literally as indicating the divine (in a broad sense) nature of poetic inspiration (pp. 95-98).

*4 "Un homme qui dort tient en cercle autour de lui le fil des heures, l'ordre des années et des mondes..."; "...le bouleversement sera complet dans les mondes désorbités, le fauteuil magique le fera voyager à toute vitesse dans le temps et dans l'espace..." (Marcel Proust, A la recherche du temps perdu, Paris, 1959; Vol. I, 5).

*5 This is similar to the aim of Mallarmé, "Donner un sens plus pur aux mots de la tribu", but without the tendency towards hermeticism.

*6 Mazars, Honneur à Saint-John Perse, 619-620. Pierre Guerre ("Dans la haute maison de mer: rencontres avec Saint-John Perse", Honneur à Saint-John Perse, 168-180) reports that in all the time that Perse was working for the Library of Congress he never borrowed a book from the collections for himself. This, of course, does not mean that he did not read. His tastes in reading were classical (Tacitus, Persius, Racine) and scientific (Audubon, naturalists of all periods, eighteenth century to modern).

VII

AMERS

In its immensity and sweep, this poem stretches to nearly unbelievable limits the fluid play of Perse's poetic thought processes and therefore also the reader's capacity to assimilate and grasp its import. Its external form is that of a Greek ode. "Invocation", "Strophe", "Choeur", "Dédidace" accumulate their varied functions and eloquent tales throughout nearly two hundred pages! If one's patience holds strong, unpressured and repeated readings reveal a firmly articulated panegyric inspiration, the whole masterfully balanced in a succession of varied rhythms, internal structures, and highly differentiated poetic voices.*1 Its composition was undertaken in 1948 while Perse was still in the United States and it was published as a whole in 1957. Chronologically it follows the series of exile poems of which three - Pluies, Neiges, Vents - initiated the highly personal form where a natural phenomenon serves not only as title with varied symbolic overtones but also as a concrete base carrying out to an impressive degree the poet's goal: fusion of subject and object.

In this case the title, Amers, is suggestively rich. The basic meaning has no exact English equivalent. It signifies the fixed points on the coast permitting navigators to chart their course.*2 So, first and foremost the poem deals with landmarks for poetic seafarers. But of course the word for sea, "mer", resounds loudly from within; and the adjective "amer" (bitter) suggests the saline flavor of seawater. Basically, Amers then continues the esthetic principle of Pluies, Neiges, and Vents with one important difference, namely, that the form and often the style of this poem do not follow the rhythm of the natural element (as do the others) but rather is structured according to the dignified Greek song of praise.

As a major composition within the whole range of that poet's work, the marine setting, symbol, and substance come as naturally as did that of the "Cimetière marin" for Valéry. Perse was born on an island in Guadeloupe, with the mystery and familiarity of the ocean surrounding him during his childhood. He voyaged far and wide on the high seas throughout his career as diplomat and later as poet. His house in France, where he now spends the summer months, is on a peninsula in the Mediterranean, perched on cliffs overlooking the water.*3 In addition, from his earliest works ocean waves, salt air, the spirit of marine exploration reappear in imagery and theme, from Eloges to Exil of which he even states that the poem's alliterations, assonance, and incantations are physically bound by the rhythm of waves.*4 More

generally, Perse explained that in a poet's philosophy: "...sa mé-
trique...qu'on lui impute rhétorique, ne tend encore qu'au mouvement
et à la fréquentation du mouvement, dans toutes ses ressources vi-
vantes, les plus imprévisibles. D'où l'importance en tout, pour le
poète, de la Mer."*5 Little wonder, then, that in the opening lines of
Amers the Poet, from the stone platform of the antique theater open
to the marine horizon, immense and green, should joyfully intone
"Inonde, ô brise, ma naissance!" Little wonder that in the final transe-
like incantation of the "Choeur" one should hear:

> En toi mouvante, nous mouvant, nous te disons Mer innommable:
> muable et meuble dans ses mues, immuable et même dans sa masse;
> diversité dans le principe et parité de l'Etre, véracité dans le men-
> songe et trahison dans le message; toute présence et toute absence,
> toute patience et tout refus - absence, présence; ordre et démence -
> licence!...*6 *

Lines which are compressed, the pitch poetically wild and redundant,
a synthesis of fluidity and contrary principles. Little wonder finally
that the immensity of the whole work should seem sanctioned by the
immensity of the Sea itself.

An explanation of the outlines of the poem and its broad aims comes
from the pen of the author himself in a letter to a Swedish writer. The
"Invocation", he explains, is a prologue in which the Poet presents
himself, defines the shape and goal of his project, salutes the Sea,
source of life and of poetic genesis. The "Strophe" presents the action
of the drama, its eight human configurations facing the Sea "pour l'interrogation, l'adjuration, l'imprécation, l'initiation, l'appel ou la cé-
lébration".*7 The "Choeur", then, embraces the collective voice to
celebrate the Sea, source of power, of knowledge, massively proclaim-
ing its role of challenge and guide in human destiny, identifying it as
"l'Etre universel". In his presentation Perse appears to attach the
most value and significance to this depersonalized, all-inclusive section. The short "Dédicace" finally, he states, liberates the Poet after
the accomplishment of his task. This exposition gives a very traditional
formal structure to the work. What is most striking is his repeated
emphasis on metaphysical aims and overtones, stressing on the one
hand the highest eternal goals and achievements of human destiny and
on the other the Sea as both a focus and a source of perpetual force.

This account does not entirely convey the force, variety, and sense
of the poem as experienced (the experience admittedly a personal one).
In the "Invocation" one first sees the Poet's extreme enthusiasm and
joy surrounded by images of light, festivity, green marine expanses.
Then his eagerness to speak and his reverence and discretion dominate
and finally the personal lyric mood gives way to a grandiose evocation
of the stage readied for the drama, peopled magnificently with Princes,
Regents, Messengers, Prophets, Magicians, Virgins, Pirates. The list
is long and noble. Of particular interest is his spontaneous avowal:
"Et comment il nous vint à l'esprit d'engager ce poème, c'est ce qu'il
faudrait dire. Mais n'est-ce pas assez d'y trouver son plaisir?"*8
This statement of motivation differs greatly from that of Perse and may

represent a truer poetic voice.

The eight sections of the "Strophe" are most original. They present diverse human groups, their aspirations, enacting rituals with the Sea as a background and as an integral part of the subconscious ebb and flow of their thoughts and of the poet's descriptions of their gestures. After a great panorama of coastal cities, their constructions, activities deployed along the waterfront, the first to speak is the "Maître d'astres et de navigation". He not only embodies ambitions of commerce, conquest, and other avid human ventures (including that of piracy) but equally those of knowledge, exploration, highest spiritual quests. Next, the "Tragédiennes" initiate action on the stage of the theatre. We see their gestures, rituals, masks and costumes; and in a final act of submission and reverence to the Sea, we see them bare body and soul, offer up their veils, ornaments, instruments as tribute and in appeal for a renewal of the ritual word, "Textuelle, la Mer". Then appear the "Patriciennes" in royal splendor, sensitive, aware of their isolation; by dream and desire they seek solace, viewing the ocean; joining the stage of the drama they find therein their tensions tempered by participation in ceremony: "Honneur et Mer! schisme des Grands! déchirement radieux..." The next section, short, is entitled "Langage que fut la Poétesse". It is a strangely beautiful, lyrical quintessence of feminine, spiritual, bitter-sweet quest for the ineffable. The following two passages evoke young girls and they complement each other. The first, "Et cette fille chez les prêtres", weaves a perceptive fusion and understanding of the lovely, evanescent, shifting sea treasures; the voice is that of a feminine spirit which is young, pure, and detached. In contrast, "Un soir promu de main divine" fills the scene with young girls who are active, ready and eager for initiation in life and love; the free spaces of the beach are a natural setting for their effervescence. The eighth section (which we will read closely) is their call across the waters to a wanderer, another "Etranger", a hoped-for suitor. Finally the ninth and longest section of the "Strophe", "Etroits sont les vaisseaux", is perhaps the most extraordinary of the whole sequence, a night of love fully consummated, a dialogue between man and woman, passionate, sweeping. This poem is one extended fusion of Sea, emotions, and bodily contours and movements. In the end, the man leaves for adventure, solitude in his heart, restless for action. "...Au coeur de l'homme, solitude. Etranger l'homme. Sans rivage près de la femme riveraine."

So the entire sequence of the "Strophe" moves from a masculine introduction, the city with its ambitious enterprise and activity, the navigator's brilliant and acquisitive mind, to a varied central section where the characters and action are of an entirely and richly feminine cast, to the sexual coalescence of man, woman, and sea at the end of which emerges again the strong male dominance. It is effective rhythmically from the imposing opening to the lyrical development to the climatic resolution. It is effective expression also, I think, of Perse's comprehension and appreciation of both the sensitive and the forceful, of the female and male human components with his final personal emphasis on the latter.

Next in sequence is the "Choeur", that hymn of glory to the Sea which enumerates and repeats in ritual fashion the multitudinous aspects of the object of its worship: Sea of divine presence, bordering on folly; Sea of celebration; Sea of exploit and action; primordial source of life and thought. After such pageantry, the brief and powerful "Dédicace" sounds a splendid culminating note when the Poet crowns his work, bows, and withdraws.

Amers VIII

"Etranger dont la voile..."

Etranger, dont la voile a si longtemps longé nos côtes, (et l'on entend parfois de nuit le cri de tes poulies),
Nous diras-tu quel est ton mal, et qui te porte, un soir de plus grande tiédeur, à prendre pied parmi nous sur la terre coutumière?

***

"Aux baies de marbre noir striées de blanches couvaisons
1 La voile fut de sel, et la griffe légère. Et tant de ciel nous fut-il songe?
Ecaille, douce écaille prise au masque divin,
Et le sourire au loin sur l'eau des grandes lèpres interdites...

Plus libre que la plume à l'éviction de l'aile,
2 Plus libre que l'amour à l'évasion du soir,
Tu vois ton ombre, sur l'eau mûre, quitte enfin de son âge,
Et laisses l'ancre dire le droit parmi l'églogue sous-marine.

Une plume blanche sur l'eau noire, une plume blanche vers la gloire
3 Nous fit soudain ce très grand mal, d'être si blanche et telle, avant le soir...
Plumes errantes sur l'eau noire, dépouilles du plus fort,
Vous diront-elles ô Soir, qui s'est accompli là?

Le vent portait des hautes terres, avec ce goût d'arec et d'âtres
4 morts qui très longtemps voyage,
Les Dames illustres, sur les caps, ouvraient aux feux du soir une narine percée d'or,
Et douce encore se fit la mer au pas de la grandeur.
La main de pierre du destin nous sera-t-elle encore offerte?...

C'est la christe-marine qui sur vos grèves mûrissait
5 Ce goût de chair encore entre toutes chairs heureuses,
Et la terre écriée sur ses rives poreuses, parmi la ronce avide et les roses vives
De l'écume, nous fut chose légère et chose plus dispendieuse

Que lingerie de femme dans les songes, que lingerie de l'âme dans les songes." *

"Et l'homme de mer est dans nos songes. Meilleur des hommes, viens et prends!..." At the end of the seventh section ("Un soir promu de main divine"), the girls, ready for love, thus introduce their lyrical summons in section eight.*9 Named in the opening lines, "Etranger",

Perse's prototype of the eternally adventurous spirit, he appears, remarkably close to shore, real, by virtue of the audible detail in parentheses ("et l'on entend parfois de nuit le cri de tes poulies"). The girls, questioning, then announce his arrival; and by their words they reveal to us the tone of pleasure, "un soir de plus grande tiédeur", with a hint of distress, "quel est ton mal", which characterize their free-winged lyrical chant to follow.

A visual setting underlies the expression of hopeful pleasure in the first stanza. Beneath the emotive message - the main sense of these lines - and beneath what may be on first reading puzzling imagery, one can see the scene clearly: bays encircled by black cliffs, the different strata of the rock lined with white traces of roosts and nesting places of seabirds; a white sail on the water, the boat's wake scoring the surface; a wide expanse of sky. It may be helpful to look closely at some of the puzzling images. "Couvaison" is semantically impertinent: it refers to a time, the breeding season, whereas one would expect a word denoting the nests themselves. The reason for Perse's choice? Perhaps it seemed phonetically and especially rhythmically more suitable than "niches". Perhaps also because its sense, the mating season, fits thematically with the main subject of the passage - love, the time for love. "Sel" to describe the white sails is of course consistent by color. But one should bear in mind also that it is a favorite word in Perse's lexicon, similar to "pur" for Valéry, whose charm for the author seems to go beyond any rational list of connotations, having its source also perhaps in aural pleasure and wide emotional personal suggestions. For Perse, the saying "the spice of life" should be modified to "the salt of life". As for "griffe", it can be explained by a spontaneous relation in visual perception. Just as the boats were seen as doves in the opening lines of the "Cimetière marin", the trace of the boat on the flat surface of the water does indeed resemble the stroke of a claw. In addition, however, the idea of the claw may be related (consciously or unconsciously) simply by the suggestion of birds already in the poet's mind, having just used the word "couvaison". In the next line, "écaille" (fish scale; oyster shell; flake of wood, marble or metal) refers in part, I think, to the sails transformed imaginatively, another touch of sea imagery, but can also be related directly to the material of which the ritual mask is made. "Masque divin" reiterates the theme of ceremony, theme basic to the entire poem, of course, and with reference here to the initiation to love. Finally, "les grandes lèpres interdites" are ambiguous grammatically - they could modify either "sourire" or "eau" - but to try to argue for one or the other would seem rather like poetic quibbling. The effect, and probable function, is to strike again the subdominant note of ill ("mal"). If the exact relation and source of images may appear ambiguous, the tone is clear: sweetness and joy, woven into the word sequence by the words "blanche couvaison", "légère", "ciel... songe", "douce", "sourire" and rhythmically prominent in the sentence, "La voile fut de sel, et la griffe légère." Here, an alexandrine whose pause falls halfway, at the traditional hemistich, catches the ear,*10 a regular, well-known, wave-like rhythm which to the English ear also falls into a familiar pattern (∪-∪∪-∪∪---) quick and light.

Freedom, release this is the thematic impetus opening stanza two.
"Plus libre... Plus libre" is the exclamation introducing the first two
lines; and the phrases which terminate each line, first "l'éviction de
l'aile", the "l'évasion du soir" and after that "quitte enfin de son âge"
all represent an act of delivrance and what is even more striking, delivrance from something in each case ("aile", "soir", "âge") which
does not seem particularly confining, in fact rather unrestrained and
unrestraining in itself!*11 So the emancipation is startlingly open
ended as well as openly begun. There is a wide sweep too in the sounds
and rhythm. The long sentence is broken at irregular intervals, the
second line quite long and slowly paced with the entire stanza punctuated
by a soft, ample internal rime: "noire... gloire, soir... noir, Soir." The
person addressed, "tu", is still the Stranger. And the final lines, particularly the last, bring him and the movement to a point of rest, not
to constrain the new found freedom but rather to permit its consum-
mation. In that last line "ancre", "droit", "églogue", "sous-marine"
contribute to the sense of stationary resolution. "Ancre", "droit" by
their meaning are stabilizing elements, "sous-marine" by weight of
its depths. The phonetic sequence of all of these words, an initial ã
providing a new sombre sound which is reinforced by the hard twinned
consonants, d͜, d͜, g͜, g͜, ("l'ancre dire le droit parmi l'églogue... ").
Lyric transport sweeps unbroken through the whole of stanza three.
The feather image had its source implicitly in "couvaisons" of the first
stanza and was used and placed in clear sight at the beginning of the
next stanza ("... la plume à l'éviction de l'aile"). This image now recalls first the sail on the water ("une plume blanche sur l'eau noire")
but it transcends any direct concrete and unrestricted metaphor. It is
repeated as a refrain, widened in scope to embody sail, bird, multitudinous winged flocks suddenly eliciting a profound emotion. It even
seems to become that emotion, disembodied, so that the searching,
sweetly anxious question of the last line, "Vous diront-elles ô Soir,
qui s'est accompli là?" is addressed to them, the feathers. Implicit
in the lyricism and the anxious sweetness is of course the desire for
love. And "dépouilles du plus fort", "qui s'est accompli là?" are probably subconscious sexual associations. "Soir" is majestically the night
of initiation.
An entirely different tone and visionary scene follow in stanza four.
The vision is of promontories dominating the seascape with the far
reaches of land and ocean felt in the sweep of the wind and smelled in
the residual scents which come from afar. "Le vent portait des hautes
terres, avec ce goût d'arec et d'âtres morts qui très longtemps
voyage."*12 And it is also seen in the sunset, "les feux du soir". All
of this is background for a sense of grandeur. The heights, the expanses and especially the unexpected figures of illustrious Ladies,
"Les Dames illustres", adorned with golden nose rings, majestic in
size and splendor. Again, as in the preceding stanza, the thoughts and
hopes about love are resumed in a question at the end, "La main de
pierre du destin nous sera-t-elle encore offerte?... " An earlier version (with the same syllabic measure) was worded, "Ta main de pierre,
Commandeur... " The Commander was probably the Stranger renamed.
While that wording introduces another person partaking of the same

dignity as the Ladies, the definitive wording using "destin" is more impersonal, less immediately forceful perhaps. Yet it closes the stanza with a broader, timeless impact.

Finally, an overwhelming, intricately woven expression of sensual presence and happiness closes the poem. Entirely depersonalized, constructed completely of images, its images are so concrete, so absolutely attributes of things present on the sea shore that it communicates with equal force both its own reality and that of the sensual dreams of the girls. The succession of tonal elements, of images is so packed and intrinsically tied within the syntax and the natural flow of that one long sentence, that I find it not only difficult but here particularly something of a critical crime to break it down. But once that risky critical game is begun it is impossible to stop. Here are the first three lines:

> C'est la christe-marine qui sur vos*13 grèves mûrissait
> Ce goût de chair encore entre toutes chairs heureuses,
> Et la terre écriée sur ses rives poreuses, parmi la ronce avide
> et les roses vives

"Grèves", "terre", "rives" all provide the solid base of earth - which is fertile. From it are conceived and ripen ("mûrissait") layers of vegetation: the flowers "la christe-marine", and "roses vives" as well as "ronce avide". The first are lovely, the second is pointed sharp and all are components of sexual fantasies, images and gestures. The sharp tone is present too in the word "écriée", by sound and sense, similarly in "avide" and by sound alone in "vives". Flesh itself, in connection with the plants, is doubly stated in the second line. There is sensual pleasure in "entre toutes chairs heureuses" and receptivity suggested in "rives poreuses".

Further, a most extraordinary poetic metamorphosis takes place between the end of the line last quoted, "...la ronce avide et les roses vives", and the next one, "De l'écume, nous fut chose légère et chose plus dispendieuse." The thorn and rose images are first directly connected thought-wise with the shore and its vegetation. However they become syntactically tied to the water, "de l'écume". Can they be metaphorically allied with foam? Perhaps the eager thorns correspond to the sharp stinging touch and taste sensation of foamy swirling sea-eddies, while the roses have possibly a visual similarity with rounded white frothy swirls. However audacious as a technique, since the lines read and can be imaginatively absorbed quite naturally, one does not find them shocking or disturbing. Certainly their intention is not to startle - as is often the case in Surrealist poetry. One cannot imagine Perse saying as did Breton at the end of his novel, Nadja: "La beauté sera CONVULSIVE ou ne sera pas."*14 Or even Valéry's idea that the poet will employ unusual techniques to "séduire, foudroyer" is far from Perse's naturally integrated poetic transformation.*15

The final note of the stanza and of the whole passage is much simpler in its statement and content. Our attention returns to familiar feminine garments and an aura of feminine day-dreams. The whole song subsides and is resumed in an impression of things light and costly, evoked as "lingerie" in the closing line. The rhythm is softly balanced in a

pair of ten syllable waves. The personal word "femme" is imperceptibly (because the phonetic change is slight) modulated into the purely
spiritual "lingerie de l'âme dans les songes" - the first noun of that
sequence is material, but light and bordering on the immaterial, and
the last two are completely incorporeal.

Considering the passage as a whole, and in comparison with the two
previously analyzed, one notes that here the voice which speaks is not
that of a narrator (as in Anabase) or of a poet, close to Perse himself
(as in Exil). The voice is rather a collective, imaginative, one is
tempted to say almost subconscious expression of the young girls.
Transcending the personal, it is less an audible voice than a thought
sequence which pours forth from within. In this, I think, Perse truly
accomplishes what he states in the letter to the Swedish writer: "C'est
l'intégrité même de l'homme - et de l'homme de tout temps... que j'ai
voulu dresser sur le seuil le plus nu, face à la nuit splendide de son
destin en cours."*16 And, here the fusion of subject and object, of
setting and experience appears as complete as in the Canto IV of Exil
but with a new and different balance. The setting is clear, stable, and
unchanging from start to finish. Also, there is no apparent passage of
time. The only element of duration is in the successive thought configurations of the mind. What is striking is the substance, dominant
and real, of the images which one might normally term metaphors but
which, although borrowing their concrete vivid qualities from the setting, exist on their own merits in the poetic scene, their imaginative,
connotative, suggestive qualities forming the basis of their body and
power.

There is yet another interesting, original feature of the passage.
Comfortingly familiar, one senses immediately the tonal unity suggested in the opening statement. It consists of warmth, pleasure,
lightness on the one hand and on the other an underlying but neither
destructive nor obtrusive sharpness, tension, a sense of ill. One is
struck, however, by the fact that there is no progression either of
theme or tone. The theme of love appears throughout with no change
either in the form of the conception or in the attitude towards it. There
is variety of tone: spontaneous immediate pleasure, then a sense of
freedom, then awareness of grandeur, then earthy fruition. But I do
not sense any particular point of emotional climax, of crescendo and
decrescendo, nor a connected tonal movement with its own inner coherence leading to a final conclusion. This is true equally of the way
in which the stanzas are put together from the point of view of idea and
imagery. Except for the recurrent marine imagery, and in particular
that of the feather, there is no "fil de logique" between the contents of
one stanza and the next. Each stanza is like a scene, emotionally coherent from within, taken from a dream sequence. No need is felt for
connection or linking on the part of the poet. Nor is the lack of same
felt as disturbing by the reader. While never remotely tied to the
Surrealist movement, Perse was nevertheless admired in a way by
Breton. As early as the First Surrealist Manifesto in 1924, Breton
described him as "surréaliste à distance". And later (1950) in an
article devoted to Perse's work he describes one line: "Lieu...plaqué
de mirages, assombri de prestiges, écartelé à l'image de ce présent,

le nôtre, entre le 'tout établi'... et le conjectural'... "*17 This commentary would be appropriate for the passage we have just read, poetry unconstrained by the need for semantically and syntactically linear forms, rationally conceived.

Amers

"Dédicace"

Midi, ses fauves, ses famines, et l'An de mer à son plus haut
    sur la table des Eaux...
--Quelles filles noires et sanglantes vont sur les sables violents
    longeant l'effacement des choses?
Midi, son peuple, ses lois fortes... L'oiseau plus vaste sur son
    erre voit l'homme libre de son ombre, à la limite de son bien.
Mais notre front n'est point sans or. Et victorieuses encore de
    la nuit sont nos montures écarlates.

Ainsi les Cavaliers en armes, à bout de Continents,
    font au bord des falaises le tour des péninsules.
--Midi, ses forges, son grand ordre... Les promontoires ailés
    s'ouvrent au loin leur voie d'écume bleuissante.
Les temples brillent de tout leur sel. Les dieux s'éveillent dans
    le quartz.
Et l'homme de vigie, là-haut, parmi ses ocres, ses craies fauves,
    sonne midi le rouge dans sa corne de fer.

Midi, sa foudre, ses présages; Midi, ses fauves au forum et son
    cri de pygargue sur les rades désertes!...
--Nous qui mourrons peut-être un jour disons l'homme immortel au
    foyer de l'instant.
L'Usurpateur se lève sur sa chaise d'ivoire. L'amant se lave de
    ses nuits.
Et l'homme au masque d'or se dévêt de son or en l'honneur de la
    Mer.*

The short last section of Amers represents in concentrated force the panegyric of the whole. Resuming a number of themes and images which characterize other passages, it is less interesting for its subject or for unusual stylistic patterns than for its inspired and colorful tonal impact. Choosing, as did Valéry for the "Cimetière marin", a moment of absolute brilliance and altitude as the temporal focus, Noon, Perse sustains that extension of temporal to near eternal throughout the three stanzas. The word "Midi" recurs as a leitmotif, the main focus of attention until at the end, the very end "la Mer" receives the last gesture of praise which is her due.

The first line in a broad gesture traces horizontally and vertically majestic temporal and spacial dimensions. First, "Midi" conveys the sight of the sun at its zenith. Then in "l'An de mer", the word sea is left uncapitalized further to accentuate a long, important duration of time. Finally, "la table des Eaux" evokes a stable, broad physical expanse. There is here, and in the other stanzas also, a shift back and forth from abstract to concrete, from the natural to the human. The sequence of people and scenes includes, apparently chosen at random, a variety of subjects. The "filles... longeant l'effacement des choses... " recall the scene, characters and disappearing traces of Canto IV from Exil. The sentence "L'oiseau plus vaste sur son erre... " gives us a bird's eye view, unlimited freedom and mastery both for the bird and for the man below. The crucial revelation of the poet's stance, however, is reserved for the last - "Mais notre front n' est point sans or. Et victorieuses encore de la nuit sont nos montures écarlates." These ornaments and attitudes denote pride, devotion ("front... or") and successful active conquest. The tone is powerful and even cruel: "fauves", "famines", "filles noires et sanglantes", "sables violents", "lois fortes", "victorieuses". It is a tone which is aggressive and moreover redundant, cumulatively emphasized in the development of the passage: "Midi, ses forges... " "Midi, sa foudre... ses fauves au forum... " The f sounds accentuate the effect of the individual meanings which have as a common ground - strength.

The second stanza is full of more particular and divinely glorified activities. "Cavaliers" and "Continent" are raised to a position of honor, capitalized; armed horsemen make the tour of the limits of their land. Again, there is a clear, colorful scene painted: cliffs, peninsulas, promontories, a foamy blue sea providing a background for the dazzling white stone temples. And the watchman from cliffs of sandstone, no doubt, orange and ochre in shade, blasts forth on his trumpet, blasts forth red (!) noon.

The sharp sound, integral to the tone of power and violence, is echoed in the next stanza by the sea-eagle's cry. Only in the final three lines does the poetic idiom touch on theme and operate a resolution. "Nous qui mourrons peut-être un jour disons l'homme immortel au foyer de l'instant." There, succinctly and with considerable poetic dignity, is the central philosophical aim of the poem. It is particularly effective because it derives man's eternal qualities not abstractly but from the base of the immediate, kindled on the hearth of the instant. To culminate the ritual, three gestures are enacted whereby in tribute three characters abdicate symbolically their functions in the poem: "L'Usurpateur se lève sur sa chaise d'ivoire. L'amant se lave de ses nuits. Et l'homme au masque d'or se dévêt de son or en l'honneur de la Mer." Gestures which add a touch of esthetic immediacy, in action. Gestures which illustrate that which Perse conceived of as a most desirable and natural motivation for his poetry, " éloges" . *18

NOTES

*1 Arthur Knodel suggests that this poem should be read several times quite rapidly and silently; and he refers to Perse's own counsel on this score which, it seems to me, is quite appropriate. In his letter to George Huppert he says: "...de telles oeuvres [les longues suites poétiques françaises] se refusent instamment à toute récitation, publique ou privée, et même à toute lecture intime faite à haute voix... " (Honneur à Saint-John Perse, 657-658).

*2 According to Bloch and Wartburg (Dictionnaire étymologique de la langue française [Paris, 1960]), the word "amer" derives from the Norman "merc" (boundary mark) which in turn came from the Dutch "merk" (limit).

*3 Pierre Guerre describes the site and the house beautifully in "Dans la haute maison de mer..." , Honneur à Saint-John Perse, 168-180.

*4 Letter to Archibald Macleish (9 sept. 1941) accompanying the manuscript of Exil.

*5 Lettre à Roger Caillois (26 janvier 1953), Poétique de Saint-John Perse (Paris, 1954), 180-181.

*6 Amers, OEuvre poétique II, 297.

*7 This letter was first published in the Swedish journal BLM in January 1959 and it is reproduced in the collection, Honneur à Saint-John Perse, under the title "Thématique d'Amers", 665-667.

*8 Amers, OEuvre poétique II, 139.

*9 This section appears to have been one of the first parts of Amers to be composed. It was at any rate the first published, entitled "Poème", in the Cahiers de la Pléiade (été-automne 1950), without the introductory lines ("Etranger... terre coutumière") and with some variants in the main text. What were to become the first seven sections of the Strophe were published in 1953 with the title Amers. And "Etroits sont les vaisseaux" (section nine) appeared in 1956. In the final version, thus, section eight serves as a short (but important) link in the development of the Strophe. Whereas, curiously, it seems to have been something of a germinal seed for the poem as whole at the outset. Information about the early versions and changes of wording is to be found in a most fruitful analysis of Perse's style and poetic aims by Albert Henry, Amers de Saint-John Perse: une poésie de movement (Neuchâtel, 1963).

*10 Marcel Raymond in De Baudelaire au surréalisme (Paris, 1952), 320-322, speaking particularly of Anabase says that the rhythm is regulated ("régie") by the alexandrine and the octosyllabic line. Valéry Larbaud also stresses the use Perse makes of the traditional alexandrine ("Eloges", La Phalange, décembre 1911; Honneur à Saint-John Perse, 32-38). One certainly does find these stable familiar rhythms in Perse's work frequently in his prosody, and, as here, they stand out prominently. But Perse uses a great variety of rhythms and it appears that needs of his poetic expression, in each particular case, are the basic determining factors.

*11 An earlier version of the last line of this stanza reads, "Que n'aille l'ancre dire le droit..." (Cahiers de la Pléiade, printemps 1948). Changing "Que n'aille..." to "Et laisses..." emphasizes the theme of release and adds to it a quality of will.

*12 The use of the phrase "ce goût d'arec et d'âtres morts" is typical
and interesting. They are both particular and rather subtle odors of
which the common denominator is a certain acrid quality. ("Arec" refers to a sort of palm tree the fruit of which we call the betel-nut.)
The inclusion of such sense perceptions gives his poetry an accurate,
concrete flavor and since this sort of image is often rough or earthy
or even slightly irritating it offsets the generally positive moral and
emotional tone which characterizes his work. Gide said, "C'est avec
de beaux sentiments qu'on fait de la mauvaise littérature." Without
such earthy qualities Perse's poetry might indeed suffer from an over-
dose of positive sentiments.

*13 Although the person or persons to whom "vos" refers is not clear,
by sound it enhances and blends with the tone of the line. Both the v
and the o are soft and serious; and the v is echoed in "grèves".

*14 André Breton, Nadja (Paris, 1928).

*15 See footnote 24, Part I, Chapter IV.

*16 "Thématique d'Amers", Honneur à Saint-John Perse, 665.

*17 These two commentaries on Perse by Breton are reproduced in
Honneur à Saint-John Perse, the extract from the First Manifesto on
p. 384 and the article, which first appeared in the Hommage International des Cahiers de la Pléiade in 1950, on pp. 53-55.

*18 Eloges is of course the title of his first published collection. Also,
Louis-Marcel Raymond reports ("Rencontres de Saint-John Perse",
Honneur à Saint-John Perse, 624-628) the poet as saying one day:
"J'aime bien l'éloge pour l'éloge; cela commande au départ un certain
ton, appelle une certaine hauteur, oblige à se situer un peu au-delà
de soi-même."

VIII

POÉSIE DE SYNTHÈSE

No explanations of human behavior or of human artistic creations, springing as they do from within the complex center of the being itself, can be simple or even necessarily free from contradictions. So much the more in the case of the poetry of a man whose knowledge and life experience is so extensive, who embodies most powerful human rational and irrational drives and ambitions. Seeking to characterize the essential traits of his work, starting with his own abstract statements and continuing by searching for reflections of these statements and for trends and cohesion in the poetry itself, I find two poles of convergent attraction which do seem paradoxical but which certainly coexist naturally on an esthetic plane. They are an equal affinity for change and for stability, for flux and for order, for the relative and for the absolute.

The two paragraphs of the letter to Roger Caillois show these two poles in the words of Perse himself. In the first paragraph he states:

Mon oeuvre, tout entière de recréation, a toujours évolué hors du lieu et du temps: aussi attentive et mémorable qu'elle soit pour moi dans ses incarnations, elle entend échapper à toute référence historique aussi bien que géographique; aussi vécue qu'elle soit pour moi contre l'abstraction, elle entend échapper à toute incidence personnelle. A cet égard, la deuxième partie de mon oeuvre publiée ne tend pas moins que la première aux transpositions, stylisations et créations de plan absolu...*1 *

Then, in the second paragraph he insists "... Je m'étonne grandement de voir des critiques favorables apprécier le poème comme une cristallisation, alors que la poésie pour moi est avant tout mouvement - dans sa naissance comme sa croissance et son élargissement final... "
To insist on poetry which evolves independently of space and time, yet which is from start to finish movement, to speak of stylization in a sphere which is absolute, yet to react against seeing his work in terms of crystallization, this does not seem entirely consistent. Perhaps in the first case he thought primarily of the finished work and in the second of the process of creation; but elsewhere even he appears to consider such a neat division into categories of process and product unrealistic. So, my aim in the pages which follow is to consider various and different aspects of the poetry of Perse which reflect these two poles of magnetism, for order and for change.

Above the varied and often obscure voices heard in Perse's poetic expression, amidst the shifting spatial and temporal environments, imposing figures appear and reappear, within one poem and in addition
as recurrent characters throughout his whole work. They are faceless,
and in a sense impersonal presences. Yet they dominate the scene.
Distinguished and named according to their functions, their names are
capitalized, their stature thus imposed poetically.

In the earliest poems they enter the scene; and even then we see several main types which are the most active and the most frequently encountered in the Persian world. For instance, in Pour fêter une enfance (1910) we see in the distance the majestic profiles of Royalty.

...Car au matin, sur les champs pâles de l'Eau nue au long de
l'Ouest, j'ai vu marcher des Princes et leurs Gendres, des hommes
d'un haut rang... (I, 27-28)*

They are products of the child's imagination, nonetheless splendid and
with the unforgettable force and clarity characteristic of dream images. In addition, there is that race of seekers, dreamers, and poets -
those who give birth perhaps to the distant Royalty but who themselves
are endowed with dignity and existence transcending the personal. In
Eloges (1910) we meet "le Songeur" and later "le Conteur", who are
born from the spirit of that small boy, the enduring person sprung
from Perse's childhood, alive in his memory and acquiring further a
poetic existence worthy of special note. Similarly, in this poem other
elements of his world are capitalized: la Maison, le Marché, le Cimetière, le Soleil. By virtue of their importance and presence within that
distant moment, they become signal parts of an ordered and durable
whole.

Later in Perse's career, as the poetry itself is less autobiographical
in inspiration, the characters become completely detached from the
author's personal life and often from that of the narrative voices. One
of the most interesting figures from the family of seekers is "l'Etranger". It was he to whom the young girls of Amers addressed their invitation to love and their tender query concerning his activities. His
mysterious presence heightened by the fact that his name introduces
the passage, he remains nonetheless an obscure, restless figure, a
wanderer, the source of hope in a sense, but with an inexplicable malaise intrinsic to his being. Similarly, in Anabase, he plays a key but
self-effacing role. He is introduced suddenly, elliptically in the opening lines of the Chanson:

Il naissait un poulain sous les feuilles de bronze. Un homme mit des
baies amères dans nos mains. Etranger. Qui passait. Et voici qu'il
est bruit d'autres provinces à mon gré... (I, 123)*

So it is he, faceless, but who comes with an offer of bitter berries,
laughs, speaks and arouses the thirst for adventure, a spirit of joyful
enthusiasm. He reappears twice more in the narrative, but rather unobtrusively, seemingly something of a companion or perhaps simply
an exceptional participant in the expedition. In Exil he figures also

among the characters, once:

> L'exil n'est point d'hier! l'exil n'est point d'hier! 'O vestiges,
> ô prémisses",
> Dit l'Etranger parmi les sables, 'toute chose au monde m'est
> nouvelle!...' Et la naissance de son chant ne lui est pas moins
> étrangère. (I, 170)*

He speaks independently from the narrative voice; but he, along with
a "Prince" and a distinct character named "Poète", seem to represent
varied aspects of the human psychic esthetic force. The "Poète" typifies perhaps the spoken word; the "Prince" incarnates the noble stance;
the "Etranger" the chosen path of exile and new experience. Georges
Poulet speaks of the "Etranger" as someone who instead of leaving is
left by his native country.*2 This was in a sense the case with Perse
himself, during World War II. Yet the "Etranger" of his poetic world,
when encountered, displays a quality of independence and choice, which
radiates openness and optimism, including perhaps a certain natural
distress concomitant with his solitary life. Particularly in Vents the
cast of characters is enlarged and there one encounters others who
embody diverse active functions of man's imagination. To take a few
examples, there is a "Narrateur", an "Emissaire", an "Enchanteur"
The latter together with the "Prince" belong not only to the world of
imaginative spirits but also to the realm of Royalty.

Characteristic of the Royalty is their distance, their height and the
way in which they reign over a scene or an atmosphere thus lending
considerable esthetic scope. In section eight of Amers they appear as
"les Dames illustres", actually high on the cliffs, motionless, re- '
splendent, an essential part of the stanza which has as its distinctive
quality - grandeur and stability. The theme of royalty is developed
into a full scale cast of personages, which are themselves the subject,
in a group of poems written at different periods (but all before 1925)
and published under the title Gloire des rois in the collected works.
In these poems, they have powerful human personalities. The Queen
(Récitation à l'éloge d'une reine) is the epitome of sensuality, concretely described. The voice of the hopeful initiate says to her "...
Reine parfaitement grasse, soulève cette jambe de sur cette autre;
et par là faisant don du parfum de ton corps..." (I, 87). Yet, she remains haughty and unapproachable, inviolable. The Prince and his
Friend engage in friendly but highly dignified and discrete conversation
and correspondence. Their friendship exists within a context of authority and management over a realm of considerable prestige. Perse's
taste for such stately figures and for their control over government
and territory come naturally - his admiration for Xenophon and Tacitus
and his own career as a diplomat have as a common denominator the
organization on a high level of peoples and states.

However, the royalty of these poems live not in the land of ordinary
human folk but in a sort of personal Olympus. And the dream-like
group of Princes seen by the child on the distant horizon in Pour fêter
une enfance are characteristic of other glimpses of royal spectors. In
the opening lines of Exil, the stage is an unbounded universe:

Et sur toutes grèves de ce monde, l'esprit de dieu fumant déserte
sa couche d'amiante.
Les spasmes de l'éclair sont pour le ravissement des Princes en
Tauride. (I, 167)*

One fine passage from <u>Anabase</u> (Canto II) depicts royal figures against
a sweeping backdrop, a silent expanse of back country, high slopes of
balm. There, the encounter seems to be purely and magnificently the
product of imagination, of the leader's day dreams. He walks ecstati-
cally amidst the Royal laundry ("la lessive des Grands")!

Nous enjambons la robe de la Reine, toute en dentelle avec deux
bandes de couleur bise (ah! que l'acide corps de femme sait tacher
une robe à l'endroit de l'aisselle!). (I, 130)*

First the gown of the Queen and then that of her daughter evoke a rich
sensual desire and joy. The dream is short but sweet; it and the laundry disappear, are dispersed by a sudden wind risen from the sea.
In all of these cases, the Royal images seem connected with intimate, introspective dream worlds - albeit worlds of extraordinary
scope. Their figures yield breadth, higher order and magical magnifi-
cence.
Another important group of "capital" characters is the one including
Priests, Priestesses, and their acolytes. Their role in the establishment of order in Perse's world is double for they not only assume god-
like proportions but they perform rites, necessary rites. The passage
from <u>Exil</u> is a particularly good case in point. Therein, the nocturnal
search for a message, the tracing of signs on the sands and their obliteration the following morning are all enacted through the auspices
of deities and religious figures. Partout-errante, the priest's court-
isan from the Sibyl's grotto is the narrator's winged messenger. The
Mendiante appears to be another mythical maiden who assists in the
ceremony. The disappearance of the words, signs gathered during the
night takes place as a ritual: "L'officiant chaussé de feutre et ganté de
soie grège efface, à grand renfort de manches, l'affleurement des
signes illicites de la nuit." What may seem simply a regular natural
event (sand patterns erased by the tide) or a chance mental phenomenon
(thoughts or dreams registered during the night and forgotten by day)
are pictured and organized metaphorically as a special and urgent ritual.
Ceremonial on a grand scale is integrally form <u>and</u> function in <u>Amers</u>.
The whole structure is structured as a choric ode. The <u>Invocation</u>,
<u>Choeur</u>, and <u>Dédicace</u> are highly formal, impersonal hymn-like strata
of verse which display an element of cosmic wonder and acclaim without, however, a particular religious commitment as in the case of
Greek poetry or in the case of Claudel; so that as a literary antecedent
one thinks of Ronsard's <u>Hymnes</u>.
These opening and closing sections are static: words are sung; actors are named but do not perform. The ritual <u>action</u> of the poem is
conferred to the successive sections of the <u>Strophe</u> (in the classical
tradition this is the movement of the chorus around the altar). These

sections are less formal in structure and tone. The "Tragédiennes" and "Cette fille chez les prêtres" are the ones closest in action, subject and tone to pure ritual, whereas others are freer poetically. However, the length of the poem as a whole is such that the clear lines of the ceremonial structure appear absolutely essential to maintain the work within the bounds of comprehension. In this case, then, ritual serves also a practical esthetic function.

Another most distinctive aspect of Perse's poetry and one which also, I think, stems from a desire to grasp, comprehend and organize, is the numerous passages of enumerations. The examples are not only plentiful but often so lengthy that it would be impossible briefly to present or analyze as a poetic phenomenon. The final Canto of Anabase should give a good idea of this idiom (I, 154-158). The leader of Anabase presents this panorama from something of a bird's eye view twice removed. He starts by saying:

> ...l'oeil recule d'un siècle aux provinces de l'âme.
> Par la porte de craie vive on voit les choses de la
> plaine: choses vivantes, ô choses
>   excellentes!

The enumeration following that introduction runs thus:

> des sacrifices de poulains sur les tombes d'enfants, des purifications de veuves dans les roses et des rassemblements d'oiseaux verts dans les cours en l'honneur des vieillards;
> beaucoup de choses sur la terre à entendre et à voir, choses vivantes parmi nous!

This series concerns people in various stages of life ("enfants", "veuves", "vieillards") and the first two mentioned are also of a ritual nature. The long list that follows includes other ceremonial actions (dedications, consecrations etc.) but also activities of day to day life - care of farm animals, preparation of food, business transactions. Then he speaks inclusively of all sorts of people and their jobs - fruit eaters, sugar merchants, flutists, dice players even "l'homme de nul métier"(!), to name only a few. He lists then those who seek a framework for life - genealogists, astronomers, book collectors. And to terminate he provides the spice of enterprise, audacious manoeuvres, plots. This enumeration, and others, combines a certain organization of presentation by categories with a great freedom of description and sudden unexpected shifts of emphasis or type. Above all, there is no moral judgement at work in his choice or in the tone of his comments. The desire and the aim is to embrace as much of the world and men as is humanly possible, to recognize and love multiplicity, variety yet somehow to arrange it poetically. The final effect is not really one of chaos but of orderly inclusiveness.*3

Certainly, the fashion in which Perse composes, according to his own explanations, includes a large measure of rational control. If the impetus is sudden and inexplicable, reason soon steps in to take over. In a recent interview he explained, "Je reconnais, intuitivement, une sort d'illumination au départ; ensuite un mécanisme rationnel."*4 And another interlocutor reports a conversation in which the poet describes his procedure. In the first stage there is a sort of argument with relevant considerations ("articulations") and the start of the poem's future development - all on one page. Afterwards each point is developed, enlarged. Successive versions follow.*5 A thoroughly methodical technique of outline and presentation in the purest French rational tradition! In the case of a poem as smoothly unfolded as Anabase, as carefully articulated as the action of the main body enclosed by the points of rest of the two Chansons, one can see that this may well have been the method of composition. Amers, on the other hand, although the main sections are clear and necessary, was composed over a long period and the inner balance of poetic argument or rhythms, quite varied, does not really appear to obey any logical necessity. But certainly, all the poems must have been carefully composed with the structure guided by lucid attention and discipline. Interestingly, a tendency for prolixity and sacrifice coexist in Perse's creative habits. If the initial plan is contained in a page, the elaboration which follows may become gigantic only to be scaled down with an unrelenting hand. To the judgment that his poems reveal an unbounded rhetoric, verbal intoxication, the author replies that on the contrary, "Je procède par soustractions, ellipses, omissions. Ma langue cherche la précision au maximum." He adds that the sixty pages of Anabase numbered originally two hundred, the two hundred pages of Vents were reduced from six hundred, and that Amers was at one stage seven hundred pages long.*6

The overall structure of Perse's poems, long or short, does indeed manifest a conscious control for form, often quite traditional in nature. Amers of course follows rigorously classical convention. The others each have their own internal structure, determined no doubt by the nature of the particular subject matter. The length of each section may vary. And within each section or Canto one may also find a number of different verse lengths. There are nevertheless certain stylistic traits which are determined not by the nature of the material but by a familiar type of poetic balance. Such, for instance, is the case in the two Chansons opening and closing Anabase, where the leader, a horse, and a tree are the common elements: the first Chanson starts the adventure and the last brings it literally to a halt (the leader stops his horse under a tree). Within the sections, too, certain conventional techniques are quite noticeable. Strophe VI of Anabase is introduced by one sentence which states the topic. Similarly in Section IV of Exil the time and atmosphere are announced at the onset and the final sentence closes the subject all the while leaving an open end, pointing to the future: "Voici que j'ai dessein encore d'un grand poème délébile... " Perse uses the same convention at the end of Anabase, where the leader mentions (for the first time) his brother the poet: "Il a écrit encore une chose très douce. Et quelques-uns en eurent connaissance."*7 In both cases the ellipsis reinforces a future anticipated yet unknown. As for the eighth section of Amers, the subject is announced in the last lines of the preceding section; and the first two sentences, set apart from the body of the poem by an asterisk, introduce not so much the theme as the situation and the tone. All of these are familiar poetic formal devices.

What is more unusual, and quite personal, is the way paragraphs, sections or stanzas are set up within each section. Sometimes the length of each internal division is varied. More frequently they are set up in blocks of roughly even length. In Neiges, for instance, there are divisions set typographically in paragraph form, roughly equal including the fact that the break in some cases falls not at a period but at a comma or even in the middle of a sentence, entirely unpunctuated. Strophe VII of Anabase is also composed of parallel paragraphs. But the other three passages we read are divided into stanzas; each have the same number of lines. In Exil IV there are three stanzas of seven lines each but the length of each line is continually modulated, usually quite long, and with the rhythm further accented or shifted by insistent questions or exclamations. The regular number of lines within each stanza is only really apparent if one studiously buckles down to count. In Amers, both "Etranger dont la voile..." and "Dédicace" are closer, visually, to lyric verse because the lines are shorter. In the first case each stanza contains four lines. The length varies greatly from a minimum of twelve syllables (the pair "Plus libre... / Plus libre... ") to twenty-five. In the "Dédicace" the three stanzas each have four lines, the second in each case set off by a dash; again the length of each line varies but they are generally fairly long, in keeping with the dignified tone. As various critics have pointed out, Perse does use, for particular effects, regular poetic rhythms - generally an even number of syllables. And there is always a rich pattern of internal rime, assonance, and phonetic modulation.*8 But these are always independent of the verse structures. So the use of balanced stanzas, the length and frame determined no doubt by the general overall tone of the poetic division, is an interesting formal feature which provides a flexible but shapely mold for imaginatively free thought elaboration.

Royalty, ritual, and rational poetic devices, all these are quite distinct if not distinctive characteristics of Perse's esthetic world. More puzzling is the insistence on the "absolute" nature of that world. In a sense it represents the highest bid for the universal. The strongest statement of the author on this score is in the "Thématique d'Amers" where he considers "...la Mer identifiée à l'Etre universel, s'y intégrant infiniment et y intégrant l'homme lui-même, aux limites de l'humain." And he asserts that this poem represents a reply to the passive nihilism of our materialistic epoch. Especially since the natural phenomenon in question is the sea, one thinks of Claudel according to whom perception and knowledge of a transcendent Being comes from direct contact with, reflection about, immersion in "les choses qui sont,"; the sea for him too represents a focal point of admiration and inspiration. By profession, diplomacy, and even by the geographical areas where they traveled and worked, settings which reappear in their artistic productions, Claudel and Perse also tread a common ground. In addition, the scope of their poetry and the tone of praise are remarkably similar. But, concerning the question of "Etre universel" a distinction must be made clear. Claudel's belief in God precedes a given experience and a given poem. In L'Esprit et l'eau (one of the Cinq grandes odes, written in 1906) where the sea is the object of descriptive adoration, Claudel invokes God directly and repeatedly,

"Mon Dieu... "; this style suggests a form of litany. And in his theory of "co-naissance" he discovers, through vital and immediate contact with experience, relations and connections which exist already, the result of some animating and homogeneous force. For Perse, on the contrary, "l'Etre universel" appears as a creation of the Poet, who finds in the sea, for instance, a multitude of symbolic relations which bind man, his life, and the world in an all-embracing unity. The absolute of Claudel is perceived in reality whereas the absolute of Perse is drawn, after the fact, from reality.

Claudel and Perse were well acquainted and the former wrote an important and admiring commentary of Vents in which his only regret is that Perse avoids the word "God". *9 This is true, of course - and for the good reason that the latter does not believe in a Divine presence. Once in an interview Perse related an occasion when, as an adolescent, he, Claudel, and Jammes were talking about religion and when his attention was more attracted by a storm outside than by the discussion: "Le feu divin m'apparaissait déjà dans l'immédiat du monde. Je n'avais besoin d'aucun intercesseur, sinon de ceux-là mêmes dont notre univers se constitue ici-bas. C'est pourquoi je n'ai jamais pu me sentir tout à fait chrétien: comme les vrais enfants des Iles, je suis sauvé de naissance... ",*10* he explained, the serious tenor of the remark tempered by a touch of humor. Sensitive to nature, its immediacy and its wonders, Perse does not conceive of God as a prime mover or a personal source of inspiration or an object of worship. If he speaks of an "Etre universel", capitalizing the substantive, and if he also uses the words "Unité" and "Continuité", I would judge that the intent is to reinforce the importance he attaches to such terms, to give them metaphorical stature in the same way that he magnifies and imposes the presence of "le Poète", "l'Etranger", or "le Prince", in the same way that through the eyes of the wondering child in Eloges the house becomes "la Maison", that in the cosmic sweep of Vents such terms as "Hiver", "l'An noir", "le Siècle" become independent poetic temporal entities, removed from particular, ordinary seasons or time units.

A passage from Oiseaux (a collection of poetic reflections, inspired by the birds of Braque, published in 1963) sheds light on the elements of Perse's own poetic world. He says that Braque's birds should receive a special nomenclature, "... Cette répétition du nom dont les naturalistes se plaisent à honorer le type élu comme archetype: Bracchus Avis Avis... "*11 They are no longer cranes of the Camargue or sea-gulls from the coast of Normandy or African herons - instead they form a new caste but of ancient lineage ("caste nouvelle et d'antique lignage"). They are related to real birds in the sense that they are inconceivable without the artist's knowledge and experience and acquaintance with particular species and more importantly single representatives of these species. Their artistic form is certainly not description nor abstraction, nor myth, nor even symbol but rather something of an archetype which contains its own truth and fidelity: "... du réel qu'ils sont, non de la fable d'aucun conte, ils emplissent l'espace poétique de l'homme, portés d'un trait réel jusqu'aux abords du surréel." They have their source in reality, take shape within another reality – that of the creative process – and then exist within their own reality which he calls here close to "surreal" and which I believe corresponds to what he terms elsewhere the "plan absolu".

As for the creative process, Perse's taste for the absolute, for order, for discipline is synthesized in the following statement which illuminates neatly various forms:

> Un poème de race est toujours frappé d'absolu. Si vous devenez le thème, vous le vivez, la langue joue son rôle dans le complexe créateur, vous atteignez le centre. Si vous devenez la mer, le vent, la pluie, vous êtes ample. Une page demain me suffira pour être la foudre, la lumière si je prends ces thèmes. On peut traiter tous les thèmes en une seule page, de la même longueur. Ce sont alors des définitions rythmées.*12 *

The poet, losing himself in the natural phenomenon to transmute, not only transcends the bounds of his own reality, his own ego but in addition reaches the heart of the substance and through language produces something endowed with the quality "absolute". Aside from that, the poet's self-assurance and the strict conception of procedure are striking. The terminology is almost that of an exercise – themes, definitions; and the goal is to carry out the project in the space of a page, of exactly the same length in each case. What this shows mainly, though, is not a didactic method but strong exigencies.

Fused in that orderly claim one perceives nevertheless two hints of the flexibility that represents the other side of the coin in Perse's esthetic temperament. For the poet to "live" the theme supposes a high degree of release and supple adaptivity. And the final cryptic point, "définitions rythmées", recalls the author's emphasis on movement – which leads us to consider this among other forces of attraction within the magnetic pole of change.

Those "rhythmic" definitions of which he speaks are quite particular, treating natural phenomena. Vents, Pluies, Neiges, Amers are all extensions of that poetic idiom, poems going far beyond, one might add, treatment in a single page. The creative process consists of losing oneself, imaginatively of course, in the thing to be described and of being particularly attentive to changes and rhythms. This is what the poet meant in the passage quoted in the preface where he defines French poetry as doing more than imitating, as being that thing itself in its movement and duration.*13 Thereby, a temporal factor is essential to the very structure of this sort of poetic expression. Returning once again to the sea as an example, Perse explains the patterns of wave and water motion which appeal especially to him: varied sounds of the waves, their expanding force, the swelling growth towards an ultimate height, the crest with a sort of stationary vertigo at the top, then a decrescendo and a silence before the formation of another wave.*14 These movements composed of varied lengths, accelerations, crescendos, decrescendos and importantly also, silences and rests appeal as a natural form for emotive language. In Amers, as we have already noted, the structure which circumscribes the whole

is not determined by the theme, nor is the expression of the parts -
with two exceptions. One is the Choeur, lengthy, redundant, where
one finds all of the recurring elements of crescendo, peak, decrescendo and rest. And, at one point of supreme identification, even
language is felt as unnecessary and somehow to be conjured away.

> ...Qu'il n'y ait plus pour nous, entre la foule et toi, l'éclat
> insupportable du langage:
> '...Ah! nous avions des mots pour toi et nous n'avions assez
> de mots,
> Et voici que l'amour nous confond à l'objet même de ces mots,
> Et mots pour nous ils ne sont plus, n'étant plus signes ni
> parures,
> Mais la chose même qu'ils figurent
> ...
> En toi, mouvante, nous mouvant, en toi, vivante, nous taisant,
> nous te vivons enfin, mer d'alliance... (II, 307-308) *

Certainly the poet must have desired and, I believe, felt this unity
with the object of contemplation; and the reader can, if he gives himself up to the power of suggestion, achieve something of the same sensation. These lines express the poetic wish; but one remains conscious
that these still are words, especially since the very expression to be
exorcised, "mot", is used repeatedly. More complete, perhaps, is the
implicit involvement through synthesis of rhythm, image, and theme
within the reciprocal metaphor (act of love - sea) in the section "Etroit
sont les vaisseaux..." Hardly in need of critical comment is the following excerpt from the opening verse:

> "...Etroits sont les vaisseaux, étroite notre couche.
> Immense l'étendue des eaux, plus vaste notre
> empire
> Aux chambres closes du désir.
> ...
> En vain la terre proche nous trace sa frontière.
> Une même vague par le monde, une même vague
> depuis Troie.
> Roule sa hanche jusqu'à nous. Au très grand
> large loin de nous fut imprimé jadis ce souffle...
> Et la rumeur un soir fut grande dans les cham-
> bres: la mort elle-même, à son de conques, ne s'y
> ferait point entendre! (II, 224-225) *

One remark is irresistible. The typographical disposition is absolutely
essential to preserve the desired rhythm. For example, in the second
line the break between "notre" and "empire" is necessary to indicate
an ever-so-slight pause before the down motion of the following words.
If the break were to come after "empire", the rhythm would be dry,
rigid - the natural suspension followed by swirl or rush particular to
wave motion would be lost.*15
    In these two passages quoted from Amers, one sees a double tech-
nique used to render the thought and sensation of movement. The use

of motion words, usually a verb ("En toi, mouvant... ", "roule... "),
is repeated with varied nuances. Also the poetic line and verse are
designed to suggest the rhythm of the natural element. Considering
the idiom in Vents one finds the same combination. In the following
passage there is a proliferation of words pertinent by sense:

> Ainsi croissantes et sifflantes au tournant de notre âge, elles
> [les forces en croissance - the winds] descendaient des hautes
> passes avec ce sifflement nouveau où nul n'a reconnu sa race,
>   Et dispersant au lit des peuples, ha! dispersant - qu'elles
> dispersent! disions-nous - ha! dispersant... (II, 18) *

In the first part, "croissantes", "sifflantes", "tournant", "descendant", "hautes passes", "sifflement" - nearly every other word in
some fashion evokes the sound and motion characteristic of wind and
windy places. In the second part the one verb "disperser" is repeated
in different forms, and here the two interjections, "ha!" and the
phrase between dashes give the sensation of sudden gusts and interrupted air currents. Such lines as these should not be read for their
verbal dictionary meanings but nearly entirely for their rhythmic patterns. Other sections are introduced in a way which also suggests
vividly not only the movement of wind currents and patterns but the
way in which they traverse enormous distances with boundless immaterial energy. The poem itself covers an incredible amount of territory - the whole expanse of North and South America including the
far reaches of the Pacific Ocean. One passage begins:

> ... Plus loin, plus haut, où vont les hommes minces sur leur selle;
> plus loin, plus haut, où sont les bouches minces, lèvres closes.
>   La face en Ouest pour un long temps... (II, 43) *

And to take one other example, successive lines and paragraphs in
another sequence begin "... Plus loin! plus loin!"; "Plus bas, plus
bas!"; "Plus vite, plus vite!" The ellipsis which frequently precedes
suggests the continuation of movement and activity. The sense of the
words, the repeated exclamations, the short staccato phonetic impact -
all this enters into a recreation of the movement and of the duration
of the "thing itself", the wind, which can indeed cover more ground,
with more alacrity than any other natural phenomenon.

Neiges is structured and styled in a most subtle and exquisite fashion
with probably a similar intention. Throughout the poem, the words are
molded into equal blocks. One cannot call them paragraphs exactly
since they do not treat separate themes or events but represent a continuous gentle descriptive flow. One thinks of the thick successive
sweeps of snow as it falls in the air and also of the subtly molded continuous contours of objects covered by snow rendered more massive
and often unrecognizable, soft anonymity. Here are two verse "blocks"
from the beginning of the poem:

> Nul n'a surpris, nul n'a connu, au plus haut front de pierre, le pre-
> mier affleurement de cette heure soyeuse, le premier attouchement

de cette chose fragile et très fragile, comme un frôlement de cils.
Sur les revêtements de bronze et sur les élancements d'acier
chromé, sur les moellons de sourde porcelaine et sur les tuiles de
gros verre, sur la fusée de marbre noir et sur l'éperon de métal
blanc, nul n'a surpris, nul n'a terni

cette buée d'un souffle à sa naissance, comme la première
transe d'une lame mis à nu... Il neigeait, et voici, nous en dirons
merveilles: l'aube muette dans sa plume, comme une grande
chouette fabuleuse en proie aux souffles de l'esprit, enflait son
corps de dahlia blanc. Et de tous les côtés il nous était prodige et
fête. Et le salut soit sur la face des terrasses, où l'Architecte,
l'autre été, nous a montré des oeufs d'engoulevent. (I, 213-214) *

Long sentences, soft sounds, words such as "affleurement", "soyeuse",
"attouchement", "frôlement", which combine a sense of light touch
with almost imperceptible movement, yet movement it is, numerous
expressions which add up to a pattern of prevalent emptiness ("fragile",
"futile", "muette", and the repeated predicates involving negatives -
"Nul n'a surpris..."). Once again, the esthetic idiom is one very close
to the "thing itself".*16 In a sense one might consider this sort of expression descriptive - it does describe, it does evoke. But where Perse
considered such verse to differ from definition or description in the
ordinary sense, and where he achieved his aim, is in the absence of
any sensation of distance, of feeling the presence of a poet who has in
mind a particular scene and who is describing it to us, the readers. It
is impossible here to abstract a triangle poet-scene-reader.
    A further instance of the high esthetic value which Perse places on
activity touches on the essence of life itself. He comments on Braque's
birds seen and transcribed by the poetic imagination. That artistic
bird appears to him as a small and succinct epitome of vitality and
movement. "Il vit, il vogue, se consume - concentration sur l'être et
constance dans l'être. Il s'adjoint, comme la plante, l'énergie lumi-
neuse." Flight, physiological combustion - in a word vital motion and
change.
    Living creatures of many kinds enter into the course of events and
images in Perse's poems. They take part in the ordinary activities of
organized human society and their living presence within the imagery
is a unique stamp of the author's idiom. Such, in Anabase, is the horse,
central to the atmosphere and action. Such are the camels, "douce
sous la tonte", mental creations having their source simply in the long
humpbacked line of desert hills. Such are the scattered, fanciful evi-
dences of birds in the imagery of Exil IV - "couvaisons", "plumes".
But the plants, insects, animals in Perse's world do not attract his
attention as symbolic of change nor do they fill the scene nearly as
dramatically in this respect as does the wide range of man's pursuits.
In Anabase we witness the concerted efforts connected with the foundation of a new city ("Au grand bruit frais de l'autre rive, les forge-
rons sont maîtres de leurs feux..."), the flavor of army life ("constructions de citernes, de granges, de bâtiments pour la cavalerie..."),
the ordinary tasks and ceremonies involved in the society of farm and
village ("les pansements de bêtes aux faubourgs, les mouvements de

foules au-devant des tondeurs... "). In Amers, the whole first section
of the Strophe deals with the organization and commercial bustle of
coastal cities, ports ("Les Officiers de port siégeaient comme gens
de frontière: conventions de péage, d'aiguade; travaux d'abornement
et règlements de transhumance.").

Restlessness, wandering exploration - action on a large and ambitious scale - of representatives of the species such as "l'Etranger"
or "l'Itinérant" or of groups of men, this is what lends the most color
and scope to Perse's poems and what represents their most striking
individual stamp. In Anabase and in Vents, the movement is continuous,
forming the thread of the plot. In the former, it takes the form of a
military expedition; in the latter a voyage with the winds, restless,
chronologically formless with intentionally freewheeling imaginative
historical anachronisms. In Anabase the aim is both adventurous exploration and constructive conquest. To impress the sedentary folk
with their spirit the cavalrymen irresistibly enthuse: " Allez et dites
à ceux-là: un immense péril à courir avec nous! des actions sans
nombre et sans mesure, des volontés puissantes et dissipatrices... "
In Vents the spirit of generous enthusiastic exploration prevails: "Là
nous allions, la face en Ouest, au grondement des eaux nouvelles. Et
c'est naissance encore de prodiges sur la terre des hommes." The
ever-present poet, too, is similar in temperament. He is a wanderer,
both in fact and in fancy. The passage from Exil IV shows him using
the supernatural powers of a fantasy figure, "Partout-errante", born
of his own psyche to extend his search into the far reaches of the
heavens.

Animating the narrative also in a narrower range of movement but
with important symbolic force are gestures: the priest who erases with
a sweep of his sleeve the traces on the night sands; and "l'Usurpateur",
the lover and the man with the golden mask whose symbolic motions
close the action and the coda of Amers. Gathered together, the whole
cast of Amers leads the earth to merge with the incessantly modulating
flux of the Sea in a votive dance:

> --et nous-mêmes avec elle [la terre] à grand renfort de peuple et
> piétinement de foule, dans nos habits de fête et nos tissus légers,
> comme la récitation finale hors de la strophe et l'épode, et de ce
> même pas de danse, ô foule! qui vers la mer puissante et large et
> de mer ivre, mène la terre docile et grave, et de terre ivre... (II,
> 302)*

Far more than mere stylistic technique, using verbs of action, nomi-
natives, and adjectives which evoke action directly or indirectly, Perse
depicts a universe in constant motion, pictures his characters as active and often, as in the last quotation, endowing their actions with
symbolic force.*17

To say, however, that this world is one characterized by change
and action is not to say also that the poetry itself necessarily consists
of movement and duration. Some important distinctions must be made.
At times, it is true, when the theme and tone are concerned with ren-
dering the "thing itself", the modulation of the poetic line reflects dur-

ation, in a Bergsonian sense as some critics have pointed out, trans-muting the intrinsic quality and natural time flow. At times, also, an underlying pattern of duration is present in a given poetic unit in a personal psychological sense. This is the case in Eloges and in Strophe VII of Anabase and of other sections also from that poem. In that strophe, one recalls, the leader absorbs with intense pleasure the sight of the desert landscape, the vast expanse, the incandescence of color and shape - an effect of the summer light and heat - with the line of hills receding in the distance, sand, smoke, clouds merging and expanding as in a dream perspective of unbounded time and space. Slowly a sense of expectancy enters his reflections and in the end comes the call to action, the urge to fare forth. Following the sense perceptions, the thoughts and imaginative abstractions of the narrator, the passage thus reflects a time sequence of mental activity in the same way as do the most typical poems of Valéry - "Le Cimetière marin", "La Jeune Parque". The action of Exil IV also takes place with reference to a time span - an imaginative quest pursued one night. But the sequence of the poetic expression is not bounded particularly by sense-perceptions nor by any repeated references, implicit or ex-plicit to particular moments. It simply starts and ends before dawn. In the beginning lines there is the reference, "Et qui donc avant l'au-be...", and towards the end, a similarly ambiguous, "Et les poèmes de la nuit avant l'aurore répudiés..." Besides, the other sections of Exil are not at all temporally defined.

In fact, the distinguishing characteristic of the internal dynamic structure of Perse's poetry is the great variety and versatility of pres-entations. One even finds as introductory lines, quite direct state-ments which one could even qualify as explicit and logical. The first. lines of Amers VIII are of this sort: "Etranger, dont la voile a si longtemps longé nos côtes... / Nous diras-tu quel est ton mal, et qui te porte, un soir de plus grande tiédeur, à prendre pied parmi nous sur la terre coutumière?" Except for its elegant diction, it is a simple question, which one might hear in the course of conversation and its function is to orient the reader as to the subject of the freer poetic passage to follow.

The introduction to Anabase is of a different nature and merits close attention. The whole section is entitled Chanson, consisting of three paragraphs. Here is the first one:

Il naissait un poulain sous les feuilles de bronze. Un homme mit des baies amères dans nos mains. Etranger. Qui passait. Et voici qu'il est bruit d'autres provinces à mon gré... 'Je vous salue, ma fille, sous le plus grand des arbres de l'année.' (I, 123)*

One is struck immediately by its elliptical qualities. One event is posed as the outset: a colt was being born. Another event follows without ap-parent relation to the first: a man puts bitter berries in our hands. The next totally elliptical statement seems to identify (ambiguously) that man: "Etranger." And the next sentence simply tells us that he was going by. Then two longer statements, joined together by ellipsis marks appear related to, if not caused psychologically by the first happenings: "Et voici que..." Without guide-lines in time and space, the total effect of the narrative is that of a very specific event – whose practical outcome is to foreshadow the future action (exploration of far lands) and whose immediate emphasis is psychological. From "à mon gré", indicating pleasure and interest at the thought of adventure, the poetic line passes by way of the ellipsis marks, which probably represent unstated or even unconscious continuation of thought to the expression in quotation marks which is yet unclear.*18 It recurs as a refrain at the end of the other two stanzas with the clarification the second time round that the daughter symbolizes (probably) the speaker's soul or spirit since it is worded as an apposition: "Mon âme, grande fille..." Unknown are the time and place, unknown is the identity of the speaker and really even the passerby. Barely suggested is the possibility of adventure. The poetic significance of other unexpected images – the colt, the leaves of bronze, the bitter berries – certainly remains a mystery at first reading and even within the context of the full poem cannot be reduced to simple explanations although their presence is certainly intentional and tonal in function. Disconnected events, unexpected images, elliptical sentences, ambiguous presentation of characters ("nous" and "je" are not identified either), ellipsis marks connecting (or separating?) two of the sentences, mysterious quotation marks – all come from the pen of a poet who feels free to dispense with simple rational linguistic conventions. Curiously, the effect, though strange, is forceful: by virtue of the short, staccato sound of the elliptical statements; by virtue also, I think, of the precise, concrete, rough-hewn imagery (colt, bronze, and bitter berries).

Considering Perse's work as a whole, a similar liberty is noticeable in the succession of verses or stanzas, their connection or lack of connection. And for the group of verses in a given section or strophe, even tonal progression obeys no fixed rules or patterns. The one qualifying remark to be made in this respect is that the author carefully indicates at the beginning and at the end theme or tone, but usually quite succinctly. Aside from that, passage from one stanza to the next takes place without necessarily a "fil de logique" either of subject or atmosphere. Again, <u>Anabase</u> is an exception: in Strophe VII there are the connective links of visual impressions and also of the changes in the leader's state of mind, from passive enjoyment to expectancy to decision. Otherwise, different motivations seem to determine the succession of verses. In <u>Neiges</u>, it is the nature of the natural phenomenon, apparently, which regulates the length of the verse. But as for content, in one verse a thought may be developed, in the next an impression, or in another a descriptive sequence may form the basis of division with little concern for explicit linking. In other words, there is no consistent thematic progression. In <u>Amers</u> VIII, a general focus of interest and tone can be defined for each stanza, and the sea and bird images provide a fine continuous thread. Beyond that, the shift from one stanza to another is unpredictable: stanza one – pleasure against a visual background; stanza two – sense of freedom and release; stanza three – sudden malaise combined with awareness of an important moment; stanza four – another scene, peopled with imaginary figures all on a grandiose scale; stanza five – earthy sensual pleasure expressed metaphorically. Some sense of esthetic balance perhaps is established in a common lyrical airy quality to the first three stanzas, the more stately and firm tone of the fourth representing something of a climax and the sensual tone of the last a down to earth movement. In any event, the form is delightfully free and unconstrained.

One is not surprised to discover the same flexible progression within the lines and from line to line. Nearly any example proves fruitful. This one is from <u>Exil</u> IV:

> Ah! toute chose vaine au van de la mémoire, ah! toute chose insane aux fifres de l'exil: le pur nautile des eaux libres, le pur mobile de nos songes,
> Et les poèmes de la nuit avant l'aurore répudiés, l'aile fossile prise au piège des grandes vêpres d'ambre jaune... *

Yet, just as Perse depends on a regular length stanza and a regular number of lines within each to present the main body of untrammeled poetic expression, so certain regular devices of rhetoric or prosody give a recognizable framework for the expression within the lines. Here several such devices are used. The impetus is given with the pair of exclamations introduced by "Ah!..." - frequent Persian expletives. Rhetorical questions or self-addressed questions are other ways of giving the reader the benefit of a familiar sentence pattern. Then there are two sets of phrases within that one line, each having a fixed syllabic count and each grammatically parallel.*19 One set begins "toute chose vaine... toute chose insane... ": Each part has twelve syllables, contains a nominative (with adjective) followed by a prepositional phrase introduced by "à" and then another introduced by "de". There is in addition a phonetic modulation from "<u>vaine</u>" to "<u>van</u>" to "<u>insane</u>" which gives another sort of continuity. Because of this continuity of sound and rhythm, one can absorb more easily the unexpected passage from the winnowing sieve of memory to the fifes of exile, both ways in which things by nature perishable or "insane" (so frightful they should perish) can be dissipated - lost in memory or diffused shrilly from abroad. The next set, "le pur nautile... le pur mobile... " has an eight syllable rhythm, is similarly grammatically parallel, and, interestingly, contains a modulation of images. The image of the nautilus floating on the open seas is a concrete counterpart of the abstract "mobile", unanchored subject of thought. The progression of the next series is much more fluid, much less logically consistent. So as T. S. Eliot counseled, one must simply proceed from one to the other without undo concern or question.*20 "Le pur nautile", as we remarked, is in a sense a metaphorical counterpart of "le pur mobile"; but it is not perishable or nearly as immaterial as are the "mobile", "les poèmes de la nuit", and "l'aile fossile". And the rest of the line, the most appealing poetic pearl, proceeds by groups of semantically unanticipated word groups: "l'aile fossile prise au piège / des grandes vêpres / d'ambre jaune." It is the middle phrase which adds the unexpected image. The fossile wing encased in yellow amber - miraculously magnified in a religious aura - suggests the yellow cast to the evening light during the hour of vesper services.*21 Such poetic liberty should indeed be a source of enjoyment rather than concern for common sense. The coherence, the poetic coherence can be found elsewhere. In the case of the stanza from which these lines are taken we saw that the unifying pattern is the disappearance of things vain or perishable with a religious trace (suggested by "vêpres" together with "cilice" and "cendre" mentioned earlier in the stanza).

As a reverse image of the absolute, one discovers in Perse's tastes and esthetic tendencies an emphasis on dissolution, on that which disappears or which seems most attractive in its least tangible condition. This predilection can be seen in a number of forms. One which we have already touched upon is his choice of natural phenomena which are changeable and unstable so that he can focus the poetic spotlight on those changes - duration and movement. Wind, rain, and snow are obvious choices of this sort. The sea also lends itself to such treatment. The following passage from Amers serves as a fine example:

L'incorporelle et très-réelle, imprescriptible; irrécusable et l'indéniable et l'inappropriable; inhabitable, fréquentable; immémoriale et mémorable - et quelle et quelle, et quelle encore, inqualifiable? L'insaisissable et l'incessible, l'irréprochable irréprouvable... (II, 298)*

Some of these qualities are actually positive, "l'indéniable" or "l'incessible" for instance. But most of them indeed reflect negative conditions, in particular a sort of untouchable state. And most of the adjectives have a negative prefix, as if the attraction lies in negation itself, like Mallarmé's Hérodiade.

As conscious of the importance of typographical presentation as Mallarmé, Perse, too, uses blanks to great esthetic advantage: between verses, between different parts of a section (introduction and poetic narrative), at the ends of lines - and the size and shape of these blanks varies according to the need. Ellipsis marks and dashes are used also to point out something unworded but important, significant absence one might say. The dash has a certain force, both connective and separative. It is used a number of times in Anabase VII. Here is one case: "Je vous parle, mon âme! - mon âme tout enténébrée d'un parfum de cheval!" It expresses a mental pause but links the two thoughts. At another point in Anabase the dash appears introducing a final section (separated from the rest by an asterisk):

--et debout sur la tranche éclatante du jour, au seuil d'un grand pays plus chaste que la mort,
    les filles urinaient en écartant la toile peinte de robe. (I, 153)*

The dash, replacing the beginning of the sentence or the description, marks a striking impetus to a striking final image. The ellipsis in Vents, subtler in effect, is used a great deal, to introduce sections and even lines within sections ("...Plus loin, plus loin"); they no doubt suggest great distances covered. Sometimes, as in that line from the Chanson of Anabase ("Et voici qu'il est bruit d'autres provinces à mon gré... 'Je vous salue, ma fille, sous le plus grand des arbres de l'année'"), the ellipsis indicates a thought process, or a mental connection, unstated and maybe unconscious. In Amers VIII an ellipsis is used twice at the end of stanzas: stanza one, "Et le sourire au loin sur l'eau des grandes lèpres interdites..." and stanza four, "La main de pierre du destin nous serait-elle encore offerte?..." Here, perhaps too it indicates a continuation of the esthetic train of thought, becoming wordless, one step further caught up in a dream world. Once it is used between lines in the middle of a stanza:

> Une plume blanche sur l'eau noire, une plume blanche vers la gloire
> Nous fit soudain ce très grand mal, d'être si blanche et telle, avant le soir...
> Plumes errantes sur l'eau noire, dépouilles du plus fort,
> Vous diront-elle, ô Soir, qui s'est accompli là? *

My impression is that this ellipsis for one thing creates a pause and for another emphasizes the sudden sensation of anguish, and reinforces that feeling wordlessly.

The ultimate gesture of disintegration for a poet, one would think, would be the negation of words or the poem itself. Perse quite willingly does so however with no apparent sense of self-sacrifice. The passage from Exil we read has this exactly as the main theme - signs, poetic messages sought, discovered and then erased as traces on the sands, with the final wish that of composing another such ephemeral poem: "Voici que j'ai dessein encore d'un grand poème délébile." Sometimes even the poem or poetic inspiration comes into being, within the sphere of natural phenomena, seemingly more truthful when wordless. At any rate, this is the sense of a line from Vents: "Et comme un homme frappé d'aphasie en cours de voyage, du fait d'un grand orage, est par la foudre même mis sur la voie des songes véridiques." (II, 82). It is as if the ultimate poetic revelation may either preexist or be beyond the structure of language.

What then is the source of the poetic voice in the works of Perse? How does language relate to the "lés du songe et du réel?" These are the key questions and delicate ones at that, since, despite the multiplicity of references to language, dreams and reality in the poetry, the references themselves are poetic and therefore usually surrounded by an aura of ambiguity.

One can say with some assurance, however, that for Perse "songe" is the source of esthetic consciousness. In essence it is disinterested, exempt from polemic function and thus it is free. In Exil IV the recurrent image of wings, soaring Muse-like maidens is very typical of the unconstrained nature of reflections which precede and prepare poetic creation. The spirit of various characters in Perse's poems who are not by precise definition poets share this quality. The leader of Anabase has an overpowering curiosity for adventure, an imagination which leads him far. The Stranger from Anabase too appears unshackled by earthly ties: "il n'y a plus en lui substance d'homme. Et la terre en ses graines ailées, comme un poète en ses propos, voyage..." (I, 140).

The "Maître d'astres et de navigation" in Amers is a poetic brother, with an eye on the far horizons, ready to follow the paths of insatiable dreams. His own description of himself is poetic rather than practical: "Ils m'ont appelé l'Obscur et j'habitais l'éclat."

Open to the influence of imagination, Perse's poet discovers a wealth of dream not only within himself, but also in the world around him. The sea not only is the object of dream but the archetype of vague but limitless dream possibilities: " Mer ouverture du monde d'interdit, sur l'autre face de nos songes, ah! comme l'outrepas du songe, et le songe même qu'on n'osa!..." Particularly in Exil, Vents, and Pluies the inspiration and message is sought and found in the thing itself - in the heavens, in the wind, on the sands. The poet, then apparently needs only receive and transmit what exists. The source is lucid, penetrating in Pluies where the opening lines present first the image of a driving storm coupled (and identified) with what Perse calls "L'Idée, plus nue qu'un glaive" and which will even shape the poem, giving it "rite" and "mesure" (I, 194). Moreover, there are a number of instances where the natural element offers a certain grammatical shape. In Exil the wind at one point utters over the whole wide world "Une seule et longue phrase sans césure à jamais inintelligible..." - with an iambic rhythm (I, 170-173). In the same poem, one section opens with the exclamation "...Syntaxe de l'éclair! ô pur langage de l'exil!" And in Amers, the waves are described as "grandes phrases lumineuses" (II, 154): the whole ocean is pictured as rich in image and rhythm (II, 296). All of these references have, of course, some metaphorical twist. But Perse did search seriously, sensitive to sight and sound, in natural phenomena for patterns to serve as a model for syntax and meter, for qualities to transmute actively so that much of his poetic expression does "apprehend" the thing itself, in its movement and duration and then serves secondarily and occasionally as a vehicle for personal sentiment, symbol, idea.

Because, perhaps, of this intimate communication between subject and object which at its ultimate point results in total fusion, there is that temptation to dispense with words, to consider them inadequate or superfluous. One passage from Amers already quoted indicates this desire to bypass language: "...mots pour nous ils ne sont plus, n'étant plus signes ni parures, / Mais la chose même qu'ils figurent..." Also in Vents he chooses "Non point l'écrit, mais la chose même. Prise en son vif et dans son tout" (II, 86). As careful as Perse is to use precise terminology, and his working habits are certainly very exacting as we have seen, there comes a point once the poem exists when the author does wish for the words to become translucent and for the reader to lose consciousness of language. In a sense it is another reflection of his taste for dissolution. A doubly reinforced trend in this direction appears in Amers where at one point an appropriately spiritual spokesman ("Cette fille chez les prêtres") first says, "Et la douceur est dans le chant, non dans l'élocution; est dans l'épuisement du souffle, non dans la diction"; she shortly thereafter shifts her tune, "Et la douceur est dans l'attente, non dans le souffle ni le chant. Et ce sont choses peu narrables, et de nous seules mi-perçues" (II, 203-204). This is about as far as one can go in a reduction to the ineffable.

But Perse the scholar and Perse the artist of precision clearly not only recognizes the usefulness of language but stakes his hopes thereon. In a passage from Neiges where the poet has just launched a spiritual adventure free from the grip of words, he does a surprising about face to announce his plan to explore all the manifestations of human tongue in a long paragraph filled with precise descriptions of an experienced linguist ("...nous nous mouvons parmi de claires élisions, des résidus d'anciens préfixes ayant perdu leur initiale..." I, 220-221). More importantly, in the opening section of Vents it is in the great tree of language that he places the initial hope for mankind threatened by disasters cosmic in scale.

For, of course, language alone can spread the poetic word, give expression to dream and coherence to the poetic voice. Moreover in the universe of Perse, one must speak of a chorus of poetic voices. One hears at times that of the child or the man himself - in Eloges, in Neiges and under the surface in Poème à l'Etrangère. One hears the voice of the wind and the rain, that of "l'Etranger", the eternal wanderer, that of a leader, a diplomat, a builder and binding the whole a voice speaking on behalf of mankind. Besides, even issuing from the mouth of a particular narrator there are different levels of voices, some directed towards fellow human beings, other more reflective and perhaps even subconscious in nature such as the lines enclosed in parentheses "(Et l'ombre d'un oiseau me passe sur la face)."

Having its source in the real, the poet, "l'Hôte de l'instant", creates his own "rêve de réel" and seeks beyond him the absolute of a "Songe incréé" (II, 162-164). Drawing his material from the wide temporal and spatial range of man's history, yet unrestricted by a particular era, a particular place, a particular event, far less to his own immediate personal experience, the poet must rely on knowledge, on memory and on imagination for the substance of his expression.*22 It is poetry of synthesis: voices are varied, order is juxtaposed with change, from reality a different unified sphere emerges retaining all the color, the odors, the rhythms and spiritual vitality of its source. This alchemy is possible by virtue of the rational and irrational structures of the mind. First, by what Perse termed "la logique du songe". And then, by means of language. The ultimate compliment he payed to Braque's birds was to say that they had ripened like words from the original sap and substance: "Et bien sont-ils comme des mots sous leur charge magique: noyaux de force et d'action, foyers d'éclairs et d'émission, portant au loin l'initiative et la prémonition."*23

NOTES

*1 Lettre à Roger Caillois (26 janvier 1953), Poétique de Saint-John Perse (Paris, 1954), 180-181.

*2 Georges Poulet, "Saint-John Perse, ou la Poésie de l'effacement des choses", Hommage International du Combat, 1957 (Honneur à Saint-John Perse, 298-315).

*3 Roger Caillois wrote an interesting article on Perse's enumerations, "Une poésie encyclopédique", Hommage International des Cahiers de la Pléiade, 1950 (Honneur à Saint-John Perse, 80-90). His analysis of the way Perse presents these series is illuminating: "Chaque terme de la série prolonge celui qui le précède par un certain infléchissement de son sens. En même temps, il introduit une nouvelle nuance, que le suivant à son tour développe et complète. Tout est jeu d'échos, de résonances et de substitutions partielles, qui établissent entre les éléments une continuité insensible, mais telle que le charme serait rompu, si elle venait à manquer."

*4 Christian Gali, "Quatre heures avec Saint-John Perse", Arts, 8 novembre 1960.

*5 Louis-Marcel Raymond, "Rencontres de Saint-John Perse", Ecrits du Canada français, 1961 (Honneur à Saint-John Perse, 624-628).

*6 Arts, 8 novembre 1960.

*7 Gide, too, liked this open-ended way of terminating a story, using it in Le Prométhée malenchaîné, Le Retour de l'enfant prodigue, and Les Faux-Monnayeurs.

*8 Good discussions of Perse's prosody are to be found in Roger Caillois' book, La Poétique de Saint-John Perse (Paris, 1954), and in that of Albert Henry, "Amers" de Saint-John Perse: une poésie de mouvement (Neuchâtel, 1963).

*9 Paul Claudel, "Un poème de Saint-John Perse", Revue de Paris, novembre 1949 (Honneur à Saint-John Perse, 43-52).

*10 Claude Vigée, "La Quête de l'origine dans la poésie de Saint-John Perse", Nouvel hommage international, 1964 (Honneur à Saint-John Perse, 345-362). There is another interesting reference to religion in the interview with Louis-Marcel Raymond (Honneur à Saint-John Perse, 624-628) where Perse states: "Si j'étais croyant, Dieu serait pour moi l'Inaccoutumé par excellence." This shows how much Perse prizes freedom and independence from ties, habits, commitments.

*11 Saint-John Perse, Oiseaux (Paris, 1963), 31-32.

*12 Arts, 8 novembre 1960.

*13 Lettre à George Huppert, Honneur à Saint-John Perse, 656.

*14 This is Perse's explanation as recalled by Louis-Marcel Raymond, Honneur à Saint-John Perse, 627.

*15 This sort of unusual division of poetic breaks, even in free verse where exigences of meter do not exist is discussed at length by Jean Cohen in Structure du langage poétique (Paris, 1966) and he says it is not so much a grammatical as antigrammatical, a deliberate deviation from the norms of ordinary discourse. In this case Perse's choice of break was determined by theme and tone.

*16 "Les images dans Neiges", PMLA, March 1955 (Honneur à Saint-John Perse, 447–456) by Arthur Knodel presents an excellent stylistic analysis of this poem.

*17 René Girard gives a philosophical interpretation to the state of flux depicted in Perse's world. Considering the historical chaos as an intentional critique of reality and comparing it with the arbitrary character of the surrealist world, he concludes that the latter denounces the whole-scale lack of reality of the ordinary world while Perse questions its historical and anthropological duration. ("L'Histoire dans l'oeuvre de Saint-John Perse", Romanic Review, Feb. 1953; reprinted in Honneur à Saint-John Perse, 548–557).

*18 The significance of passages in quotation marks in Perse's work is an interesting question. Perhaps they represent a particularly personal, inward-directed, dreamy sort of reflection.

*19 Although at times the rhythm of Perse's expression is like that of Claudel by virtue of being patterned on natural rhythms such as that of waves or of human respiration, this is not always the case. The rhythms in Perse's poetry are varied, often suggesting conventions of rhetoric, often quite traditional (alexandrines, octosyllabic lines), and often seemingly obeying some inner necessity, following the flow of subconscious esthetic mental currents.

*20 T. S. Eliot, Preface to his first translation of Anabase (London, 1930).

*21 This image is discussed by Roger Caillois in his Poétique de Saint-John Perse, 23.

*22 Georges Poulet, in a chapter of his book Le Point de départ (Paris, 1964) describes Perse's part as a sort of simultaneous whole of events resembling a backdrop, but not fixed or immobile, on the contrary, movable with almost spatial qualities.

*23 Oiseaux, 24.

PART THREE

BENJAMIN PÉRET: L'HOMME INVENTE

L'oiseau vole, le poisson nage et l'homme invente car seul dans la
nature il possède une imagination toujours aux aguets, toujours sti-
mulée par une nécessité sans cesse renouvelée.*1

As absurd, as gratuitous, as irreverent and willfully playful as the
work of Benjamin Péret may appear, it is essential from the start to
realize that his views on the role of poetry, on the nature and possibilities of human existence, even on the methods of composition have
a highly serious and positive intellectual base. Unlike André Breton
or Louis Aragon fellow Surrealist authors, Péret did not write many
polemical esthetic essays. But, the preface to his anthology of Latin
American myths shows, not abstractly but with an appealing spontaneous intelligent enthusiasm, that for him imagination, creative, imagination, is man's unique and precious gift within the whole wide world
of nature.

Péret shared the basic tenets of the Surrealist movement according
to which man's inner thought processes, "le fonctionnement réel de la
pensée", should be brought to light, enjoyed, used directly in creative
methods, according to which separation of conscious and unconscious
expression and behavior is undesirable and unrealistic, considering
that dreams and reality are related and should be seen and portrayed
in interaction. Personally fascinating to him were the primitive mentality and the spontaneous expressions of ordinary people in the form
of slang (argot) or old regional dialects because, there, thought and
reactions to experience are formed and expressed unfettered by reason
and logic. Equally typical was his utter faith in language as true and
natural formulation of such prelogical thought. And this certitude even
goes so far as to place poetic language at the very base of human communication. Admitting that the invention of language was first due to
the need for communication of a practical sort, he insisted that once
basic pragmatic needs are satisfied language then becomes poetry, a
means of relating man to the world. In a primitive society, myths tie
man spiritually to his environment; the hope for the salvation of modern man in an industrialized society is to regain that natural spontaneous expression thus to recover a sense of individual freedom, to
gain knowledge of himself and of the world.*2

As for himself, the role of poetry is neither destructive nor gratuitous. He rejected vehemently the Dada movement in that it lead to a
dead end. Proposing to destroy artificial existing forms of expression,

using words completely arbitrarily, it ended up disintegrating itself. Instead, Péret looked to the future hopefully, free of preconceptions or any particular goal: "Je quitte les lunettes dada et prêt à partir, je regarde d'où vient le vent sans m'inquiéter de savoir ce qu'il sera et où il me mènera."*3 This enthusiasm and openness to suggestion, direction, and goal remain constant in his creative temperament. His method of writing was a remarkably pure form of what the Surrealists termed "écriture automatique". He would improvise a poem when and where the spirit urged - at a café, using any bit of paper at hand, for example, a page torn from a magazine, following his train of thought with few subsequent revisions. The kind of inspiration he cultivated and relished was a sense of the marvellous ("merveilleux") which he said can be found anywhere, in the simplest circumstances or objects - the contents of a drawer for instance. One can't consciously seek it or make it ("fabriquer"); what is necessary is to be "on vacation" and then the marvelous will find you.*4

All of this indicates that Péret does consider language as highly meaningful, as expressing most naturally in its prelogical form man's spontaneous feelings and perceptions which spring from and bind him to the world.

To enjoy his poems is simple. But since for him poetry was not merely play or pleasure, we may justifiably want to appreciate them and understand them intelligently. For this, the poet himself gives us few clues. One small indication is that he placed value judgements on the work of others, mentioning in a letter to Breton that he thought a book of poems by Arp was on the whole very fine except for the last few poems which were considerably less successful.*5 One other potential clue is a stanza of a poem from the earliest collection, Le Grand Jeu. This must be prudently interpreted since it is itself poetic. Nonetheless, it deserves attention for its mention of circular structure and for the concept of natural currents.

L'homme découvre la poésie circulaire
Il aperçoit qu'elle roule et tangue
comme les flots de la botanique
et prépare périodiquement son flux et son reflux*6 *

NOTES

*1 Benjamin Péret, "Introduction", Anthologie des mythes, légendes et contes populaires d'Amérique (Paris, 1960), 9-10.

*2 These ideas are presented at length in the aforementioned "Introduction" to the anthology of Latin American myths. That "Introduction" was reprinted in a small volume published by Pauvert (Paris, 1965) under the title "La Parole est" of an essay therein which deals with poetic theory vehemently disassociating art from political polemics.

*3 Benjamin Péret, "A travers mes yeux", Littérature, no. 5 (octobre 1922), 13.

*4 "Introduction", <u>Anthologie des mythes, légendes et contes populaires d'Amérique</u>, 15-16.
     The main sources of biographical material about Péret are the presentation by Jean-Louis Bédouin in the Seghers edition (Paris, 1961) including selected poems and the study by Claude Courtot, <u>Introduction à la lecture de Benjamin Péret</u> (Paris, 1965).

*5 Courtot, 44-46.

*6 "Le Mariage des feuilles", <u>Le Grand Jeu</u> (1928; rpt. Paris: Losfeld, 1967), 152.

IX

"ON SONNE"

On Sonne

Un saut de puce comme une brouette dansant sur les
    genoux des pavés
une puce qui fond dans un escalier où je vivrais avec toi
et le soleil pareil à une bouteille de vin rouge
s'est fait nègre
esclave fustigé
Mais je t'aime comme le coquillage aime son sable
où quelqu'un le dénichera quand le soleil aura la forme
    d'un haricot
qui commencera à germer comme un caillou montrant son coeur
    sous l'averse
ou d'une boîte de sardines entr'ouverte
ou d'un bateau à voiles dont le foc est déchiré

Je voudrais être la projection pulvérisée du soleil sur la
    parure de lierre de tes bras
ce petit insecte qui t'a chatouillée quand je t'ai connue
Non
cet éphémère de sucre irisé ne me ressemble pas plus que le
    gui au chêne
qui n'a plus qu'une couronne de branches vertes où loge un
    couple de rouges-gorges
Je voudrais être
car sans toi je suis à peine l'interstice entre les pavés
    des prochaines barricades
J'ai tellement tes seins dans ma poitrine
que deux cratères fumants s'y dessinent comme un renne
    dans une caverne
pour te recevoir comme l'armure reçoit la femme nue
attendue du fond de sa rouille
en se liquéfiant comme les vitres d'une maison qui brûle
comme un château dans une grande cheminée
pareille à un navire en dérive
sans ancre ni gouvernail
vers une île plantée d'arbres bleus qui font songer à
    ton nombril
une île où je voudrais dormir avec toi*1*

From a sequence of disjointed images comes an unmistakable revelation of intimate sensations, of love. And even the impression of a first reading includes the certainty of important constants within rapidly shifting nuances of feeling and within a kaleidoscope of images which assume a vivid reality on their own. A basic recurring theme is the desire for something resembling a nest, "un gîte". The overall tone is irresistibly light and joyous.

Although subordinate to the free flow of sensation, a concern for form is also evident. The poem is divided into two stanzas. The first has an introspective, tonal emphasis and appears to explore carefully thoughts and feelings which are particularly immediate - the irrational here and now. The second includes more awareness of self in relation to the future, expressing wishes; and the syntax reveals a more self-conscious thought process, often close to reason. A great boon for the reader is the fact that, with a few exceptions, Péret follows regular sentence forms, omitting of course all punctuation except to indicate the beginning of a new sentence with a capital. Also helpful is the fact that the lines are cut at quite normal grammatical pauses. There are even few grammatical ambiguities and, despite logical absurdities, modifying phrases, successive conditional clauses can always with a little effort be syntactically related.

The short quick ring of the title, "On Sonne", alerts the reader, prepares him for the equally fast bouncy pace of the first line. This is no chance phenomenon but an opening which sets instantaneously a light, happy tone. Small at first, jump of a flea is likened to the bouncing of a wheelbarrow, two agile movements: that of the dance suggests happiness and then mentioning knees suggests a human physical quality. Although the sequence is set up in terms of a simile, and with a logical ground (the jump of a flea _does_ resemble the bounce of a wheelbarrow), the effect is not really to compare but to double the effect and to draw the reader into a full visual mood of participation. There are no verbs in the first line, frankly an ellipsis; here it perhaps represents an urgent need to register an immediate impression - pure sensation unrelated to event. You _see_ the flea and then you _see_ the wheelbarrow. From then on nearly all the images impress themselves visually first, intellectually afterwards. So, with the tone set and full reader participation assured, Péret finishes by making the flea disappear and stating just what is really on his mind - thinking of, talking to the woman he loves and saying that he'd like to find a comfortable spot where he could live with her ("un escalier où je vivrais avec toi"). The last half of that sentence ("et le soleil pareil à une bouteille... esclave fustigé") is similarly pure atmosphere. There is a progression from sunlight to color ("vin rouge") which then turns quite nasty and violent, evoking a thrashed slave and the rhythm is short and abrupt. It all has passionate, sexual overtones.

"Mais je t'aime comme le coquillage aime son sable..." With a definite conjunction of opposition, there is a shift to the whole long statement of love, more precisely a description of _how_ he loves her. In the first comparison, "comme le coquillage aime son sable", there is the same natural intimate cosy feeling as at the end of the first sentence. And after that, there is a flight into fancy of future possibilities, of

future conditions and events. The section, "quand le soleil aura la
forme d'un haricot qui commencera à germer comme un caillou montrant son coeur sous l'averse", has a theme of fecundity ("germer"),
which is very typical of Péret's world, and also of continued warmth
("soleil", "coeur"). The last two lines are connected grammatically
with the conditional clause, "quand le soleil aura la forme d'un haricot... ou d'une boîte de sardines... ou d'un bateau à voiles... "; but that
connection seems gratuitous. There is perhaps however an underlying
tie in another direction: the pebble which shows its heart, the open
can of sardines and the boat with the torn jib all have in common an
opened up or vulnerable quality.

The main lines of the second stanza are much clearer in a formal
sense for it consists principally of two statements of wish ("Je voudrais être... "; "Je voudrais être... ") and then a long sentence which
starts as a descriptive explanation ("J'ai tellement... ") and ends up in
a series of pleasant dream-like free associations. In this part, the
lover's consciousness is clear and forceful: "Je" introduces three of
the sentences and an emphatic, ego-centered "Non" launches the second statement.

Here, the woman he loves suffuses all his thought and feeling, is
close, necessary, physically and spiritually. There is a real physical
closeness which finally results in an imagined and desired fusion of
the two. The first wish, "Je voudrais être la projection pulvérisée du
soleil sur la parure de lierre de tes bras", has a delicate, warm visual beauty. The second, "ce petit insecte qui t'a chatouillée quand je
t'ai connue", reminds one of that first character, the flea. In both
cases, particularly the second, Péret's feeling for the insect is not
that of an entomologist, one feels sure, but almost of empathy.

Suddenly, and to our surprise, there is a forceful negation, "Non...",
which, despite its vehemence, is playful and absurd. There is no apparent reason for it. Its effect mainly, I think, is to reinforce the
sense of self, of will. There is perhaps a tonal resemblance between
the mayfly made of iridescent sugar and the sun's pulverized projection (but perversely this is what the poet denies!). More interesting,
important to the total pattern of the poem and another fine visual design is the green tree-top with the robin's nest.

Now comes the second, "Je voudrais être", which leaves the reader
up in the air, because, for lack of punctuation, one doesn't really know
whether he stops short of saying exactly what he would like to be or
whether he is saying simply that he wants to be, existentially. But the
next statement is unequivocal saying "car sans toi je suis à peine l'interstice entre les pavés des prochaines barricades", he expresses
with direct imagery how absolutely important she is to him, necessary for him to feel that he fills any substantial place at all.

Physical union, imaginatively formed and transfigured, is the subject of the last long sentence, beginning quite concretely, "J'ai tellement tes seins dans ma poitrine... " The images which follow are not
unconnected and trace a rich tonal path. First the breasts undergo
metamorphosis into smoking craters and the sense of being contained
internally (in his chest) is also magnified poetically into the immensity
of a cavern. All this manifests a desire to receive, to absorb; and then

follows another image of a hollow object made to enclose a human body: "pour te recevoir comme l'armure reçoit la femme nue..." The next succession of events has as a common theme disintegration, sensually powerful, conveying a sensation of erotic transport. First becoming liquid ("en se liquéfiant"), then burning ("comme les vitres d'une maison qui brûle") and finally drifting off ("pareille à un navire en dérive"). But when one reads the poem, the events, or our interpretation of them, are really subordinate to the rapidly painted images: a burning house which changes into a castle burning in a big fire place, suddenly shifts to the wide seas (the twisting burning flames perhaps suggesting swirling waves) and the human construction (the castle) becomes a ship. From the line "pareille à un navire en dérive", the development of thought is undistracted and leads to a sure haven, a magical island with blue trees where the lover rejoins the woman he is dreaming of. The last line, "une île où je voudrais dormir avec toi", restates happily the wish for an intimate place of union and rest. One cannot help thinking of the resemblance to Baudelaire's "Invitation au voyage". In a sense, Péret's paradise, albeit clearly imaginary, is closer because his dream world is real and present – thus containing more assurance of fulfillment than that of his nineteenth century predecessor.

Amidst surprise images, the two patterns mentioned at the start emerge clearly. They form a sort of atmospheric line which gives cohesion in an otherwise nonsensical chain of thought. The first, desire for a comfortable spot for two, is expressed in the following phrases: "un escalier où je vivrais avec toi", "une couronne de branches vertes où loge un couple de rouges-gorges", and the final very definitive statement "une île où je voudrais dormir avec toi". I would add to these the image, "comme le coquillage aime son sable", which evokes a natural resting place and comfort. The second pattern, lightness and happiness, is really what gives the poem its unique quality and appears throughout in images as well as in spirit and rhythm. Here are some particular phrases which contribute to the total picture: "Un saut de puce", "une brouette dansant", "la projection pulvérisée du soleil", "ce petit insecte qui t'a chatouillée", "cet éphémère de sucre irisé", "un navire en dérive", "une île plantée d'arbres bleus". The source of the effect in each case may be different. In the case of the jumping flea and the dancing wheelbarrow it is principally movement. But the flea and the little tickling insect and the mayfly appeal also by virtue of their size, their minuscule dimensions. The sun's pulverized projection, the iridescent sugar and the blue trees on the other hand seem to me attractive in this way because of a visual quality involving bright light and color.

Particularly striking in Péret's poems is the intricate and shifting rhythm and progression of tone. Whether this was spontaneous, conscious, or unconscious in the creative process seems to me in a sense irrelevant, since the effect on the reader is unmistakable. In the first line, for instance, the light tone comes partly from the images we have mentioned but also, I think, from the rhythm of the word groups. Traditional prosodic analysis (in terms of syllabic count), I feel, is not the best tool for Péret's creations but rather a phonetic sense of groupings and accents where the sounding board would be popular speech.

That first line breaks naturally into four phonetic rhythmic groups:
"Un saut de puce - comme une brouette dansant - sur les genoux des
pavés." If one were to take the Parisian accent as a base,*2 one would
then have the first two groups consisting of three short words with one
longer accent at the end ("un saut de puce") accompanied by a rise in
intonation. The third group would be similar except that there is an
extra short slightly accented syllable in the last word, "pavés". That
line certainly has a cheerful lilt! As for the general introduction of
theme and tone in the beginning (desire for nest; lightness), this continues at least up to the first words of line three ("et le soleil"). Then
the tone changes to one with suggestions of passion. It is significant
no doubt that the next two lines are abrupt ("s'est fait nègre / esclave
fustigé") - a brief violent interlude. The pace of the last sentence of
the stanza, four lines long, is slow and without any striking rhythmic
qualities. But there is a perceptible shift of tone. The emotional warmth
of the statement of love likened to the shell in the sand is followed by
the suggestion of physical warmth - the sun's beneficent effects - including the idea of liberation and of fecundation. The verb in the future
suggests the certainty of a prediction, "un haricot / qui commencera
à germer". However, the last two lines and images somehow are different. They are parallel grammatically, about equal in length, contain negative concepts of damage (the opened sardine can, the torn jib)
and when read aloud I think the reader's voice would slacken and fall.
So the end of the stanza represents a natural break and a tonal low
point.

The contrast is great at the outset of the second stanza. For immediately the thought expressed as well as the images are strong and
positive: "Je voudrais être la projection pulvérisée du soleil sur la
parure de lierre de tes bras..." Throughout the stanza a succession
of long carefully elaborated images alternates with statements of
judgment or desire, highlighted rhythmically. The third line is simply a monosyllable of negation, "Non", where one instinctively adds
an exclamation mark to the oral expression.*3 Similarly short and
eloquent is the line after the robin-nest image, "Je voudrais être".
In a sense it represents the emotional center of the stanza and perhaps
of the entire poem, isolated and selfsufficient, low-keyed but representing a precious existential truth. After that, once again, one very long
sentence leads to the end of the poem, going through modulations of
idea and tone. First, four lines ("J'ai tellement tes seins... du fond de
sa rouille") describe with a sudden, brief passionate expansion in the
image, "deux cratères fumants", how he feels filled, fulfilled with
the body of the woman he loves. Then, there is a series of disjointed
similes changing, shifting, which suddenly at the end leads to something which represents the narrator's deepest desire, discovered and
stated succinctly with an air of restful finality - an island for two.
From the point of view of the thought sequence (a succession of similes)
the resolution comes abruptly. But there are other indications, minute
but important, which prepare imperceptibly the close of the poem.
One, at the end of the next to last line reintroduces a corporal image.
The blue trees, says the narrator, recall "ton nombril". Thus we return to the thought and presence of the lovers. The other indication

appears in the phonetic series: "vers une _île... ton nombril / une île".
At the beginning and end of that penultimate line the same sound, i, is
repeated and it assumes the place of prominence - in sound
and in theme - at the beginning of the last line, where the discovery
occurs. One can indeed call this "poésie circulaire", for the desire
for a comfortable place for the lovers to live, expressed at the beginning is imaginatively reached at the end.

At this point, a word about interpretive method is in order. What I
have done is first to seek without preconceptions any constants of tone
and subject within the whole poem, isolating these patterns with no
necessary regard for logical syntactic sequence and then to look for
progression (sequentially) of rhythm, movement, phonetic relationships and semantically suggested tone. The matter is delicate because
in this sort of poetry many words, images, grammatical sequences
are purposefully absurd (in contrast to the poetry of Valéry and Perse).
Interesting and helpful in this regard is the evidence of Péret's method
of composition.*4   He wrote very rapidly and with really very few
changes. Often he would write so fast that in order to render a word
legible he would have to go back, write over it or write it again more
carefully. Sometimes he would write one word, cross it out, put down
an alternative next and then cross that out and return to his first
choice. For instance, the line of one poem in manuscript form reads,
"... célèbre, solide, célèbre..."*5   He wrote nothing in the margins
and apparently made no major revisions of form. One habit of note is
that some changes have to do with rhythmic balance - changing phrasing
or words, for instance, to establish syntactic equilibriums (repetitions
or sequences of conjunctions). This shows that he was indeed concerned about form. As for the nature of changes of single words, there
seem to be two sorts of choice. Sometimes, as in the example cited
above, the change seems to deal with meaning: a tortoise which was
"célèbre" appeared more fancifully desirable than one which was
"solide" - perhaps because tortoises can be solid but are infrequently
famous. In another case, the change is less original but similarly determined by sense. He changed the title of one poem from "Passagers
de première classe et leurs yeux ronds" to " Passagers de première
classe et leur teint frais". Here it is a simple shift from one physical
quality to another. But in another example the change is radical: a
poem first entitled "Ma main sous une pierre" was changed to "Ma
main dans la bière". But in this case the rhythm remained the same
and also the final rime ("pierre", "bière"). Another example is the
substitution of "cloche" for "roche"; and still another involving a more
complex sequence where tense, rhythm and rime were all preserved
was a line, "nous arrêterons les marées", altered to read "nous boule-
verserons les allées".*6. What conclusions can one draw? Mainly
that Péret was concerned both with sound and with sense. Sometimes
it appears as if he would opt for the more unusual sense; but still the
particular reason for a particular choice usually leaves open an immense area of speculation for the critic. If the poet apparently followed
the dictates of imagination, instinct, and subliminal concern for form,
the critic then can only do likewise.

NOTES

*1 Un Point c'est tout (1947; Paris: Losfeld, 1971), 183-184.

*2 The Parisian accent is characterized by a quick lilting rhythm and by the elision of practically all mute e's. This would radically change the measure since according to the rules of traditional prosody the mute e does count under most circumstances.

*3 Perhaps the absence of punctuation is really desirable and natural. The poet confidently leaves the words themselves, the sense and feeling behind them, as the whole set of pointers for oral expression.

*4 Most of Péret's manuscripts are unavailable, many probably lost. However, in the collection of the Bibliothèque Doucet there are some, mainly from the early collection, Le Grand Jeu.

*5 "La Pêche en eau trouble", Le Grand Jeu.

*6 "La Pêche en eau trouble" and "Le Quart d'une vie", Le Grand Jeu.

X

"A MI-CHEMIN"

A Mi-Chemin

Le vieux chien et la puce ataxique
se sont rencontrés sur le tombeau du soldat inconnu
Le vieux chien puait l'officier crevé
et la puce disait
Si ce n'est pas malheureux de s'accrocher des petites
   merdes avec des rubans rouges
sur la poitrine
Jadis les poireaux pourris ne rougissaient pas d'être pourris
les bouts de bois toussottant et crachottant
faisaient des corbillards très convenables
avec une odeur vénéneuse de champignons d'église
et la moustache ne servait qu'à balayer
Maintenant les sources de vieux poils jaillissent entre les pavés
et tu les adores vieux général
car ils viennent du crâne d'un curé
qui n'a pas d'os
qui n'a pas d'yeux
et qui se regarde dissoudre dans un bénitier *

Péret's numerous love poems, such as the one just analyzed, have a
great range of tone and theme voicing joyousness, bliss, tenderness,
shared adventures, also anxiety, concern about communication,
worries of loss. "A Mi-Chemin" shows quite another side of the poet's
temperament, his anti-establishment views, to use modern terminology, or in traditional terms his particular hate for the military and
the clergy, a part of his general scorn for bourgeois values.*1 This
poem, actually, is mild compared with others, especially those from
the collection Je ne mange pas de ce pain-là which dates roughly from
the same period*2 and where there are no holds barred on invective
and obscenity and where, with a few exceptions, the bile impairs the
effectiveness of expression. In those poems, he would usually take a
particular person or event as a spring-board, either from the past
(Jeanne d'Arc, Louis XVI) or the present (a politician such as Briand,
a military figure such as marshal Foch). Other targets were Gide's
"conversion" to communism, hypocritical patriotism ("Hymne des
anciens combattants patriotes"), a Eucharistic congress in Chicago,
international politics, fiscal problems - the perennial instability of
the franc ("Ci-gît le franc betterave sans sucre..."). Actually, the

most successful of his political satire is to be found not in his poetry but in his free-style prose, usually short humorous, impossible adventures. In <u>Mort aux vaches et au champ d'honneur,</u> one of the collections of this improvised prose, there is for instance a delightful satire of the Chambre des députés, "Ici l'on se rase gratis", written in the form of dialogue with extraordinary characters such as Mlle Lanterne, Mlle Démolie, Lohengrin, le Ministre de la Rage de Dents and so forth. Their elocutions touch on such vital problems as alcoholism, police brutality, abortion, military security (formulated in terms of an arms race involving "les bicyclette-boomerangs"). This particular story and another in the form of a series of letters, "Mes belles histoires se suivent mais ne se ressemblent pas", rival Rabelais in their social satire, verve, humor and imaginative style.

Politics were not simply an intellectual concern for Péret. In fact he and Aragon (in a different direction) were those of the Surrealist group for whom political action was part and parcel of their lives. In 1926, along with others of the group, he became interested in Communism and worked for a time for <u>L'Humanité.</u> Joining the leftist communist opposition in 1929, he continued throughout his life within that orientation and, with Breton, met Trotsky in Mexico in 1937. With no fixed residential roots, he lived at different times in Paris, of course, and in Brazil (when he was married to a Brazilian singer in 1931, returning there again in 1955). He went to Spain during the Civil War where he joined the Republican forces. Throughout World War II he stayed in Mexico. He was constantly engaged in political activities which on occasion led to arrest or expulsion.*3 However, despite some of his poems and stories which satirize capitalist society, on a theoretical level he separated literature and politics, vehemently opposing a conception of artists as serving a given social institution. He maintained that the poet should be free from political (or religious) control or bias and should constantly be alert to criticize, to preserve, and even to incarnate true human freedom, individual and social.*4

"A Mi-chemin", whose title remains a puzzle to me, is an uncomplicated poem as far as its message is concerned. The idea of scorn for the military and the church comes through loud and clear. It is interesting, however, as an example of a form combining poem and story and for certain very typical style and thought patterns. On the most direct and superficial level it is a jocular tale, almost child-like in its simple setting. But, one recalls, Péret values highly that which is naive. Right away we are introduced to the characters, an old dog and an ataxic flea who just happen to meet on the tomb of the unknown soldier; the rest of the poem relates what the agitated flea has on its mind, reflecting of course what he thinks of his comrade, the old dog, and certain very scornful attitudes about matters of general interest. Although the characters themselves share a quality of debility which clearly is intended to indicate the author's attitude about the sort of people one finds in the military and ecclesiastic arena, and although having the dog stinking like an "officier crevé" puts him in a bad light, or more precisely, in foul air, although these negative qualities are evident, still the first line, "Le vieux chien et la puce ataxique", contains a residual tone of warmth - an underlying sympathy for the creatures themselves. Describing the flea as ataxic is a nice and accurate touch, because fleas are by nature a bit shaky.

After hearing about the meeting in the first sentence, we then listen to the flea's speech, three sentences, containing directly expressed opinions in very conventional language but with a generous sprinkling of absurd conditions. The very first expression, "Si ce n'est pas malheureux", sets the tone, in caricature, of condescending, supercilious bourgeois judgments, the sort of thing which comes into ordinary conversations all the time. In fact, this quality in Péret's writing has as literary ancestors Flaubert's <u>Bouvard et Pécuchet</u> and the work of Alfred Jarry. It also foreshadows closely the same sort of parody and techniques of Ionesco and Beckett. Despite its conventional phraseology the whole introductory statement by the flea is not only critical of the tradition of military decorations but downright irreverent by virtue of the unaffected inclusion of the four letter word.

Next comes a description of the way it was in the good old days ("Jadis...") compared with present conditions ("Maintenant..."). The list of examples from the past is fairly detailed. The fact that "...les poireaux pourris ne rougissaient pas d'être pourris" shows how, then, people (translating the leeks anthropomorphically) were satisfied with their condition; "les bouts de bois...faisaient des corbillards très convenables..." emphasizes how important ceremonies took place properly; and "la moustache ne servait qu'à balayer" suggests that everything was in its right place, had its reasonable social function. Of course, the bitingly critical tone is laid on thick by the leeks being "pourris", having the bits of wood "toussottant et crachottant" and having the hearse exude "une odeur vénéneuse de champignons d'église". This pattern of debility was introduced at the beginning by the state of health of the characters themselves. The inclusion of odors ("le vieux chien puait", "une odeur vénéneuse") makes it all the more forceful and immediate, inescapable also because while one can close one's eyes to unpleasant sights, close one's mind to unpleasant ideas, bad smells are hard to avoid and physically quite intolerable. But, as in the first sentence, the slashing satire is tempered by the harmless and even humorous nature of the subjects - "les poireaux", "les bouts de bois", and "la moustache".

In the last sentence, the flea's strong feelings lead him away from comparison to direct attack. There is perhaps a semantic tie, the old hairs deriving from the idea of the mustache. The first part, "Maintenant les sources de vieux poils jaillissent entre les pavés", introduces a stronger overtone from the verb, "jaillissent" - evoking sudden, violent movement. Then, the flea addresses his companion directly and scornfully, "et tu les adores vieux général". The last part becomes even more vehement:

car ils viennent du crâne d'un curé
qui n'a pas d'os
qui n'a pas d'yeux...

The feeling is accentuated by the incisive rhythm starting with "du crâne d'un curé": five short, sharp syllables (if one drops the ə of crâne as a Parisian would) with the hard consonants d̠ and k̠ repeated.

The next two lines, the only short ones of the poem, both abrupt, four syllables in length, punctuate the attack. Their effect is to destroy him morally and physically bit by bit - suggesting that he is spineless and blind. The last line disposes of him entirely by making him witness his own dissolution and, of all appropriate places, in a holy-water basin, an ultimate insult.

All told, this poem has a very direct impact. It consists of four simply defined sentences, not exactly equal in length but close enough to make their individual rhythm stand out clearly. The overall tone is unambiguous. The tonal and phonetic rhythms follow a relatively simple line: introduction of scene; statement of irreverence, short, negative in tone but low in key; longer accumulation of the atmosphere of decay; a quick destructive windup. Of particular note is the absence of metaphors. So that nothing distracts from the force of the judgments. For judgments they are. From the statement of opinion, "Si ce n'est pas malheureux...", to the comparison of past and present and finally the explanation implicit in the use of the conjunctions "et" and "car" near the end. Although most of the conditions, events, combination of actors and actions are absurd, it is no chance that the syntactic framework emphasizes judgment and cause and effect. Conventional, and Péret appears to suggest "rotten", type of reasoning and expression is exactly the target of this poem.*5

NOTES

*1   These attitudes are expressed unambiguously in his reply to the last item of a questionnaire for the "Nouveau dictionnaire des contemporains". The item reads: "Particularités: déteste les curés, les flics, les staliniens et les commerçants." A photographic copy of the whole questionnaire is reproduced in Bédouin's presentation published by Seghers.

*2   Je ne mange pas de ce pain-là was first published by Les Editions surréalistes in Paris, 1936. "A Mi-Chemin", O.C., tome 1 (Paris: Losfeld, 1969), 43.

*3   Primary sources about his life are rare. A few letters from Péret to Breton written during the years 1936-1947, some when Péret was in Spain during the Civil War, others when Breton was in Mexico and several when Péret was in that country give something of a first-hand view of his personality.

*4   The essay, "Le Déshonneur des poètes", deals with this subject. It was written in Mexico in 1945 and vociferously attacks a volume of Resistance poetry, "Honneur des poètes", published in Rio de Janeiro. Loys Masson, Pierre Emmanuel, Louis Aragon, Paul Eluard are all targets of his attack.

*5   J.H. Matthews emphasizes this anti-rationalistic attitude and corrosive humour in his introduction to a bi-lingual collection, Péret's Score (Paris, 1965) and at length in an article, "Mechanics of the

Marvellous: The Short Stories of Benjamin Péret", L'Esprit créateur
Vol VI, No. 1 (spring 1966), 22-30.

XI

"SOLEIL ROUTE USEE..."

Soleil route usée pierres frémissantes
Une lance d'orage frappe le monde gelé
C'est le jour des liquides qui frisent
des liquides aux oreilles de soupçon
dont la présence se cache sous le mystère des triangles
Mais voici que le monde cesse d'être gelé
et que l'orage aux yeux de paon glisse sous lui
comme un serpent qui dort sa queue dans son oreille
parce que tout est noir
les rues molles comme des gants
les gares aux gestes de miroir
les canaux dont les berges tentent vainement de saluer les nuages
et le sable
le sable qui est gelé comme une pompe
et projette au loin ses tentacules de cristal
Toutes ses tentacules n'arriveront jamais à transformer
    le ciel en mains
Car le ciel s'ouvre comme une huitre
et les mains ne savent que se fermer sur les poutres des mers
qui salissent les regards bleus des squales
voyageurs parfumés
voyageurs sans secousses
qui contournent éternellement les sifflements avertisseurs
    des saules
des grands saules de piment qui tombent sur la terre comme
    des plumes

Si quelque jour la terre cesse d'être un saule
les grands marécages de sang et de verre sentiront leur
    ventre se gonfler
et crier Orties Orties
Jetez les orties dans le gosier du nègre
borgne comme seuls savent l'être les nègres
et le nègre deviendra ortie
et soutane son oeil perdu
cependant qu'une longue barre de cuivre se dressera comme
    une flamme
si loin si haut que les orties ne seront plus ses enfants
mais les soubresauts fatals d'un grand corps d'écume

salué par les mille crochets des eaux bouillantes
que lance le pain blanc
ce pain si blanc qu'à côté de lui le noir est blanc
et que les roches amères dévorent lentement les chevilles
    des danseuses d'acajou
mais les orties ô mosaïque les orties demain auront des
    oreilles d'âne
et des pieds de neige
et elles seront si blanches que le pain le plus blanc
    s'oubliera dans leurs dédales
Ses cris retentiront dans les mille tunnels d'agathe du matin
et le paysage chantera Un Deux Trois Quatre Deux Trois Un Quatre
les corbeaux ont des lueurs d'église
et se noient tous les soirs dans les égouts de dieu

Mais taisez-vous tas de pain le paysage lève ses grands bras
    de plume
et les plumes s'envolent et couvrent la queue des collines
et voici que l'oiseau des collines se retrouve dans la cage de l'eau

Mais plumes arrêtez-vous car le paysage n'est presque plus
    qu'une courte paille
que tu tires
C'est donc toi fille aux seins de soleil qui seras le paysage
l'hypnotique paysage
le dramatique paysage
l'affreux paysage
le glacial paysage
l'absurde paysage blanc
qui s'en va comme un chien battu
se nicher dans les boîtes à lettres des grandes villes
sous les chapeaux des vents
sous les oranges des brumes
sous les lumières meurtries
sous les pas hésitants et sonores des fous
sous les rails brillants des femmes
qui suivent de loin les feux follets des grands hérons du
    jour et de la nuit
les grands hérons aux lèvres de sel éternels et cruels
éternels et blancs
cruels et blancs *

Cosmic breadth, archetypal images, spiritual anguish, these form a
constant serious thread of subject and atmosphere from the very beginning of Péret's artistic production, particularly striking as they
are interspersed with poems of social satire, with others of a light,
playful vein. This work comes from a group of six short pieces published first in 1924, entitled Immortelle maladie. Péret and the other
Surrealists had discovered Freud early - the immense force, wealth,
and value of the subconscious aroused their curiosity, entered into the
theoretical framework of the movement and was the area explored in

the experiments involving hypnotic sleep and in the creative method "écriture automatique". Was Péret also familiar with Jung's work? Very possibly.*1 In any case a strong archetypal imagination was intrinsic to Péret's temperament and that sort of imagery was what came to the surface when he participated in experiments of hypnotic sleep during those years. There is an account of one such experiment and Péret's reactions are interesting in this regard. In a state of hypnosis, he was asked various questions. One was, "where are you going?" to which he replied: "Où on me mènera (puis) là où les hommes tombent morts, morts, comme tombe la neige." More questions followed about where that country was. Péret pointed, said that it was a planet far away from earth. And when asked what he saw there, he replied: "Une grande lame bleue... une grande lame bleue... qui roule, qui roule...(A partir de ce moment le visage de Péret prend une expression d'extase qui ne le quittera plus jusqu'au réveil. Il est tout à son étonnement, il rit aux anges)."*2 * This psychological domain revealed is certainly cosmic in scope.

Later in his life, after he had discovered the ancient cultures of Latin America and Mexico, he pursued traces of the primitive imagination, published a collection of Latin American myths, translated a Mayan religious chronicle. Two of his most successful original creations of his later years, Histoire naturelle, a chronicle of the creation of the world and Air mexicain, a long poem, reflect those personal imaginative forms enriched by experience and reflections about the primitive mentality.*3

"Soleil route usée pierres frémissantes", is a nameless poem, set in a nameless country. Before our eyes a gripping sequence of events takes place. Normal objects appear ominous. Anxiety pervades the air, at times subdued, elsewhere strangely and wildly distressed. The form suggests the long, sometimes seemingly endless pace of a nightmare where the observer is absorbed at each step and at first may feel unable to foresee an end, but eventually views the experience as a whole. Yet form there is. Two parts of roughly equal length and rhythmical impact are followed by a short interlude which relieves the tension. A final fourth section, with its own special tempo, leads to the particularly forceful final image.

The first line, dispensing with verbs and any relational semantic elements (prepositions, articles, adverbs) evokes a bright barren landscape suffused with an active uneasiness - "pierres frémissantes". Evoke is too mild a word: the sight is elemental and compelling. Two events take place, the first one on a particular day, "le jour des liquides qui frisent". Initially, a storm strikes a frozen world; then the storm disappears, the world becomes unfrozen. In this introductory part, ending roughly with the shorter line, "parce que tout est noir", where the prosody and the implied sentence structure indicate a break, the sense of hidden unrest is already strong. Two archetypal images reinforce that sense, "le mystère des triangles" and "un serpent qui dort sa queue dans son oreille": both shapes have hidden ambiguous significance (the triangle and the circle) and the snake has unmistakable overtones of evil. Furthermore the words "soupçon" and "mystère" state the presence of something unknown and directly disquieting.

The two verbs "dont la présence se cache" and "l'orage aux yeux de paon glisse sous lui" elaborate that sensation.

Next comes a series of superimposed images, shapes in the darkness: "les rues molles comme des gants / les gares aux gestes de miroir..." In form this resembles the scenes of Dali, in tone those of Chirico: places all seemingly deserted and with their outlines and gestures softened, altered, rendered ominous. The streets are soft as gloves, the stations whose gestures only reflect themselves, canals trying in vain to greet the sky and the sand, even with its tentacles reaching out and upwards also makes hopeless attempts. The short line, "Car le ciel s'ouvre comme une huitre", offered strangely as an explanation is somehow reassuring. It represents, too, the second point of rest rhythmically speaking after the first shorter line, "parce que tout est noir". Perhaps it is significant that both are offered as explanations - reasons all too infrequent in a distressing world of uncertainty. But the negative tone reappears directly, syntactically, in the following line, "les mains ne savent que se fermer". The last lines accent the theme of restlessness and of wandering. "Voyageurs parfumés / voyageurs sans secousses" are eternally tracing the same path. The travelers, the warning whistles repeat the theme of wayfaring which was introduced from the start in the phrase "route usée" and reinforced by "rues", "gares", and "canaux". The end of the section is sketched with a soft downward motion, "...qui tombent sur la terre comme des plumes". The main elements of this whole section, in retrospect, include a wide scene, universal proportions ("monde", "terre", "soleil", "orage", "ciel", "mers") where there are traces of human wandering - roads, streets, and canals. The atmosphere from the start has an anxious cast and one is aware particularly of a feeling of powerlessness: "gelé", "rues molles", "gestes de miroir", "les canaux... tentent vainement", "voyageurs... qui contournent éternellement" supported by the two negative constructions, "n'arriveront jamais" and "ne savent que se fermer".

The tone of the second part becomes immediately sharp and violent. Introduced by a conditional, "Si quelque jour la terre cesse d'être un saule", it swells to apocalyptic proportions. Indeed, although that first conditional seems mild and even perhaps unlikely, what follows, stated in the future tense, feels inevitable, really so vivid that one forgets altogether that grammatically it is only hypothetical. The hidden mystery becomes highly ominous: "les grands marécages de sang et de verre sentiront leur ventre se gonfler." Swamps of blood swell and the cry breaks out, "Orties Orties". Nettles, the English equivalent, although denoting something unpleasant and prickly does not seem as bad as "Orties!" Phonetically, in French, there is a wild tone to that word and it is repeated twice and then sounds like an imprecation in the angry, insulting command that follows, "Jetez les orties dans le gosier du nègre...", a command composed of short violent lines. And then comes another awesome event, "une longue barre de cuivre se dressera comme une flamme". From the swelling of the swamp's bellies, to the voice shouting, expansion continues - a sharp vertical thrust like a flame, far and wide ("si loin si haut..."). It is accompanied by another heat image, "eaux bouillantes", and followed by violent, destructive actions ("soubresauts fatals", "les mille crochets...que lance", "roches amères dévorent"). Several of the lines give the impression of something resembling a strange lyrical satanic orgy.

> ...des danseuses d'acajou
> mais les orties ô mosaïque les orties demain auront des
>   oreilles d'âne...

Totally absurd from a rational semantic point of view, the emotional effect is powerful. Dance is first suggested by "danseuses"; an unbridled tempestuous rhythm ("mais les orties ô mosaïque les orties"), then evokes excited movement. This is heightened by a phonetic intensity in the word "mosaïque"*4 with the shrill i preceded and followed in "ortie", and also by the sense of imprecation already pervading the word "ortie" because of the previous passage where it appeared.

In this section too there are several shorter lines which relieve the tension, "que lance le pain blanc" before, and further on "et des pieds de neige". Both nouns, bread and feet, are harmless by nature; but mainly it is their whiteness which is heartening and this is dwelt upon smoothly in the line that follows "et elles seront si blanches que le pain le plus blanc s'oubliera dans leurs dédales". However, the respite is brief for the anguished cries are heard again, like the resounding pleas of someone lost in a labyrinth. The "dédales" become "tunnels"; not just several, they are multiplied into thousands. This line is interesting phonetically: "Ses cris retentiront dans les mille tunnels d'agathe du matin." Up to the first break ("ses cris retentiront") there are two sounds which come across emphatically, first the sharp i of "cris" which swings and modulates to the booming, low õ of the last syllable of "retentiront" - both sounds perfectly onomatopoetic evoking shouts resounding in the tunnels. The last part of the line is composed of a long series of more evenly accented and neutral syllables, the one exception being the i reappearing in "mille". Considering the line as a whole, there is a high frequency of staccato consonants, five with t d, and g. That line stands out as a supreme climax, stressing the tone of anxiety. At the end, dismal ideas return. The "lueurs d'église" are hardly reassuring, especially considering Péret's "dim" view of the church. "Les égouts de dieux" have similar dark overtones. "Les corbeaux"*5 and "les soirs" are further black notes. Just as the first section ends with a downward movement, so this one descends, drowning, into the depths of gutters.

The bread, the feathers, and the landscape figure again as principal actors in the short third section. But the tone changes radically. "Mais taisez-vous...", a voice urges a return to silence. As rescue from the depths, the first two verbs, "lève" and "s'envolent", lift upwards and three words evoking the bird image - "plumes", "queue", and "oiseau" itself - add to the lighter touch. The end, however, returns our attention to a stationary position. "...Voici que l'oiseau des collines se retrouve dans la cage de l'eau."

The same voice speaks to open the fourth section, "Mais plumes arrêtez-vous car le paysage n'est presque plus qu'une courte paille." The wide open settings of the first two parts disappear, shrink. For a moment the person through whose eyes we have seen this nightmare-like film, seems partially to regain consciousness and discover some truths about what he has witnessed. The unique human being of the poem, "fille aux seins de soleil", he thinks may embody the landscape. This is also the first reappearance of the sun which bathed the scene at the start. He then describes, exactly - with no "nonsense" - that landscape in a series of adjectives strung out line by line: hypnotic, dramatic, frightful, glacial, absurd and white. After that, a more irrational frame of mind takes over, for he pictures the landscape as going away "comme un chien battu", going away to hide. The next series of parallel lines is very typical of Péret's poetry, more so than the preceding description of the landscape which was entirely reasonable:

sous les chapeaux des vents
sous les oranges des brumes
sous les lumières meurtries
sous les pas hésitants et sonores des fous
sous les rails brillants des femmes

These words are illogical in sequence. But certain patterns tie them together. The final nouns of lines one and two and then lines four and five are related, "vents" and "brumes" have to do with weather, while "fous" and "femmes" are human beings. Also, "les pas hésitants et sonores" and "les rails brillants" echo the pattern of byways and wanderers from the first section. And each line seems to guide us farther and farther away, fleeing into the distance as is suggested by the next line, " qui suivent de loin les feux follets... " But the last extraordinary image returns us to the vivid immediacy and the distressed tone of the beginning. It leads to the end in a series of four rhythmically contracting lines:

qui suivent de loin les feux follets des grands hérons du
    jour et de la nuit
les grands hérons aux lèvres de sel éternels et cruels
éternels et blancs
cruels et blancs

If not archetypal, the herons have the stature of mythical figures by their size but mainly because of their attributes. They reign over day and night and they partake of the eternal. To think that they have lips of salt is not comforting. If "sel" for Perse represented a healthy sign of challenge and life, their salty lips suggest a torture similar to that suffered by the victim of Camus' tale, Le Renégat. Eternal, cruel, and white, these qualities are forced upon us as immutable, their presence becoming frighteningly stationary as they are slowly repeated in unrelenting pairs. Interestingly, the powerful third line, "les grands hérons aux lèvres de sel éternels et cruels", resembles in its rhythmic and structural pattern that equally forceful line in the second section, "Ses cris retentiront... " There is an initial short group of words at the start which modulates from a sharp vowel to end with a low nasal phoneme followed by a longer series with a repetition of more equal, neutral sounds. Here, the first part has a pair of such modulations: "les grands hérons" swinging first from e̱ to ã and then from e̱ to ɔ̃.

Throughout the line there are e and _ sounds repeated and linked in
the last part by a pattern of r and l sounds. The mysterious hostile
presence sensed at the outset of the poem is disclosed in all its white
horror. The end is not only rhythmically stationary but tonally frozen -
eternal.*6

NOTES

*1 Freud, of course, was the principal source of psychoanalytic
thought for the group. I have not found any mention of Jung by Péret.
However, Tzara mentions his name in an article "Essai sur la situation de la poésie", Le Surréalisme au service de la révolution, no.4,
1931. A number of Jung's articles were published in French scientific
journals, the first in 1913. L'Analyse des rêves was published in Paris
in 1909, Métamorphoses et symboles de la libido in 1924, Essais de
psychologie analytique in 1931. It seems probable that Péret was acquainted with his ideas.

*2 "Récit de sommeil hypnotique", Littérature, no. 6, nov. 22, 12-16.

*3 Péret prefaced his translation of the Mayan chronicle, Le Livre
de Chilám Balám de Chumayel (Paris, 1955) with an essay combining
historical background and personal impressions of visits to archeological sites. Air mexicain was published in 1952 in Paris by Librairie
Arcanes. Histoire naturelle (Ussel, 1958) is beautifully illustrated by
his friend the artist, Toyen.

*4 The phrase "ô mosaïque" has something of the strangely attractive
exotic ring as does the famous line from Racine's Phèdre, "La fille de
Minos et de Pasiphaé".

*5 According to Jobes' Dictionary of Mythology, Folklore and Symbols,
the crow in French and Italian tradition is a symbol of misfortune, in
the Greek tradition a bearer of ill-tidings the symbol of longevity. On
the modern scene, the crow appears ominously evil in the films of
Ingmar Bergman.

*6 One is reminded of the atmosphere of "Le vierge, le vivace..." by
Mallarmé. Bédouin relates that Péret told him that some of his early
unpublished poems were inspired by Mallarmé (p. 25). Temperamen-
tally the two poets seem unrelated. But each, in his own way, did indeed "peindre non la chose mais l'effet qu'elle produit".

LE GRAND COEUR DE LA NATURE

Fired with the enthusiasm of the Surrealist project to liberate the human spirit from social restraints and rational intellectual bonds, Péret
and his poetic world is best viewed within the context of that literary
movement's esthetic and psychological conceptual framework. He joined
the group in 1920, its early formative stage and his appearance is sig-
nalled with an appropriate air of mystery in Breton's Nadja.*1 What
is most unusual, in that group where dissidence and defection were
the rule rather than the exception, is that he remained within the inner
circle, close to Breton until his death. Péret was less inclined to formulate abstractly modes and aims of poetic creation, but certainly he
was influenced by the theoretical pronouncements of the others and,
indeed, although his poems never received wide public acclaim, they
were and are most highly regarded by those sensitive to the Surrealist
ideal, the "happy few" so to speak.*2
    The central poetic aim of the Surrealists was both optimistic and
ambitious. The tone of optimism is particularly striking in the First
Surrealist Manifesto (1924) which sets forth the goal of reconciling
objective experience with the inner world of feeling and thought. Breton's definition of "surréalité" is precisely this: "une résolution future
de ces deux états rêve et réalité en apparence contradictoires."*3 In
subsequent documents he elaborates on this basic tenet. The Second
Manifesto (1930) widens the elements of experience to be reconciled
to include life and death, the real and the imaginary, the past and the
future, the communicable and the incommunicable.*4 And in a particularly interesting later essay, Situation surréaliste de l'objet (1935),
he approaches the question from the point of view of plastic arts posing
the aim of expressing visually internal perception, that is, using concrete forms from the outside world but considering them and translating them as integrated by the imagination in an inner mental world.
This, of course, excludes representational art and also relegates
rational and speculative thought processes to the background presuming
to render the pleasure principle stronger than the reality principle.*5
Freud's influence is obvious.
    As for the means to discover and approach this goal, both in general
experience and in artistic creation, attention is focused on the thing
itself, that inner world, conceived from the start interestingly in temporal terms, in terms of thought process. Discovering and expressing
this thought process becomes the means to the end. The famous definition of the First Manifesto makes this quite clear:

Automatisme psychique pur par lequel on se propose d'exprimer, soit verbalement, soit par écrit, soit de toute autre manière, le fonctionnement réel de la pensée. Dictée de la pensée, en l'absence de tout contrôle exercé par la raison, en dehors de toute préoccupation esthétique ou morale.*6 *

Amplifying this premise, Breton endows this area of human experience with an ontological superiority and also mentions dreams and free association as its main manifestations. Later Breton conceded that some element of control would enter into the picture in art, saying, "Un minimum de direction subsiste, généralement dans le sens de l'arrangement en poème."*7 This concession is of considerable importance for the critic since it introduces the key notion of structure.

Equally essential to the whole picture is the Surrealist's faith in language. Here, positions vary somewhat. Breton and Aragon manifest a striking, and surprisingly traditional, confidence in verbal forms and expression. Although they dismiss purely logical expression as insufficient (in poetry), there is no apparent doubt about words having meaning, about words accurately expressing thought and feeling. Breton has an almost teleological view in this respect: "le langage a été donné à l'homme pour qu'il en fasse un usage surréaliste."*8 The method is simply to trust instinctive judgment, to let the words flow freely and one will unquestionably achieve the desired lucidity. Aragon, in his Traité du style, goes so far as to insist that Surrealist writing is fully coherent and rigorous. If the meaning flows from within and if each word can not be explained simply by its dictionary definition, each word is nonetheless irreplaceable and the text as a whole will exhibit interrelated content and form. Furthermore, one is invited to make value judgments. Says Aragon, "Si vous écrivez suivant une méthode surréaliste de tristes imbécilités, ce sont de tristes imbécilités. Sans excuses."*9 This, together with his and Breton's suggestion that logical and grammatical analyses of Surrealist texts should be enlightening, leaves the critic encouraged, of course, but indeed awed by the difficulty of the task*10 given the atypical use of meaning within normal syntactical forms. Tzara was perhaps more honest in a sense, or at least more willing to admit the elusive nature of Surrealist language. The central figure of the early Dada movement, he himself recognized later that reducing poetry (words) to a simple succession of sounds had lead to a dead end although it had served the important purpose of emphasizing the volatile nature of meaning, the "capacité de fuite de la signification des mots". *11

Péret, as we have already remarked, shared Breton's faith in language as an unambiguous vehicle for poetic thought, with an individual emphasis on primitive and popular forms of expression as revealing more of instinctive, unconscious grasp of the world. Such expression escapes, never having experienced, the dualistic conception which values logic more highly than reason. But aside from an expression of faith in language untouched by rationalism, Péret does not go into detail about practical matters of writing. He does, however, indicate something about the source of poetic inspiration and links it directly with experience. In his preface to the anthology of Latin American myths he describes it in terms of a sense of the marvellous

which one can encounter at any time, any place and which is ready to
explode like a time bomb if only one is sensitively tuned to the possibilities. Here is an example he gives:

Ce tiroir que j'ouvre me montre, entre des bobines de fil et des
compas, une cuillère à absinthe. A travers les trous de cette cuillère
s'avance à ma rencontre une bande de tulipes qui défilent au pas de
l'oie. Dans leur corolle se dressent des professeurs de philosophie
qui discourent sur l'impératif catégorique... *12 *

The starting point is a very ordinary external perception, a simple
drawer containing simple objects. The development springs from the
free play of the imagination and contains its own truth. It is not absurd,
it has its own reality - a "surréalité".

Further on in the same essay he discusses in detail the mechanism
of the formation of images starting from an even simpler external perception. In 1940, in a prison at Rennes, a particular series of images
occurred to him as he was lying on the floor, looking at a window which
had just been painted over. He saw the face of François Ier, a bucking
horse, a tropical landscape like those of le douanier Rousseau. These
images would reappear and sometimes undergo transformations. What
is interesting is the fact that Péret gives a symbolic interpretation for
each image, all having to do, he said, with a "violent appétit de liber-
té tout naturel dans ma situation". The images stem directly from his
past experience: the portrait of François Ier suggested history books
in school where as a youngster he felt similarly imprisoned; the bucking horse symbolized his vain protests and recalled his service in an
armored division in World War I; the tropical forest involved a more
complicated chain of associations having to do with experiences in
Mexico.*13 The conclusions to be drawn from this explanation are
important for the reader. If the raw material, the initial image for
poetic expressions comes from the outside world, the force governing
the formation of images is emotional in nature, personal of course.
And the images have a particular symbolic meaning which also is very
personal drawn from the life of the poet. Once again the reader is reassured to know that an apparently gratuitous series of images likely
contains definite symbolic significance, but he is also faced with limitations. Since the source of imagery is so very personal, the reader
can not ever expect to attain full comprehension. Yet that is true of
all human communication in literature or in life.

This being the case, the practical course is simply to examine what
is available, the poems. Since Péret himself (and the other Surrealists) stresses the importance of immediate experience as the starting
point, it should prove illuminating to consider initially just how the
outer world is reflected in his work. Immediately striking is the fact
that the impetus for many poems is an event, or an idea, or a feeling.
The collection, Je ne mange pas de ce pain-là, provides the most obvious examples of political situations and actions which serve as the
subject of particular poems. The problem of the instability of the
French franc, a Eucharistic Congress in Chicago, these are instances
we already mentioned. Another which is even more circumstancial is
a poem entitled "6 février".*14 Here are some excerpts:

Vive le 6 février
grogne le jus de chique
vêtu en étron fleurdelysé
Que c'était beau
Les autobus flambaient comme les hérétiques d'autrefois

...
Vive le 6 février
et vive le 7
J'ai hurlé pendant deux jours
A mort Cachin A mort Blum
Et j'ai volé tout ce que j'ai pu dans les magasins
dont je brisais les vitres*

...

Although this poem contains its share of unexpected characters and actions ("grogne le jus de chique... "), it tells of a specific event including realistic details such as the burning of buses and even including the author's own actions.

Also personal in nature, and exhibiting a form with traditional overtones, is an early poem, "Le Quart d'une vie", written possibly when Péret was around twenty-five, composed of twenty-six short stanzas. Although the syntactic sequences are nonsensical, although the imagery is simply playful and often gratuitous, there is a personal tone. The first persons, singular and plural recur; there are indications of time past, time present, and time future. A melancholy air, mainly ironic, is noticeable. It ends thus:

...
Sa destinée fut courte comme une sueur
Ma soeur
as-tu vu ma pipe
Ma pipe est morte
et mon grand oeil est sans saveur

One is reminded of Les Testaments of Villon;*15 and in certain ways the two poets do resemble each other. Both led a life of vagabondage, of protest against existing society. Both also had a taste for the vernacular, for the earthy and used it spontaneously and colorfully as a poetic idiom. Even if this poem ("Le Quart d'une vie") was primarily intended as a satire of traditional forms, there remains a substratum of authentic sentiment which, perhaps unconsciously, attenuates the negative, destructive aim.

A good many of Péret's poems have as inspirational force a frame of mind or a subjective feeling. Some are dedicated to particular people and one of these, addressed to René Crevel, shows both a depth of understanding and an ability and urge to express feeling through poetry. Crevel was one of the original Surrealist group, of an unhappy temperament, who exhibited over a number of years self-destructive symptoms and who committed suicide by hanging. In the collection De Derrière les fagots (1934) a poem, "S'Ennuyer", starts with these lines:

Quand les montagnes têtent les serpents qui les étouffent
et les bêtes de sang somment l'électricité
d'aller se faire pendre ailleurs
la poussière amalgamée sur les nouveaux-nés
se fend de haut en bas... *

The title is clearly not absurd, the tone of suffering and desperation announced at the outset is developed and reinforced. Péret, too, experienced moments of anxiety, of fear and expressed these quite personal subjective sensations directly in a number of poems mainly found in the collections dating in the thirties. From this period also come the most sensitive love poems, especially the collection Je Sublime where a vast range of feelings - tenderness, warmth, passion, total joyous absorption, abandon - all find a spontaneous poetic outlet. "On Sonne" is only one of a number which show the free, light play of such personal warmth. The open quality is particularly striking after having seen in the work of Valéry an expression less personal through its drive to extract the essence of human emotions and psychological patterns and in the work of Perse portraying passions on a broad cosmic metaphorical level. In a sense, despite the nonsensical syntactic groupings, Péret's poetic expression often exhibits a more direct kinship with traditional lyric verse by virtue of its origins in personal sentiment, romantic in nature.

But, if frequently the initial inspiration for a poem is an idea, an event or a feeling, such a traditional characteristic is more than compensated for by the case with which the author launches into fantastic adventures. The title of his first published collection is, significantly, Le Grand jeu. A spirit of playfulness, a taste for the ridiculous and pinpricking humor prevail, more so than in his later works. Also, particularly in the stories which date from that period, and in most of his poems throughout his life there is a refreshingly childlike enthusiasm for adventure. The Surrealists in general admired Lewis Carroll and much of the curiosity and that author's taste for pursuing unlikely trails is very similar to the way Péret's imagination can be carried away on an escapade at the drop of a hat in even rather serious poems. The starting point, the initial image or situation may still well be grounded in something immediate, like the example he gave in his preface - the contents of a drawer; but there is no telling what may follow in the way of encountering strange characters, strange situations and strange actions. A passage from "Soleil route usée..." shows how this can happen even in the most anguished atmosphere:

...
mais les orties ô mosaïque les orties demain auront des
   oreilles d'âne
et des pieds de neige
et elles seront si blanches que le pain le plus blanc
   s'oubliera dans leurs dédales
Ses cris retentiront dans les mille tunnels d'agathe du matin...

Suddenly those frightful thistles are seen as about to sprout donkey ears, feet of snow thus to furnish a labyrinth where the white bread will wander, lose itself and cry out. Very often Péret will relate such a sequence of bizarre events in the future tense, usually introduced by a conditional or adverbial clause ("Si..."; "quand..."). But although the interlude is posed as hypothetical, the situations are so vivid that they seem real or at least inevitable. There is another such passage in "On Sonne":

> ...je t'aime comme le coquillage aime son sable
> où quelqu'un le dénichera quand le soleil aura la forme
> d'un haricot
> qui commencera à germer comme un caillou montrant son
> coeur sous l'averse...

Sun, rain, germination, although posed as a future condition, appear in the context as a natural and unquestioned occurrence. The action of that poem furthermore leads afar – ending happily on an island forested with blue trees, a haven for lovers. This characteristic of the poetic imagination of Péret is very different from that of Aragon who spoke scornfully of the trips of Baudelaire, Rimbaud, and Gide, considering freedom and flights of fancy an illusion, emphasizing that no paradise of any sort exists.*16

The sharp clear outside world not only usually furnishes the starting point for Péret's poems, it also provides characters, qualities, in short, situations which are very life-like except for the impossible subjects of action, relationships, and occurrences. Active figures, the heroes of Péret's universe can be almost anything. Occasionally they are people – mainly in the stories. Very often they are animals, birds or insects: herons, parrots, crows, mayflies, other little insects; the dog and the flea, heroes of "Mi-Chemin", reappear as actors in other poems too. Sometimes parts of the human body are the main characters as in a poem, "Le Genou fendu", which starts out: "L'épaule indifférente / et la bouche malade / sont tombées sur les épines..."*17 But inanimate objects appear and also engage in action. Péret is especially fond of food, often vegetables – carrots, radishes, artichokes – and bread which plays such an important role in "Soleil route usée". The title of the main collection of short stories is naturally, <u>Le Gigot sa vie et son oeuvre</u>.*18 In the case of animals and food, the tone in which Péret speaks of them is usually very fond, even affectionate. Natural phenomena are called upon frequently to act too: rainbows, the sun, rocks, stones. One poem starts impressively: "Tandis que le rocher surplombant la mer / admirait sa mâle prestance..."*19 That sardine can we read of in "On Sonne" often figures prominently. Even abstract nouns can perform: "les nombres élevés", "les fractions infinitésimales", and one which I like especially, "les adverbes sauvages".*20

Péret's world is packed with action – this we will analyze later. It is also complete with qualities of color, sound, and smells. "A Mi-Chemin" is an example where smells were used to impress on the reader the idea of decay ("le vieux chien puait l'officier crevé"; "une odeur vénéneuse de champignons d'église"). Voices, cries make themselves heard forcefully as in "Soleil route usée..." ("Criez Orties Orties"; "ses cris retentiront"; "le paysage chantera"). Other noises

made by objects also accompany the narrative: "les sifflements avertisseurs des saules"; "...la mâchoire inférieure d'un tigre qui me dé-
chire lentement avec un affreux bruit de porte enfoncée..." renders
the atmosphere horrifying in another poem.*21 Colors are sometimes
used specifically to paint a metaphysical atmosphere. This is the case
in the long poem, "Dernier malheur dernière chance", written in
Mexico, and in "Soleil route usée..." where, in the first section, one
line alone darkens the whole scene - "parce que tout est noir", and
where in contrast the color white evokes the glacial, frozen stillness.
One line of that poem is particularly interesting because both colors
appear in a description: "ce pain si blanc qu'à côté de lui le noir est
blanc." It is a sort of play of contrasts where opposites disappear or
are in some sense fused. Sometimes colors are used quite simply in
descriptions. There is the peaceful "couronne de branches vertes où
loge un couple de rouges-gorges", and the "île plantée d'arbres bleus"
in "On Sonne". Blue and green seem generally to be favorite colors of
Péret, ones he found esthetically pleasing and restful. Blue, one recalls, figures in the report of that happy hypnotic conversation. There
are occasions when Péret uses colors more unconventionally. One
interesting example is a poem from <u>Dormir dormir dans les pierres</u>
where a stanza begins: "Souffle ô corne un azur sombre et verbal..."
"Azur" is impertinent semantically as the object of "Souffle ô corne"
and one of the adjectives is similarly unexpected, but the line is forceful imaginatively, I feel, just because of "azur" and "verbal". A bit
further on in the same poem is the sequence: "Assise flamberge assis
vents / La mer se décolore et le rouge domine / Le rouge de mon coeur
est le vent de ses fles..."*22 Here colors are used much more arbitrarily; but they retain strongly their visual impact. Eluard who is
well known for his own verbal color magic wrote an introduction for a
collection of verse by Péret, signalling an image (from a poem with
heated negative political import) which combined sound and color: "le
cri strident des oeufs rouges." His remarks include the comment that
such clear images convey perfect understanding ("compréhension parfaite") of things out of the ordinary, substituting for dull common
sense a new sort of logic, "liée à la vie non comme une ombre mais
comme un astre".*23

  Not only Péret's images display this different sort of logic. His entire world, where reigns supreme that taste for simple surprise or
biting absurd irony, that readiness to launch into strange adventures,
that willingness to expose himself and to be guided by a dream-like
state even though it may be a source of terror as well as ecstasy, this
world is not in the least formless and arbitrary but on the contrary
exhibits a structure of its own. To understand this, it is helpful to
know how Breton conceived of the "fonctionnement réel de la pensée".
In a fairly recent essay,*24 he explains the difference between Joyce's
interior monologue and Surrealist thought. The former, he says, remains in the naturalist tradition, seeking a flux of sensations and
thoughts from many points of view directly related to experience and
tending to imitate closely life in the immediate. The latter, in contrast,
is concerned solely with the flow having its source deep in oneself. It
is personal in nature and one must not seek to direct its course other-

wise it will dry up, vanish. Two striking characteristics of this "automatisme psychique pur" are for one thing its luminous intensity and for another the fact that it expresses itself verbally with few neologisms, without distortions of syntax and vocabulary.

This luminous quality is nicely illustrated by an early poem of Péret, "La Boîte aux lumières".*25

> Elle est pleine d'un coton léger
> qui s'envole au moindre bruit
> qui crépite au moindre vent
> qui s'ennuie à la moindre pluie
> et qui tue pour le moindre désir
>
> Cela ne peut pas continuer ainsi
> Il tombe sur le pied de mon voisin
> une mousse de nuages
> qui est verte
> Ce sont des épinards
>
> Il tombe sur la tête de ma voisine
> des cailloux de fourrure
> dont elle fait ses délices
> Ce sont des souris *

The title of this poem is directly the source of its inspiration. It reminds one of the drawer whose ordinary contents can lead one's imagination far and wide. This box of lights, full of weightless cotton, evokes movements and actions which are equally weightless, free, ready to take place at the least simple cause ("au moindre bruit... au moindre vent... à la moindre pluie... pour le moindre désir"); the causes themselves are nearly or totally immaterial. The first stanza is thus plain description. The next starts out in a way which is quite typical of Péret's thought process. Into a description or the account of an adventure, he introduces, naturally but pertinently, his comment or his spontaneous reactions. Here he says, "Cela ne peut pas continuer ainsi..." And, breaking the spell and the initial rhythm, he proceeds ostensibly to reverse the motion. The idea of weightlessness and rising drift ("s'envole", "crépite") is changed to the concept and the occurrence of falling, which introduces the second two parallel stanzas, "Il tombe... Il tombe..." Yet, despite the surprise or light shock for the reader due to the unexpected comment and despite the downward pointing verb, a number of light tonal elements continue. "Mousse", "nuages", "verte", "fourrure" are by quality light. The "épinards" and the "souris" are light by virtue of humor. And "délices" echoes the happy hopeful quality of "désir" from the first stanza. The contents of "la boîte aux lumières" indeed engenders thoughts which are luminous.

As for Breton's statement that the expression of automatic thought follows regular grammatical patterns, Péret's poetry not only follows true to form but even emphasizes in many cases specific syntactic nuances - qualifying phrases, conditional and causal clauses, conjunctions of coordination or opposition. In the case of one poem we examined closely, "A Mi-Chemin", the syntactic framework very clearly is ironic in intent. First the statement, "Si ce n'est pas malheureux

de s'accrocher des petites merdes..." parodies the superficial and
self-righteous tone of bourgeois conversation. Next come the two sentences comparing the past with the present: "Jadis les poireaux pourris ne rougissaient pas d'être pourris..."; "Maintenant les sources de
vieux poils jaillissent entre les pavés..." Again the author uses common references to the past as somehow better, more orderly than the
present to make fun of the unrealistic quality of such judgments and to
satirize what he considers rotten conventional attitudes about religion.
The opening adverbs, "Jadis" and "Maintenant" serve to sharpen the
critical blade. So that the basic syntactic presentation has a negative,
destructive aim, taking the form of an anti-rationalistic, anti-bourgeois
weapon.

But this is not always the case. Although a patterned syntactic presentation may have a negative twist as in "Mi-Chemin", although some
constructions may be gratuitous or simply a recognizable frame on
which to hang fantastic or absurd statements or adventures. I think
that a careful study of Péret's work would show that in most cases the
grammatical frame has a very definite meaning within the context of
the tone, scene or problem which represents the core of the poem.
Taking another poem already analyzed "Soleil route usée...", one can
see several distinct cases where this is so. For instance, the use of
the conjunction of opposition, "Mais", to introduce both the third and
fourth sections is certainly not arbitrary. Recalling that the contained
anxiety expressed in the first section was developed and raised to a
very intense and depressing pitch in the equally long second section,
one can see for one thing that some release of tension, some event or
action is necessary to counteract an emotionally unbearable build-up.
So the opening lines, "Mais taisez-vous tas de pain le paysage lève
ses grands bras de plume", and "Mais plumes arrêtez-vous car le
paysage n'est presque plus qu'une courte paille" serve that psychologically necessary purpose. Furthermore, within the frame of reference of the narrative the change is even quite reasonable. In the first
case, the landscape (which is after all a central figure in the story)
makes a reassuring gesture - it raises its long arms seeming harmless because they are feathered. In the second case, again, the landscape is reduced to the small and innocent dimensions of a "courte
paille". So, to hear a voice come out of the blue calmly to command
silence and stillness is not in the least unreasonable but rather a welcome and plausible relief. And the sentence which follows closely,
"C'est donc toi fille aux seins de soleil qui sera le paysage..." is similarly not too surprising under the circumstances. Although the girl,
addressed affectionately, has appeared from nowhere (as did the preceding calming voice), the whole expression conveys the notion of discovery, sudden but not too impossible, and once again clear and reassuring. The tone is succinct, evoked simply by a limpid explanation,
a sudden insight, "C'est donc toi".

Even more characteristic of Péret's presentation of events is the
frequency of cause and effect relationships and of intentions. In "Soleil
route usée..." there are several examples although they are not developed or used centrally in the poem's total structure. They are quite
directly meaningful however and therefore merit comment. Both are

from the first section. (In the analysis of that poem I commented that they stood out as short lines and were reassuring since they were the only explanations given in a sequence where the atmosphere was mysterious and full of apprehension.) The line, "parce que tout est noir", derives unambiguously from the preceding statement, "...un serpent qui dort sa queue dans son oreille". It explains why the snake is asleep; and it leads into a more detailed description of the scene. The other causal statement, "Car le ciel s'ouvre comme une huitre", comes in between two negative statements and gives a reason and a background for the state of powerlessness. The preceding line, "Toutes ses tentacules n'arriveront jamais à transformer le ciel en mains", indicates an intention, a desired attempt but one which is destined to be fruitless. The sky remains out of reach, eludes the manipulative grasp of the tentacles by self-controlled movement of its own, opening like an oyster. Helpless, the hands (which have strangely materialized anyway) are reduced to a simple holding action, "les mains ne savent que se fermer sur les poutres des mers".

In other poems causal relations figure more prominently. In "A Demain",*26 a poem in which the key preoccupation is with problems of all sorts, some nonsensical, others of an obvious social nature whose proposed solution contains revolutionary overtones, such causal relations occur in nearly every line. Here is a part of the first sentence which immediately hammers away at the theme.

Que meure le blé noir si les dents du moineau
n'attirent pas les alouettes
si les lumières du vin blanc n'obscurcissent pas les
    miroirs anciens
si les lacets des souliers ne guident pas les papillons
    le soir
quand la pluie tombe comme un pendu
dont la corde s'est rompue
parce que le voisin se battait avec sa femme
à cause d'une horloge qui s'obstine à rire avant de sonner
pour signifier à ses propriétaires que le monde est renversé
que les sources demain chasseront les hommes à courre... *

From the start there is a black almost apocalyptic tone, the basic problem being that "le monde est renversé". If such negative conditions persist, a day of judgment is inevitable ("Que meure le blé noir si..."). The only remedies are violent. Suggesting, "les sources demain chasseront les hommes à courre", the author offers the first of a number of even more vengeful acts designed to destroy an unacceptable social order. Besides such obvious causal constructions such as "Que... si... si...", "parce que", "à cause de", "pour", lines such as "quand la pluie tombe comme un pendu / dont la corde est rompue" imply conditions underlying other states or happenings. The whole poem presents a situation of which the elements are frequently absurd but which is tightly bound together, causally connected. The principle which governs the poet's presentation of such a situation appears to derive from an intuitive judgment of the reality he sees, translated into the "surréalité" of the poem and formulated by a sense of righteous indignation. This comes close to Wittgenstein's inquiry about the origin of causal statements where he concludes with the question: "Can one ask: 'How do you know what you do is because of this, or not because of this?' And is the answer perhaps: 'I feel it'?"*27 These thoughts seem particularly relevant because they have to do with the explanation of causes of human behavior as does Péret's poem.

But the action in Péret's world is not limited to human actions or to the interpretation of events, of natural (or unnatural) occurrences. For the author is well aware of the limitations of human perception, of the extent to which what goes on in the world where he lives is unpredictable - the real world, the dream world or the fusion of the two in the world of "surréalité". Chance events are the rule rather than the exception. In one of his best fanciful stories, Il était une boulangère, naturally at a dramatic moment, the author interrupts the narrative to state: "Si court que puisse être l'intervalle entre la pensée et l'acte, il y a toujours place pour un événement, petit ou grand. " *28 In contrast to the poems his stories have human beings as central figures; and the drama consists exactly of states of mind, thoughts, actions, events and reactions repeated and developed nonsensically. Indeed, it is the sudden events, interrupting our chain of thought, or the hero's inexplicable events, even impossible events which keep the action moving at a rapid pace and constitute a good part of the charm probably for the author as well as for the reader.

Temporal patterns in the poetry of Péret, aside from their pleasurable surprise effects, form a very basic and complex structural background and therefore merit particular attention. Although all of his poems are anchored to the present occasion and have an immediate impact, even when certain passages are related in the future or conditional tense, the poet is acutely conscious of time as such, not abstractly but as an acutely lived experience. One early poem, "Une île dans une tasse", could be described as a kind of nightmare in time.*29 It opens:

Les siècles de charbon les lanternes de colle sèche
les pertes de temps les chutes d'eau
se succèdent et se perdent dans l'allée grise qui mène
aux îles sanglantes
il n'y a pas plus de temps que d'eau... *

The poem continues, without further references to time, but without escaping from the sensation of horror set by the initial revelation of time viewed as sequence doomed to loss with the underlying water metaphor giving the passage of time a concrete visual sense. Such intuitions, cosmic in scope, are clearer in his later poems. In "Dernier malheur dernière chance" a black eternal danger, "une menace d'an mil", pervades the entire narrative. One short sequence ends the long first section in a pessimistic tone similar to the passage quoted above.

...le chant de la bouilloire amoureuse des tropiques
s'effaçait comme midi
balaie son minuit crépitant de siècles sans mémoire*30 *

Again, speaking of great periods of time, centuries, the poet pictures them as somehow unfathomable ("sans mémoire") and in addition suggests that time by nature is destined to oblivion, is swept aside ("s'effaçait comme midi / balaie son minuit...") as are all other things.

Time past slips from the mental grasp but time present offers other compensations. The immediacy of the moment can be a source of surprise and delight. Chance events, as he said, may interrupt what one has planned or intended. transpiring, interceding between the thought and the act. Also, the immediate present or a particular moment offer something the mind can grasp. The second section of "Dernier malheur dernière chance", in sharp contrast to the temporally evasive end of the first section starts out with "D'une minute à l'autre le froid maigre drapeau des ciels taillés en rose..." Attention suddenly alerted, the reader is ready and waiting for further action, which does indeed resume vigorously. The introductory line of "On Sonne" creates the same effect in a different way. When one reads, "Un saut de puce comme une brouette dansant sur les genoux des pavés", one is riveted to quick, instantaneous action. Although time is not mentioned, the mind pictures this as taking place here and now. The poet's and the reader's mind can be totally and restfully absorbed in the present.

There is rarely a chance even to contemplate or reflect peacefully for the reader is more often than not witness to action, rapid-fire action. Sometimes events are dramatic and even violent, as in the second section of "Soleil route usée..."

   ...une longue barre de cuivre se dressera comme une flamme
   si loin si haut que les orties ne seront plus ses enfants
   mais les soubresauts fatals d'un grand corps d'écume
   salué par les mille crochets des eaux bouillantes
   que lance le pain blanc...

Besides the action verbs "se dressera", "salué", and "lance" other words suggest movement or direction - "flamme", "si loin si haut", "soubresauts fatals", "écume", "eaux bouillantes". Added to the continuous seething motion of flame and water are the specific, precipitous acts of shooting up and throwing.

Other motions or happenings may be more subtle but nonetheless closely following one upon the other, the poetic expression a constantly shifting sequence of occurrences. Usually the verbs appear within the lines grouped or cut as normal syntactic sequences. One poem however is interesting in that it emphasizes the verbs by using them to introduce the lines.

   Du fond du granit qui cache son secret de lichen
   sous un clinquant de saltimbanques
   encerclant une équipe de lutteurs transis de froid
   sous leur vêtement de pince à épiler
   émerge une lueur triste de lampe à pétrole qui serait une chatte
   guettant les cicatrices essoufflées du mur
   ermite barbu qu'une vaste plaine plantée de conques marines
   rapproche des troncs qui l'ont banni
   mais isole des banques dont les cloches qu'il n'entend pas
   hantent son sommeil peuplé de hanches
   flottant dans un vent d'aurore qui lui rend des satins mats... *31*

Far from sudden or violent, these verbs include both active and continuous subjective states ("guettant", "hantent") and equally continuous and active though rather subdued happenings in the outside world ("encerclant", "émerge", "rapproche", "isole", "flottant"). This is a subtly blended amalgam of things, states and occurrences objective and subjective, an example of how Péret in his own fashion achieved the Surrealist goal, fusion of apparently contradictory areas of reality.

Explicitly, even, Péret speaks of time as inseparable from motion, and as being rhythmical and cyclical. There is a love poem in which the tone is not simply light and gay as in "On Sonne" but where the same sweetness and sense of being totally absorbed is mixed with a touch of distress. The theme of time is an integral part of this poem, introduced in the third line, "et les scies du temps grincent leur chanson de charbon", and recurring in the second stanza where the poet says:

si je t'aime c'est que le sol est carré
et le temps aussi
et cependant je ne ferai jamais le tour de temps
car le temps tourne comme à la roulette...

Further on comes the theme of the tide:

Marées de mes erreurs où mîtes-vous nos vents

. . .
ô mon amie
vous qui êtes ma marée mon flux et mon reflux
vous qui descendez et montez comme le dégel... *32 *

This concept of continuous motion, of time and human relations as turning, ebbing and flowing is not gratuitous. It closely resembles the idea of the lines from "Le Mariage des feuilles", quoted at the beginning of the chapter: "L'homme découvre la poésie circulaire / Il aperçoit qu'elle roule et tangue... "

The serious nature of these ideas seems to me evident since the structure of Péret's poems shows exactly these qualities of continuous motion and periodic change. In some cases the verbs themselves create and elaborate the movement. The last line of "A Mi-Chemin", where the priest "se regarde dissoudre dans un bénitier", does just this - completing the theme of rottenness and decay, disposing neatly of the objectionable figure and ending the poem in disintegration.

In "Soleil route usée... " states and movements are more highly developed. The first section opens with a stationary theme, the world is frozen; it continues with certain expanding gestures ("projette", "tentacules", "le ciel s'ouvre"); and it eventually leads to a hopeless circular wandering ("voyageurs... qui contournent éternellement... ") and finally a falling motion ("saules... qui tombent... comme des plumes"). The events in section two are more complex involving expansion, desperate shouts, transformations; but the final line where the crows "... se noient tous les soirs dans les égouts de dieu" repeats in tone the descending motion of the first, leading the reader into the depths of divine gutters where he meets death. The third stanza rapidly reverses these trends, silencing the shouts and changing the direction upwards ("le paysage lève ses grands bras de plume / et les plumes s'envolent"). The last stanza arrests all motion except for the cease-less, hopeless wandering. It starts out with the command, "Mais plumes arrêtez-vous..." The two long parallel series of verbless phrases, one describing the landscape and the other indicating a num-ber of hiding places also contribute to a motionless state. The final lines describing the herons, eternal cruel and white, by the rhythm of their syntax, by the connotations of the adjectives achieve a fixed im-mutable effect which echoes the frozen world of the beginning. Here, the different states - motionless, rising, falling - are for the most part rendered directly by verbs although the pace of the grammatical sequences, particularly in the last stanza, also contributes to the ef-fect.

"On Sonne", despite the straightforward subject of love, presents an extremely subtle and intricate variation of states. It starts of course with movement pure and simple - jumping and bouncing. And the long last sentence of the first stanza ("Mais je t'aime comme le coquillage aime son sable où quelqu'un le dénichera...") develops the notion of germination and of the state of being opened and vulnerable. And in the very last lines the idea of an ocean trip also evokes motion - not only the trip itself and eventual rest but a sense of rolling and tossing, partly by the line "pareille à un navire en dérive", also by the short, suspended succession of lines. However, physical motion is not the sole structural element of this poem. More subtle, and more essential, are the rapid shifts of tone which here represent the lover's emotions. In the first stanza he is happy and light at first ("un saut de puce..."), then briefly but violently passionate ("...une bouteille de vin rouge / s'est fait nègre / esclave fustigé"), next warm, expanding, vulnerable. In the second stanza the rhythm of expression is irregular, strong, light, happy images and feelings interspersed with interruptions, sud-den short contradictions and one line where he even reduces his own being to minuscule proportions at the thought of her absence ("car sans toi je suis à peine l'interstice entre les pavés..."). Then the tone rap-idly undergoes changes - expanding, receiving, melting, burning - floating happily at the end. The physical motions, the shifts of intimate human feeling, the esthetic rhythms - all these woven together - take place in a given and irreversible temporal sequence. In two of the three poems analyzed one finds also a clear pattern of circularity. In "Soleil route usée..." and in "On Sonne", the state reached at the end is reminiscent of the conditions of the opening scene. Certainly, the underlying intention, conscious or not, must have been esthetic in nature, what Breton meant when he spoke of "arrangement en poème". But if regular poetic rhythms and circular construction are charac-eristics of Péret's work, they are quite different from similar traits which one finds in the case of Valéry. Whereas both follow the changes and developments of states, physical and emotional, Valéry's poems and the psychological sequences within them reflect repeated and re-peatable occurrences. Péret's psychological narratives are unique and very individual; one cannot imagine ever encountering the same charac-ters involved in the same chain of events or even remotely similar ones in his poems, in his abstract thought or in his life.

With the passage of time in Péret's world the reader views not only familiar shifts of feeling and familiar or unfamiliar actions but changes far more radical in nature. These are changes of the very nature of the actors, the objects or the scenery. They involve transformation of the essence of being. Metamorphosis is an ordinary and an essential occurrence in his tales and poems. Of the three poems analyzed, "Soleil route usée..." contains the clearest examples of this phenomenon. In the second part a number of transformations take place, all in connection with the nettles. The author suggests that if you throw the nettles in the black man's throat, "le nègre deviendra ortie et soutane son oeil perdu". And after the copper bar shoots up high enough, the nettles, having unbeknownst to us turned into children, "les orties ne seront plus ses enfants / mais les soubresauts fatals d'un grand corps d'écume". Finally the nettles are destined to have donkey ears and feet of snow and at that point they undergo a more unobtrusive but more definitive change becoming a labyrinth. These transformations are mainly related to the tonal shifts of the poetic sequence.

In Péret's tales the extraordinarily frequent mutations are more playful, often quite arbitrary and highly ingenious. One prose work, however, treats the most fundamental universal subject in which every event involves change, the first change from nothingness to being - creation of the cosmos. The title is Histoire naturelle. It has four parts, written at different times (from 1945 to 1958), covering the classic natural divisions: Part I entitled "Les Quatre éléments" discusses the nature and powers of earth, air, water and fire; Part II deals with "Le Règne minéral", Part III "Le Règne végétal"; Part IV, "Le Règne animal" presents the vast drama of the birth of the animal kingdom ending with the creation of man. The whole work radiates optimism. The poet's typical, inexhaustible sense of humor prevails free from bitterness. A good deal of the account is sheer fancy such as the description of water in which the reader is told that in the state of rain, water turns into earthworms when it penetrates the soil and subsequently becomes crude oil of which there are a number of varieties - "le pétrole unicorne, le pétrole velu" and so forth. The last sequence of "Le Règne animal" dealing with the creation of man and woman manifests, beneath the playful surface, a warm, gentle confidence:

> ...j'ai taillé l'homme dans un pruneau. Il était encore minuscule mais j'avais confiance dans le temps qui lui permettrait de grandir, d'ailleurs, il me l'avait promis. A peine l'homme avait-il commencé à respirer qu'il se dressait sur ses jambes et cria 'Et ma femme? Où est-elle?' 'C'est à toi de la trouver', lui dis-je. Et, ayant recueilli du miel qui coulait d'une ruche, il façonna sa femme.[33]

The author, confidently assuming the role of a benign creator, brings to life the first man. Then, with faith in time and in man's intentions, the author withdraws, leaving him free to act independently.

The concept of natural transformation was not exclusively Péret's but a general feature of the Surrealist orientation towards life and art. Anna Balakian deals with this subject in an article entitled "Metaphor

and Metamorphosis".*34 As a background for her discussion she points
out the essential difference between the theory of correspondences to
which Baudelaire subscribed, which involves a dualistic conception of
nature and implies transcendance, and the theory of hermetics and
alchemy where change and metamorphosis are a basic feature. She
then analyzes the philosophical framework of Breton's world view
where only one reality exists and according to which the act of interpreting reality actually consists of transforming it. Two points she
makes about Breton's works are equally applicable to Péret. First,
life is pictured as becoming, as a continuous process. Thus metamorphosis and all changes of form are natural. They have a positive orientation and are directed towards the future. Even death is included in
this scheme as a prolongation of this sort of natural transformation,
albeit beyond comprehensible limits. Interestingly, death as such
hardly figures in Péret's world: accidents or acts of violence which
would be mortal in the real world usually simply lead to strange transformation or speedy inexplicable resurrections.*35 But there is one
interesting passage about suicide in an early tale, La Brebis galante
(1924):

> J'entends par suicide cette subite conscience de soi-même qui nous
> fait désirer devenir navet ou pelle à charbon, encore que j'aie une
> représentation insuffisante des métamorphoses que peut subir le
> corps d'un suicidé pour aboutir au stade définitif de navet ou de pelle
> à charbon.*36 *

There is a serious undercurrent of these reflections despite the unusual nature of the change envisaged. A sudden lucid consciousness of
self accompanies an awareness of death and change after death as natural but also in the realm of the unknown.

The second point has to do with imagery. She indicates that within a
philosophical framework, where interpreting reality actually consists
of changing it, the word "comme" loses its sense of identity to assume
a meaning of actual transformation. Several lines from "On Sonne" illustrate vividly this process. Reading "et le soleil pareil à une bouteille de vin rouge / s'est fait nègre / esclave fustigé", one's attention
is caught up not so much by the analogy (bright light) but by the violence suggested by the image red wine (red as violent in tone; wine-
drunkenness) because it leads directly to the violence of the whipped
slave. So that the sun is in a sense left behind, more a starting point
than a thing whose presence remains at the end of the thought sequence.
Similarly the statement "comme un château dans une grande cheminée /
pareille à un navire en dérive" has a cognitive value which is entirely
linear. For the image of the castle in a chimney derives from the preceding image of the burning house. It has logical connection with the
tossing ship by virtue of motion. The ground of the two images is
mainly important as a psychological bridge. But the passage from one
image to the other is significant not so much because of the descriptive
connection but because the tossing ship becomes the focus of interest
for the action that follows. For practical purpose of reading the poem,
the castle is indeed transformed into a ship. These lines could easily

have been composed as an example to accompany Breton's statement
concerning the irreversible nature of images:

> Elle [l'image analogique] se meut, entre les deux réalités en pré-
> sence, dans un sens déterminé, qui n'est aucunement réversible.
> De la première à la seconde, elle marque une tension vitale tournée
> au possible vers la santé, le plaisir, la quiétude, la grâce rendue,
> les usages consentis.*37 *

Besides being clearly irreversible in nature, Péret's ship also manifests that quality of vitality and of optimistic direction suggested by
Breton.

The Surrealist chief also emphasizes the arbitrary, fortuitous nature
of such analogies, insisting that the value of the image depends on its
special sudden light and that the degree of success depends on the extent to which the connection is arbitrary and even bordering on hallucination. All of these remarks have as a backdrop Reverdy's famous definition of imagery, the "rapprochement spontané de deux réalités très
distantes dont l'esprit seul a saisi les rapports".*38 Breton's refu-
tation of Reverdy's definition is actually more one of emphasis than of
contradiction. For while Reverdy states that a connection does exist,
albeit distant, Breton only denies that the connection is <u>conscious</u>. The
former even says that the images are juxtaposed spontaneously by the
poet and also that they seem far removed. So Breton's argument appears rather specious. Still, the important point in both cases is the
element of surprise and of originality. Valuing the unexpected is
certainly not exclusively a Surrealist phenomenon. Even Valéry, who
exacted from himself an almost superhuman goal of coherence and
whose style includes many classical images affirms the pleasure and
importance of surprise. In his personal notes he says, "Pour me
plaire... il faut que l'idée, la pensée, l'expression, le <u>motif</u> me <u>sur-
prenne</u>... Le génie serait-il la possibilité de se surprendre."*39

Regardless of theoretical discussions about whether Surrealist images are fortuitous or clearly meaningful, it is worth examining sequences of Péret's poetry to determine the nature of his imagery as
experienced by the reader. To start with, one should note that many
of his images are hardly absurd at all, very imaginative, very evocative but not really very shocking. In one love poem he says of his mistress: "...tu passes comme un courant d'air chargé de rosée aux ailes
de lampe qui file."*40 Her passage thus is simply like a breath of
fresh air, luminous, quickly passing. Another is perhaps more original but not shockingly so. In a more anxious mood he explains, "Mais
tu n'es pas là / et l'écureuil de tes yeux grignote la capucine de ma
tête."*41 The image of a squirrel nibbling away at a nasturtium is
superimposed (in grammatically parallel form) on his mistress'
eyes which he sees in his imagination, which he can't get out of his
mind. There is perhaps an ever-so-slight element of hallucination,
but not frightening or overwhelming, and at any rate not unlikely in a
poetic context.

In contrast, a considerable number of arbitrary elements do appear
in the following lines from "Soleil route usée..."

> Mais voici que le monde cesse d'être gelé
> et que l'orage aux yeux de paon glisse sous lui
> comme un serpent qui dort sa queue dans son oreille
> parce que tout est noir...

Certainly the qualifying phrase, "l'orage <u>aux yeux de paon</u>", is unrelated to the noun it modifies or to the other elements of the passage. In fact the entire event of that line, the peacock-eyed storm sliding under the unfrozen world as a whole is not particularly coherent in the circumstances. Yet, mention of the storm is not a complete surprise since it has been already introduced in the second line ("Une lance d'orage frappe le monde gelé"); and the action of sliding under is semantically connected with the verb in the preceding line ("la présence se cache..."). The image of the serpent does have some tie with what it follows since snakes can slide. But this snake is not sliding, it is motionless, sleeping. More important, I think, is the fashion in which it fits into the poem in a broader sense. The image of the snake and, especially a snake made into a circle, sleeping with its tail in its ear, reinforces the patterns of mythical imagery with mysterious foreboding overtones already present in the introductory lines ("pierres frémissantes", "oreilles de soupçon", "le mystère des triangles"). Moreover, the theme of sleep leads into the next lines describing the darkness and nightmare-like setting. This suggests why it is important to consider not just the sense of a single word or word group but to look for their relevance in larger word groups - sentence, section or full poem. And this is consistent with the view of Frege and Wittgenstein that a word has meaning only as part of a total word group - if one adjusts the conditions to include the possibility that in poetry semantic relationships are not necessarily bound in the normal syntactic order.*42

The final lines of that first section of "Soleil route usée..." are interesting for different reasons:

> ...
> qui salissent les regards bleus des squales
> voyageurs parfumés
> voyageurs sans secousses
> qui contournent éternellement les sifflements aver-
>   tisseurs des saules
> des grands saules de piment qui tombent sur la terre
>   comme des plumes

Although the travelers appear rather strangely in apposition to sharks, they pertain to the theme of travel and wandering, a key theme of the secti and of the whole poem. Why they should be "parfumés" and "sans secousses", is difficult to see. It is not reasonable that the travelers should go around the "sifflements avertisseurs"; but the whistles do also relate to the theme of travel despite their impertinent syntactic function and despite the improbable fact that they issue from willow trees. Then, the willows which recur as the next subject are inexplicably of red pepper, certainly a surprise image which perhaps in a jokingly banal way adds spice to the expression. The last part of the sentence, a relative clause ("qui tombent sur la terre...") is typical of Péret's style. Relative clauses frequently are used to expand the action, to give it added impetus and often an entirely new twist as is the case here. It is conceivable, but unlikely, that willows might fall to the ground. However, in view of the final image, one's doubts are resolved, for feathers do fall, slowly and softly. This a fine example of the principle already suggested whereby images can be presented not in terms of comparison but rather of transformation. This characteristic especially suggests that the best way to read this poetry is first to progress simply from one phrase to the next, not asking oneself too many questions immediately about logic, simply absorbing one image, one event after another and accepting them initially on their own grounds, even taking the improbable for granted. Many of the images are forceful visually and should be experienced and appreciated primarily as such. The pump which projects into the distance its cristal tentacles, the sky opening like an oyster are images of this sort. And the great red-pepper willow trees falling like feathers could be translated into a film idiom where the falling trees would become drifting feathers. It would resemble the work of Paul Klee in animated form.

Following the sequence of thought exactly as Péret composed the poem, and in a sense "reliving" the chain of associations with their accompanying visual, auditive, and emotional effects, one can then proceed to a second reading in which emotive patterns and lines of structure can be isolated and perceived as a coherent whole.

In the eyes of Péret metamorphosis has a particularly profound significance because for him it is allied with an inherent and tenacious optimism combined with the strong desire actively to contribute to a better world. He expresses these thoughts in a preface to a book devoted to the artist Toyen in connection with the spirit underlying her painting; but they are equally applicable to his own temperament and his own artistic production. The exterior world remains the source of art but it is only one element in the composition of a "complete" world, a better world. "Toute l'oeuvre de Toyen, he says, ne vise pas à autre chose qu'à corriger le monde extérieur en fonction d'un désir qui s'alimente et s'accroît de sa propre satisfaction."*43 Through metamorphosis, the changes wrought by the poetic imagination, a new world comes into being, one which is coherent and entirely new ("l'ensemble formant un monde entièrement neuf"). He even envisages in this essay the world of the artist as resembling that of the first creator of the universe, where from a state of chaos and of unstable forms a new existence takes shape. This is exactly what Péret took as explicit subject matter in <u>Histoire naturelle.</u> And a passage from the chapter on the vegetable kingdom of that book demonstrates his faith in a possible universal harmony:

Rien ne permettait de supposer qu'un jour l'harmonie régnerait, lorsque le ciel parut s'éclaircir et l'orage s'éloigna...un arc-en-ciel étincela au-dessus de la terre fascinée. La végétation comprit et, sans se rechigner, chaque plante occupa sans bruit le coin qui lui était destiné.*

Such an ambitious project, the creation of an entire cosmos from chaos is not, however, really the main aim of Toyen or Péret. It simply illustrates the latter's natural comprehensive optimism. More down to earth is his description of the source and development of poetic thought which was mentioned at the outset of this chapter, where he defines the "merveilleux" in terms of the imaginative possibilities inherent in simple objects such as the contents of a drawer. The essay on Toyen also emphasizes the fact that if the exterior world is not the only factor involved in the esthetic process it remains the starting point. The example he gives in this case is the perception of a bird's song which can lead to the resurrection of a submerged city. And the bird song is not a negligeable factor. Fernand Alquié in his penetrating study, Philosophie du surréalisme, emphasizes the extent to which for the Surrealists, as opposed to the French Romantic movement, real life is in the here and now, close at hand ("la vraie vie est là"). That bird song is important in and of itself. Certainly, in Péret's poems the creatures he tells about have a colorful and warm immediacy.

This does not exclude the possibility of dissatisfaction with the world as it is. In fact, Alquié poses just such dissatisfaction as being at the origin of metaphysical speculation in general.*44 For Péret and the other Surrealists the revolt was directed on the one hand against the constraints and injustices of the existing social order and on the other hand against the limitations and insufficiencies of rational thought and expression. It is certainly true that there is a strong negative streak in Péret's work ranging from invective against all aspects of bourgeois society to a more subtle but clear aim to satirize and destroy rational patterns of thought. But if the revolt springs from a desire for a better life, that desire in the case of Péret in its positive form in the long run overshadows the flippant, bitter, and often simply destructive drive.

Ultimately what mattered the most to him was that sense of the "merveilleux", which for him represented as much an object of faith as a source of esthetic gratification. The contents of the drawer, the bird song are examples he took at random from his own experience. But such simple perceptions are at the basis of the best of which man is capable, what he calls "conscience poétique du monde". In an article on superstition, he describes this consciousness, primitive in nature, at the origin of myths and of ritual (before it is corrupted by organized religion), as being both a belief and capacity for feeling.*45 As example he gives "la mélancolie qui l'empoigne [l'homme] à la vue de la neige éteignant tout bruit, flocon à flocon" or "l'enchantement que lui procure le muguet de mai". As important as the initial perception are the feelings spontaneously aroused and they run the gamut of man's innermost and powerful emotive capacities from the pleasant, "l'enchantement", to the disturbing, "l'épouvante", "l'angoisse", as well as the less threatening, "la mélancolie".

This is very similar to Lévy-Bruhl's well-known concept of "participation mystique", which Jung incorporated in his theory of the archetypal imagination, whereby primitive man integrates and fits natural phenomena into his world view first by totally emotional identification in experience. In the case of Péret, the emphasis is esthetic, although there is also an underlying sense of faith; in addition he introduces the idea of mission. Political and social changes are necessary and inevitable to better the human condition; yet the ultimate salvation will include recapturing the freshness and freedom of the primitive imagination. He describes the artist's role in the following fashion: "La véritable mission de l'artiste - peintre ou poète - a toujours consisté à retrouver en lui-même les archétypes qui sous-tendent la pensée poétique, à les charger d'une affectivité nouvelle, afin que circule entre ses semblables et lui-même un courant énergique d'autant plus intense que ses archétypes actualisés apparaîtront comme l'expression la plus évidente et la plus neuve du milieu qui a conditionné l'artiste."*46 * This was written late in his life, after his experiences in Latin America and Mexico and his studies of primitive civilizations and myths. In the preface to his translation of the Mayan religious chronicle he comments admiringly: "De toute évidence, ce peuple [maya] n'entretenait pas avec le monde extérieur de simples rapports de nécessité, mais chaque homme adhérait par toutes les fibres de son être, qu'il n'avait pas songé à dissocier au bénéfice exclusif de la raison."*47 * As we have seen in the early poem "Soleil route usée..." the poet very naturally transposes imaginative sequences where sensitivity to the world about him shines through, in an unearthly, timeless setting, with exactly that current of energy of which he speaks linking the real and the imaginary and establishing a bond between himself and the reader.

That sensitivity, however, is not confined to poems of cosmic breadth. It suffuses his entire work, even, negatively, the areas of bitter social and political satire. The "merveilleux" serves to start off improbable adventures. It is responsible for the spontaneous charm of his imagery and of his unexpected transformations. It permeates the lyricism of his love poems joyfully and somewhat impersonally in "On Sonne", with a more intense and personal tone elsewhere. It is responsible, I think, for the value and the attraction of Péret's poetry as a whole - in that is the source of that original and pervasive tone and uninhibited expression of feeling. Wittgenstein posed the possibility that it is a feeling which gives a sentence (but not each word) "meaning" and "truth".*48 In the sentence "Oh, if only he would come!" which the latter gives as an example, the force would derive more from the clear word or the syntactic arrangement. In the absurd world of Péret, where semantic sequence and rational connections are consistently scrambled, feelings, precisely, are the source of the expression and remain coloring the verbal sequence to give it depth and coherence. This is so even in a simple and nonsensical tale where the main characters are a narrator and a certain M. Charbon, where the author refers without a trace of self-importance to "le grand coeur de la nature, celui qu'on trouve parfois sous les jeunes champignons après les pluies d'orage..."*49

NOTES

*1 The first encounter is related thus. One evening there is a knock on the door, an unknown woman comes in, asks for an issue of Littérature, announces the arrival of an acquaintance. "Mais qui me donnait-on charge ainsi, plus que chimériquement, d'accueillir, de conseiller?

Quelques jours plus tard, Benjamin Péret était là" (pp. 26-27 of the 1963 edition; Nadja appeared first in 1928).

*2 For instance, in the essay, "Situation surréaliste de l'objet", Breton cites a poem of Péret as one where the depth of feeling the wealth of intuition and the verve of combination are carried to greatest heights (Manifestes du surréalisme [Paris: Pauvert, 1962], 322-324). It was Eluard who wrote a friendly, perspicacious and elogious preface for Péret's collection of poems, De Derrière les fagots. One of the most moving (although perhaps exaggerated) tributes is the reply of Philippe Soupault to a negative judgment of Pierre de Boisdeffre in a radio interview reported in Arts (no. 878, 18 juillet 1962). De Boisdeffre: "Aragon et Eluard sont des poètes de portée universelle. L'oeuvre de Péret est une panoplie de petit ingénieur..." Soupault: "Et vous auriez parfaitement tort! Moi, je donnerais toute l'oeuvre d'Eluard pour un seul poème de Péret."

*3 Manifestes du surréalisme (Paris: Pauvert, 1962), 27.

*4 Manifestes..., 154.

*5 Manifestes..., 325-333.

*6 Manifestes..., 40.

*7 Lettre à Renéville, NRF, 1 mai 1932; reprinted in Le Point du Jour (Paris, 1934).

*8 The quotation of Breton is from the First Manifesto (Manifestes, p. 48). There was furthermore, despite the experiments with hypnosis, a strong tendency to value lucidity as such. Breton, himself, never took part in experimental hypnosis. Both he and Aragon took a dim view of drugs. They, Eluard and Péret as well, wrote their poems in a state of full consciousness.

*9 Aragon, Traité du style, 191-192.

*10 An interesting article by Robert Champigny ("Analyse d'une définition du surréalisme", PMLA, Vol. LXXXI, no. 1 [March 1966], 139-144), exploring the semantic problems of the statements in the First Manifesto, indicates certain of these difficulties.

*11 Tristan Tzara, "Essai sur la situation de la poésie", Le surréalisme au service de la révolution, no. 4 (décembre 1931), 15-23.

*12 Anthologie des mythes légendes et contes populaires d'Amérique, 15-16.

*13 Anthologie..., 16-20.

*14 This poem is based on the parliamentary crisis, an attempted coup d'état by the right wing, riots which took place on that date in

1934 triggered by the Stavisky affair.

*15 Besides "Le Quart d'une vie", other poems in Le Grand jeu have the flavor and form of medieval or popular verse. The principal intention is no doubt satirical as is the case in the joint production of Péret and Eluard, 152 Proverbes mis au goût du jour (Paris, 1925). Still a positive lilt and flavour survive the travesty.

*16 Aragon, Traité du style, 84 and 93.

*17 Le Grand jeu, 185.

*18 Courtot (59-60) describes Péret as a "bon vivant" who follows his inclinations rather than ceremony. He had a passion for lobster. On excursions in the country he would spend hours picking wild strawberries, for instance, and one evening he appeared with a great quantity of artichokes to which he had helped himself in some farmer's field.

*19 "Tournez à gauche", De Derrière les fagots, 31.

*20 "Vent du nord", A tâtons, 200-201.

*21 "Où es-tu", Un point c'est tout, 193.

*22 "Dormir dormir dans les pierres", 45-49.

*23 Eluard's color imagery centered on the words themselves, their power to evoke not things but sensations and mental connotations, as illustrated by the well-known lines: "La terre est bleue comme une orange / Jamais une erreur les mots ne mentent pas."

*24 "Du surréalisme en ses oeuvres vives" (1953), Manifestes du surréalisme (Paris, 1962), 355-363.

*25 Le Grand jeu, 192.

*26 De Derrière les fagots, 33-34.

*27 Philosophical Investigations, 2nd ed. (N.Y.: Macmillan, 1967), 137e. The whole note reads:
"'I am leaving the room because you tell me to.'
'I am leaving the room, but not because you tell me to.'
Does this proposition describe a connexion between my action and his order; or does it make the connexion?
Can one ask: 'How do you know that you do it because of this, or not because of this?' And is the answer perhaps: 'I feel it'?"

*28 Le Gigot sa vie et son oeuvre (Paris, 1957), 115.

*29 Le Grand jeu, 196-197.

*30 Dernier malheur dernière chance, 159.

*31 "Mille regrets", Feu central, 87.

*32 "Nue nue comme ma maîtresse...", Dormir dormir dans les pierres, 59-61.

*33 Histoire naturelle, 31.

*34 French Studies, XIX (Jan. 1965), 34-41.

*35 An interesting exception is a short story, "La Dernière nuit du condamné à mort" (Le Gigot sa vie et son oeuvre, 91-94). It is told in the first person, anonymously, and with a good many absurd details. The atmosphere and much of the setting has an authentic ring of personal anxiety resembling a real nightmare. It ends with the execution.

*36 La Brebis galante (Paris, 1959), 29.

*37 La Clé des champs (Paris, 1967), 136.

*38 Breton's discussion of this subject is in the First Manifesto (Manifestes du surréalisme, 51-53). Reverdy's definition is in Le Gant de crin (Paris, 1927), 34.

*39 Paul Valéry, Cahier VI (Paris, 1958), 179.

*40 "Nébuleuse", Jeu sublime, 139-140.

*41 "Pour ne rien dire", Un point c'est tout, 189.

*42 Philosophical Investigations, 24e.

*43 Benjamin Péret (avec André Breton et Jindrich Heisler), Toyen (Paris, 1953), 24.

*44 The study of Fernand Alquié, La Philosophie du surréalisme (Paris, 1955), is exceptionally thorough and thought provoking. Professing particular admiration for the doctrines of Plato, Descartes, and Kant, Alquié also values the Surrealist venture in that it lucidly doubts and questions aspects of "le Monde objectif". Yet he is careful to recognize that the Surrealists do not pose or suggest the existence of a transcendent world. Although the "surréel" casts doubts on and changes what we know as day-to-day reality, it still remains immanent to the world in the broader sense.

*45 "Le Sel répandu", Le Surréalisme en 1947 (Paris, 1947), 21-24.

*46 "Wilfredo Lam", Médium, no. 4 (janvier 1955), 1.

*47 Le Livre de Chilám Balám de Chumayel, 35-36.

*48 Philosophical Investigations, 146e.

*49 "Qui perd gagne", Mort aux vaches et au champ d'honneur (Paris, 1953).

PART FOUR

RENE CHAR: TRANSMETTRE TA PART DE MERVEILLEUX DE
REBELLION ET DE BIENFAISANCE

Optimism, violence, freedom from traditional constraint, awareness
of the force of the subconscious, all these characteristics of the Surrealist spirit inform the poetic world of René Char. They are natural
to his temperament and they were reinforced during the years when he
participated in their activities and contributed to their publications.
Yet it would be a gross error simply to consider him a Surrealist or
even one who left the movement but continued to write in a similar
vein. Born in the Vaucluse (a region in Southern France between the
Rhône valley and the lower Alps, rich in history, tradition and a gently
ascetic natural beauty), Char has remained profoundly rooted to the
people and the land, while nurturing wide intellectual interests and
contacts. Particularly after 1936 when he consciously elaborated a
poetic idiom rigorously consistent with his own life, certain traits become increasingly preponderant which distinguish him radically from
the Surrealist group. Of these, I think the most important are on the
one hand a continuous urge to discover and transmit the full weight of
reality and on the other hand rationally and seriously to search, pon-
der, and elaborate a new order. The first includes the imaginative,
generous sweep of Surrealism. For instance, a poem, "Commune
présence" (written during the period of reevaluation), continues to
urge the inner poet: "Hâte-toi de transmettre ta part de merveilleux
de rebellion de bienfaisance."*1 Still, for him the primary concern
is not to invent but to discover and to penetrate what he sees and feels.
He speaks not of "surréalité" but incessantly and unambiguously of
reality itself. "Celui qui invente, au contraire de celui qui découvre,
n'ajoute aux choses, n'apporte aux êtres que des masques, des entre-
deux, une bouillie de fer."*2 Among his life-long and exacting speculations about esthetics the following is luminously inclusive:

Dans le tissu du poème doit se retrouver un nombre égal de tunnels
dérobés, de chambres d'harmonie, en même temps que d'éléments
futurs, de havres au soleil, de pistes captieuses et d'existants
s'entr'appelant. Le poète est le passeur de tout cela qui forme un
ordre. Et un ordre insurgé.*3 *

Human anxieties and hopes woven into poetry in the shape of devious
paths and comfortable enclosures, this is the esthetic substance molded
by a mind with a Promethean passion for resurgent order.

NOTES

*1 René Char, <u>Le Marteau sans maître suivi de Moulin premier</u> (Paris, 1945), 98.

*2 René Char, <u>La Parole en archipel</u> (Paris, 1962), 76.

*3 René Char, <u>A une sérénité crispée</u> (Paris, 1951), 44.

XIII

"DECLARER SON NOM"

Immediately moving and gripping, Char's poems are exceptionally
difficult to understand and explain in depth although incontestably that
depth exists. Far from consciously hermetic, the elliptical nature of
his work stems from an urge for succinct and exact expression of
emotions and experiences completely personal in origin but transfused
with broad human generality by the process of esthetic alchemy. In
order to approach his work in the most direct fashion, I have chosen
first a group of three poems where the dominant spirit is fresh and
simple even though the underlying texture is intricate and deeply
thoughtful. Simplicity can be deceiving also in a chronological sense
and such is the case here. His poems are often hard to date. A few
were written at a particular moment; others were written and rewrit-
ten over a period of years, in other cases it would seem that the initial inspiration reached far into the past but that the formulation into
poem occurred after many years had passed. "Déclarer son nom",
appearing first in an anthology in 1960 is certainly not an early work
for he did not attain such limpidity until after World War II. "Chaume
des Vosges" is dated 1939 in the text of the anthology in which it first
appeared, Fureur et Mystère (1948). "Madeleine à la veilleuse" was
written in 1948.*1 Roughly speaking, they all date after his association with Surrealism.

Déclarer son nom

J'avais dix ans. La Sorgue m'enchâssait. Le soleil chantait les
heures sur le sage cadran des eaux. L'insouciance et la douleur
avaient scellé le coq de fer sur le toit des maisons et se supportaient ensemble. Mais quelle roue dans le coeur de l'enfant aux
aguets tournait plus fort, tournait plus vite que celle du moulin
dans son incendie blanc?*2 *

Radically different from the Surrealist taste for surprise effects and
for a generous sprinkling of consciously absurd images and sequences,
Char's creative habits - from the choice of title, to the selection of
words singly, in groups and in the entire coordinate sweep of each
poem - reveal a conscious sensitivity and concern for exact expression. In this he resembles Valéry and Perse. Char, in addition, takes
pleasure in grouping poems and choosing a title which captures some
perhaps evasive but essential spiritual thread which is common to all.
In one recent inclusive anthology, Commune présence, he even re-

groups and renames poems which appeared previously at diverse moments.*3

"Déclarer son nom" figured first under the group title, Au-dessus du vent, part of a larger collection. The latter title suggests a quality of calm detachment, having passed through wind currents, rising, attaining a certain altitude and perspective. Such a quality at any rate typifies the poem, "Déclarer son nom", and it is a detachment which must have evolved over the passage of time, the emotion of the child recaptured in maturity. Finally, to comment the title of the poem itself (descending from the heights), it marks the straight-forward expression of the core of the child, the core of the person whom he becomes. It is significant certainly that Char chose this poem to open Commune présence.

Before entering the world of feeling and thought, it should be helpful to point out certain factual landmarks. The opening lines themselves are of a reassuring precision, a boy of ten, absorbed and enriched by the river passing through the town. "J'avais dix ans. La Sorgue m'enchâssait." The river, La Sorgue, is wide and meandering as it flows through the fields past the village named l'Isle-sur-Sorgue because, at that point, the river divides in a circuitous route through grassy lands later to merge and flow into the Rhône. The sun is inescapable, a summer sun no doubt because of its peaceful effect (in the third sentence) and also perhaps because of the heat which apparently is in part responsible for the sensation of arrested time and motion suggested in the following sentence ("L'insouciance et la douleur avaient scellé le coq de fer...") and finally because of the blinding quality evoked by the last words "incendie blanc". And there is the village - rooftops, weather-vane, and further on the mill - simple human constructions blending integrally with the natural components of the scene.

Memory or imagination? Both very likely enter into that intense moment related in the poem. The reality of the poem poses its own time, an instant of bright pleasure and tension.

A great number of Char's poems are prose poems. This comes naturally as a form of expression since, although the initial impetus for a poem may be a memory, an event or a feeling, the fashion in which his mind models the material is thoughtful in the strict sense. That is, the concrete elements and the feelings are grasped by the mind, ideas about them are developed and expounded in linear sequence, one reaction following the other, each occupying its necessary place in relation to the rest. He speaks of "la ligne de vol du poème",*4 and I think this illustrates well that sense of linear development. Besides, it is quite apt in this case because it conveys also the sense of perspective and soaring over experience. To read his poetry, then, one is bound to follow carefully the linguistic sequence which is meaningful exactly in the way that Péret's sentence patterns are not.

Tonally this poem has three stages. The initial one consists of three statements: "J'avais dix ans. La Sorgue m'enchâssait. Le soleil chantait les heures sur le sage cadran des eaux." The first two - mainly because of their rhythm, equally short and decisive - have that ring of clarity and immediate frankness suggested by the title. This is so particularly for the opening sentence, which relates a simple fact.

The first word, a frank "I", and the expression of age, "dix ans",
have a direct childlike certainty and naïve egotism. Immediately after
that he melts into the surroundings, peacefully, naturally. "La Sorgue
m'enchâssait. Le soleil chantait le sage cadran des eaux." A succession of soft phonemes s and ∫ contribute to a sense of lightness and
peace. This is rendered more brilliant and more precious by the unusual word "enchâssait". Its multiple meanings all fit into the context
of the poem. The primary sense is religious indicating carefully to
preserve a relic in a special container. This enhances the theme of
cherished memory. Its secondary meaning is to mount, to put permanently in a setting and usually evokes a precious stone. One of the
words given in connection with this usage by Robert is "encadrer"
which echoes the word in the third sentence "cadran" both etymologically and by the suggestion of being framed, enclosed.*5 So the total
impression of these lines is that of the past preciously preserved,
bathed in peaceful rich luminosity.

A shift of scene, tone, and viewpoint catches the reader's attention
in the following sentence: "L'insouciance et la douleur avaient scellé
le coq de fer sur le toit des maisons et se supportaient ensemble."
Perhaps a natural perception underlies this remark, that of intense
heat, which gives the sensation of everything made motionless and
shimmering as if from tension. It is the same sensation Valéry conveys in "Le Cimetière marin" reinforcing the idea of fixation, absence
of motion, and passage of time by signalling the precise moment of
noon. The word "scellé" of course is what specifies the motionless
nature of the scene; and "coq de fer" enhances that tone by its hard
phonetic and connotative values. But the main emphasis here is on another level, an ethical and emotional one, intentionally transposing
the scene into human terms. "L'insouciance et la douleur" reflect an
awareness of pitfalls and pain beyond that initial peaceful realm or
perhaps even springing from the same natural causes and offering a
glimpse of life beyond the calm embrace of the river. The main verb,
which comes at the end, "se supportaient ensemble", also contains
both physical and moral overtones - mutual contact which maintains
a given state, either literally (holding each other up) or figuratively
(bearing with - emotionally).

The last statement moves to break even more radically with the
preceding ones in a number of ways. The conjunction "Mais" is the
first sign of change. It foreshadows the change from immobility to
movement. The image of "la roue" dramatically denotes the contrast
and the verbal phrase repeated with slight variation "tournait plus
fort, tournait plus vite" accelerates the tempo. Again, the components
of the sentence combine subjective and objective elements. There is
the child's heart which is "moved" by the experience. There is the
mill wheel revolving in the fiery light. One cannot even say that this
effect is achieved by imagery. Even though there is a comparison between the wheel of the child's heart and that of the mill, both the child
and the mill are there, in the surroundings, not imagined but real.

Aside from the accelerated tempo and movement, another change
takes place in this last part which develops a spiritual tension already
introduced by the words "insouciance" and "douleur". Heightened lu-

cidity is evident in a number of ways. First, the child is described as
watchful. The French expression "aux aguets" has no exact English
equivalent: it denotes a sensitive immediate alert quality almost primitive in nature since it derives from a term in old French designating
lying in watch for an enemy. Transposed into the intimate psychological
domain, it suggests consciousness of some external menace and a natural reflex concerning the security of the ego. In addition, there is a
marked break in the narrative stance for now, instead of being absorbed
in memory, the poet is speaking from the present. Still identifying
himself with the child, he comments on the force of the recalled emotion, magnified doubly by the way in which that comment is expressed -
as a question, and one which has the force of an exclamation, a discovery and a thrust towards the future since, unanswered, it leaves
one in a state of expectancy. To conclude, the emotion and the strong
natural light of the sun which was evoked in the opening lines are integrated in one powerful final verbal explosion, "incendie blanc".

This poetic moment, past and present combined, real yet transmuted
by the imagination is remarkably similar to moments described by
Proust in A la recherche du temps perdu. For him, the involuntary
memory was the natural means of recapturing the plenitude of such
moments from the past. In his experience, that mental phenomenon,
memory, stirred by some immediate perception similar to another
such perception in the past (the taste of a cake, the feel of a napkin)
would preserve intact and later resurrect the total emotional and physical impact of a scene and time, including details of the surroundings
but more importantly the full force of old desires and pleasures.*6
The scene evoked by Char in this poem is more narrowly delineated
in time and place than the vast psychological panoramas of Proust; it
is bathed in the same passionate clarity.

Chaume des Vosges

Beauté, ma toute-droite, par des routes si ladres,
A l'étape des lampes et du courage clos,
Que je me glace et que tu sois ma femme de décembre.
Ma vie future, c'est ton visage quand tu dors.*

"Chaume des Vosges" is a poem with a long history. First published
in the 1948 edition of Fureur et mystère, it appeared with considerable
changes in the 1962 edition of the same collection. Significantly, since
the author rarely situates his poems in time, it bears the date 1939.
Yet a number of important details - the same date given, a winter setting and the warm haven, a sense of being away from home (dépaysé)
together with a sense of discouragement relate it to another poem,
"Donnerbach muhle". Most fortunately for the critic, the poet himself
indicates in a rare mood of creative retrospection that the latter work
goes back to the winter of 1929 when he was in military service in the
Vosges, indeed far from familiar surroundings.*7 So the setting and
the personal emotional overtones have their source quite far in the
past. But events in subsequent years, perhaps the pre-war tensions
dominant in 1939, and possibly also shifting personal anxieties, all
combined to form the definitive poetic substance.

Regardless of the real details from which that substance stems, what is striking - and essential - is that the poem as it stands radiates intense emotion which attains a classically sculptured generality. Both are equally important, the warmth and the esthetic anonymity.

This poem is structured in lines of roughly (but only roughly) equal length. The divisions are important as each line enunciates a particular thought and a particular tone. Claudel expounded a theory of versification according to which the length of a line would follow a natural cycle of spiritual and physical rhythm with a sense of pulse and respiration fused with spiritual expression.*8   Char's rhythm here is determined also by natural forms but the key factor is quite intellectual. It is interesting to note that although the first three lines are grammatically only one sentence, each line really expresses a thought, complete and important in itself, then united by the wish, "Que je me glace..." which has its source in the total complex of the preceding individual conditions.

The central figure of the poem, in a sense its subject, is announced simply at the start, "Beauté". Woman? Muse? Incarnation of esthetic pleasure? It is an abstract noun but it is not abstract in conception. The ambiguity certainly is intentional and inclusive. The line as a whole has a somehwat rigid, staccato rhythm, broken by commas separating shifts of mental attention and punctuated by relatively explosive consonants d̲ and t̲ ("Beauté, ma t̲oute–d̲roite, par d̲es rout̲es si lad̲res"). The last word, "ladre", is strong and really is responsible for the main tone. Meaning variously leprous, parcimonious, sordid, it carries a broad unpleasant sense of menace consistant with and reinforced by the alliterative sequence just mentioned. If there is also a sense of rigidity, it is certainly not due to insensitivity but rather a need to conjure up a bracing attitude to face a hostile world. In this case it takes a visual form: Beauty, erect against a horizontal background of ominous paths.

The second line provides a comforting contrast, continuing the theme of travel because of the word "étape" and indicating a welcome place of rest. The words "lampes", "courage", and "clos" reinforce the sense of warmth, a very human warmth. That sense furthermore was announced in the title: "Chaume", a thatched roof, made of straw warmed and weathered by the sun, simple peasant building material. Phonetically also the title suggests warmth, because of the soft consonants ʃ and ʒ and the elongated vowels o̲: of both main words ("Chaume des Vosges").*9   Also the word "chaume" is close phonetically to the French word for warm, "chaud". This second line because of the added verbal strength of the title and because also perhaps of its inner glow, literal and figurative, represents the tonal core of the poem.

The third line is curious in that it combines elements of acceptance within a vocabulary of chilly overtones. The poet is speaking directly, intimately to Beauty. He addresses her with the familiar "tu" and with the tenderly possessive "ma" (as in the first line), inviting physical and spiritual union. However the two most uncommon words, "glace" and "décembre" introduce the notion of humanly hostile elements, winter and cold, which echo the sense of menace in the first line. And there is a curious aura of desired but in a sense helpless yielding.

The early version of the poem has "Ecroule-moi" instead of "Que je me glace" which is a stronger expression of submission, commanded, even, rather than wished for. But the last line is set off as a separate sentence thus, in a way, indicating that the poet has regained control and comprehension. It is simple, intimate, and - most importantly - hopeful. "Ma vie future, c'est ton visage quand tu dors." Oblivious of all exterior hostile forces, immediate peace reflected in the sleeping woman's expression and echoed by the tender gaze of the poet, seems to symbolize in fact and not abstractly or with self-conscious literary intent, hopeful orientation towards the future. It reaffirms in a very personal way the warm, positive element of the title and of the second line. Nonetheless the ultimate poetic effect depends upon the background of hostile elements, a background which has been subtly presented as near equilibrium: lines one and three with negative overtones, lines two and four plus the title tipping the balance towards warmth and hope.

Madeleine à la veilleuse

Je voudrais aujourd'hui que l'herbe fût blanche pour fouler l'évidence de vous voir souffrir: je ne regarderais pas sous votre main si jeune la forme dure, sans crépi de la mort. Un jour discrétionnaire, d'autres pourtant moins avides que moi, retireront votre chemise de toile, occuperont votre alcôve. Mais ils oublieront en partant de noyer la veilleuse et un peu d'huile se répandra par le poignard de la flamme sur l'impossible solution.*10 *

This poetic narrative is as personal in nature as are "Déclarer son nom" and "Chaume des Vosges". In all three the poet's presence is on the verbal surface, not just implied but explicit in the main statements. As in the others too, the focus of attention is on people: in the first, the double image of the poet (child and man); in the second, the poet with Beauty incarnate; in this one, it is the poet in a moment of respectful intimacy and profound painful empathy with the young woman of La Tour's painting. In a sense, the relationship poet woman here is the reverse of that in "Chaume des Vosges", for in the latter case Beauty was the stronger and the active, soothing partner whereas in this case it is the poet who embraces feelingly yet discretely and immaterially, the figure of the girl in distressed reverie.

For La Tour, a seventeenth century artist, Char has a close almost brotherly regard. The painting of Madeleine is typical of all of his work in that, although the subject may be religious, the settings are always simple - unadorned ordinary surroundings. His characters are similarly plain human beings; and, most interestingly, candles are the sole source of light. The first two characteristics apply equally to Char's poetic world. Besides, candlelight as well as fire have considerable symbolic weight in his esthetic views. The range of significance is vast. In the present instance, two points are pertinent. One is that for Char, I would surmise, light - poetic and artistic light - is not the equivalent of knowledge so much as something resembling a constant flame which enlightens, literally "sheds light on". The other has to do with the effect on the subject. Speaking of the candle in another painting of La Tour, Le Prisonnier,*11 Char says: "Au fond du cachot, les minutes de suif de la clarté tirent et diluent les traits de l'homme assis." This is exactly the case in the painting of Madeleine. Her gaze is drawn directly to the steady, soft, but penetrating flame and the light baths her face fully, the clothes and flesh of her torso brightly but partially. Her hand resting on the skull on her lap benefits mercifully from the lower shadow.

Once again, as in "Déclarer son nom", the author speaks simply and directly of an intensely lived esthetic moment. He speaks from the present, yet all the verbs are hypothetical: conditional, subjunctive or future. The impression of certainty must come then from emotional conviction of understanding, of desire and sympathy. Two immediate elements are declared at the start: "Je voudrais aujourd'hui..." so there is no doubt who is speaking nor when. The poet is speaking - now. And the parallel sweep and emphasis of the first double sentence set the tone and theme. Both parts start with "je" and end with explicit mention of the human condition - in the first case "souffrir" and in the second the primordial cause of that anguish, "mort". The thoughts enunciated in the slowly paced intermediate phrases in both cases seek through sympathy, wish, and will alone to attenuate that suffering. The hesitancy with which the words seem to be pronounced reveals the force of involvement and the difficulty of finding adequate words of comfort. One could read the first sentence, for instance, with the following oral halts: "Je voudrais/aujourd'hui/que l'herbe fût blanche/pour fouler/ l'évidence/de vous voir souffrir." The breaks after "voudrais" and "fouler" are perhaps optional but the others are clear either by grammatical grouping or by imagery and meaning. For instance, the sequence "que l'herbe fût blanche" is unusual both in the context of the picture and in the strange concept of grass turning white. Similarly the word "fouler" makes one pause to reflect even though "l'évidence" is clearly the object of the verb. The slow, interrupted pace continues throughout, probably a function of the poet's feelings and his own difficulty in expressing that feeling, with the effect, totally uncontrived, of communicating to the reader those very sentiments. Can those unusual expressions be accounted for? The thought of whitening grass is perhaps fitting in that for grass, normally green, fresh and alive, to become white is a contrast startling enough to counteract the sight of a young girl's misery. "Fouler" (trample, crush), likewise, is a very strong expression pitted against an equally strong pain at the sight of pain.

The second part of the sentence, expressed grammatically as an extension of the first (following a colon), combines a tone of tenderness with hard fact: "...je ne regarderais pas sous votre main si jeune la forme dure, sans crépi de la mort." Discreetly, the poet would like to avoid the evidence of death, a hard smooth shape so incongruous with the girl's hand gently resting upon the hollow-eyed skull. His respect is indicated by reserved intent, an impersonal (but not cold) form of address, "votre", and by tenderness revealed in the words "main si jeune" - taking particular note of the hand and remarking almost familiarly on its innocence. The following sentence represents a considerable jump in the thought sequence, not unrelated, but something that puts the reader on his mettle. Char once exclaimed, "Salut

à celui qui marche en sûreté à mes côtés au terme du poème."*12
This is meant to be encouragement but it shows also the author's
awareness of the challenge - a challenge encountered frequently in his
work. The first words, "Un jour discrétionnaire", indicate another
time, in the future, and a moment which appears both highly significant and beyond ordinary control. The adjective "discrétionnaire" remained opaque to me for some time. It is an unusual word and one
which has primarily a judicial sense (the unlimited power of a judge
to take initiatives and to render judgments) with a figurative extension
of arbitrary or unlimited decision. Since it is commonly used to modify a noun signifying "power" its use here, following "jour", is strictly
speaking impertinent. Poetically, I think, its function is to stress as
strikingly as possible the inevitable nature of an event resembling a
day of judgment. Possibly also, there is an unconscious retrospective
semantic echo of the tone of discretion elaborated in the preceding
sentence. The rest of the statement is quite clear, however, phrased
in the future with a tone of something ineluctable, indicating how the
scene will be altered by the act of passion, a desire which the poet
shares no less, and how the girl's reflections, that still reverie partaking of the absolute, will be interrupted.

The last sentence is stated as a resolution, yet the ultimate note is
one of an unresolved fact. Most of it is clear in a realistic sense. It
continues to use the elements of La Tour's painting: the lamp with a
tall pointed flame against a nocturnal background, an oil lamp with the
wick and the oil clearly visible, painted carefully in a transparent glass
container. So when "they" leave the room, taking Madeleine aside, the
flame will continue to burn. Its intensity is rendered in the poem by
the image of the dagger, "par le poignard de la flamme". Through the
flame, a bit of oil will spread over (smoothing imperceptibly?) what
the poet calls "l'impossible solution". The sense of resigned but dis-
appointed finality is evident. The exact reference is not. What solution?
Absolution of sin? The impossibility of fathoming death through thought?
Accepting the imponderable, one can at least find assurance in the
overall tone of acute, pained sympathy. The words "souffrir", "fouler",
"forme dure", "mort", "avides","poignard de la flamme", explicitly
combine to evoke the distress, an atmosphere which that initial wish
expressed subtly and analogically, "Je voudrais...que l'herbe fût
blanche" combines and translates that feeling with original force and
sharpness. Sympathy is indicated in part by the details the poet notices
concerning the girl's body and dress ("votre main si jeune", "votre
chemise de toile"). More striking still in this respect are the gestures
of the poet - the wishes proffered generously in the first sentence and
the admission of his contained desire in the parenthetical phrase further on ("d'autres pourtant moins avides que moi"). The unique quality of this poem, I feel, resides behind the verbal whole, in the clear
mental gestures which render the poem an intimate act.

There is a curious sequel to this poem. Immediately after having
finished writing it, the author was returning home late one winter
evening after visiting a friend, and on the way was approached boldly
by a girl, thin, pale, with an intense light in her eyes. His first reaction was not to respond; but something about her curiously direct plea

for momentary companionship along the deserted streets attracted his curiosity. In the course of their conversation he learned that her name was Madeleine. The encounter was brief but deeply moving and reminiscent of other occasions when, after finishing a poem which had been extremely difficult to compose, a similar adventure had occurred where the creation had appeared "verified" by experience. As he explained it, "L'accès d'une couche profonde d'émotion et de vision est propice au surgissement du grand Réel." In this respect, Char maintained and even developed the Surrealist uninhibited openness to experience including the possibility of chance happenings which may turn out to be highly significant. The author's description of this particular experience, short but humanly and poetically touching, closes thus: "La réalité noble ne se dérobe pas à qui la rencontre pour l'estimer et non pour l'insulter ou la faire prisonnière. Là est l'unique condition que nous ne sommes pas toujours assez purs pour remplir."*13

NOTES

*1 The Bibliographie des oeuvres de René Char de 1928 à 1963 by P. A. Benoit (Paris, 1964) is useful for the detailed chronology of the publication of Char's works and for mention of certain variants.

*2 La Parole en archipel, 129.

*3 René Char, Commune présence (Paris, 1964).

*4 René Char, Fureur et mystère, nouvelle édition (Paris, 1962), 116. From the wartime diary, Feuillets d'Hypnos.

*5 Here are the principal meanings of "enchâsser" given by Robert (Dictionnaire alphabétique et analogique de la langue française, Paris, 1966): "1 Mettre (des reliques) dans une châsse... - Fig. Conserver précieusement, avec piété. 2 Par ext. Mettre dans une monture. V. Monter; encastrer, sertir. Enchâsser un rubis dans une boucle..."

*6 What is particularly interesting about the nature of the Proustian memory is that there is a clear esthetic dimension which is closely bound with the desire, experienced as the one surely permanent emotion and which is equally closely connected with certain primitive sensations such as heat and light. I studied this in my book, L'Evolution de la mémoire involontaire dans l'oeuvre de Marcel Proust (Paris, 1966). In Char's poetry desire is equally central to the esthetic perspective but oriented principally towards the future.

*7 In his commentary of the poem, "Donnerbach muhle", in the Arrière histoire du poème pulvérisé (Paris, 1953) Char describes the setting as a wooded isolated region in the Bas-Rhin where he was stationed for military service in 1929. For purposes of comparison, here is the text of "Chaume des Vosges" as it appeared in the first edition of Fureur et mystère (1948), 186:

Beauté, ma toute droite, par les routes d'étoiles,
A l'étape des lampes et du courage clos,
Dans l'absurde chagrin de vivre sans comprendre,
Ecroule-moi et sois ma femme de décembre.

*8 See Claudel's Réflexions et propositions sur le vers français.

*9 When, in an interview with Char, I mentioned what had occurred to me as the phonetic connotations of the title, he replied that the sound of the words had not entered into his choice of title. If not consciously determined, the effects do exist for the reader.

*10 Fureur et mystère (Paris, 1962), 224. The title of the subgroup which includes this poem is "La Fontaine narrative".

*11 These reflections are from Feuillets d'Hypnos (Fureur et mystère, 138-139). During the years in the maquis, Char had a reproduction of that painting hung on his wall, near at hand, a visible embodiment of suffering and hope. Two other passages about La Tour are especially interesting, one also in Fureur et mystère (p.69) and another from a recent poetic group, Dans la pluie giboyeuse (Paris, 1968), 27-28.

*12 This line is near the end of a particularly forceful early poem, "Fenaison" (Fureur et mystère, 34-35).

*13 This episode is related in Art bref (Paris, 1950), 20-21; it is dated 27 janvier 1948 which permits us to date the poem, "Madeleine à la veilleuse", roughly at the same time.

XIV

"CHANSON DU VELOURS A CÔTES"

Chanson du velours à côtes

Le jour disait: "Tout ce qui peine m'accompagne, s'attache à moi,
se veut heureux. Témoins de ma comédie, retenez mon pied joyeux.
J'appréhende midi et sa flèche méritée. Il n'est de grâce à quérir
pour prévaloir à ses yeux. Si ma disparition sonne votre élargissement, les eaux froides de l'été ne me recevront que mieux."
La nuit disait: "Ceux qui m'offensent meurent jeunes. Comment
ne pas les aimer? Prairie de tous mes instants, ils ne peuvent me
fouler. Leur voyage est mon voyage et je reste obscurité."
Il était entre les deux un mal qui les déchirait. Le vent allait de
l'un à l'autre; le vent ou rien, les pans de la rude étoffe et l'avalanche des montagnes, ou rien.*1 *

The external form of Char's poems varies immensely. In all his mature works, the sources are eclectic; the wealth of French literary
tradition can be sensed entering into the wide range of poetic structure.
The dense, multifaceted dream-like sequence of the Surrealists, typical of his early poems, reappears occasionally in later years. A short,
bejeweled, visionary type of prose poem often recalls Rimbaud, a predecessor whom he admires particularly. There are light tenuous, lyrical poems (the love poems of Visage nuptial for instance) which remind
one of Verlaine. And then there are some forms which have not only
titles but a naïve rhythm and line revealing a literary ancestry of
French medieval verse. A rather long poem, "Fête des arbres et du
chasseur", a dialogue between guitars and a hunter, renews the trouba-
dour tradition through the style and inspiration of present day Catalan
folk music.*2 The poem, "Chanson du velours à côtes", retains this
same popular, earthy spirit and also the use of dialogue between two
poetic voices, although the verbal form is that same linear poetic prose
which bears the author's individual stamp.
The underlying theme of "Chanson du velours à côtes" should be
viewed against the background of a poetic and metaphysical principle
which represents a basic feature of Char's thought, namely the interaction and close-knit complementary relation between adverse elements, adverse forces. Heraclitus was natural classical mentor in
this respect (and in others too), as an influence and as an intellectual
companion. In a series of notes and poetic reflections, "Partage formel", Char speaks of the philosopher's predilection for "la fusion de
ces contraires", noting that "Il voit en premier lieu en eux la condition

parfaite et le moteur indispensable à produire l'harmonie."*3   In the poet's own terms the interaction of contrary elements maintains the unique character of the adversaries' mutual differences but modifies the aloofness and the rather fierce violence of the Greek philosopher's outlook with a humanistic and humane desire for reconciliation. Another reflection, this one from the notebook kept during the years spent fighting in the Resistance, Feuillets d'Hypnos, formulates that idea in the following fashion: "L'effort du poète vise à transformer vieux ennemis en loyaux adversaires... "*4   And, in fact, one group of poems is united under the title, Les Loyaux adversaires. This group does not include "Chanson du velours à côtes" (written at a later date) but that might well have been the case.

Two speeches plus a poetic commentary: the form of the poem is simple, the consistent tone of tension and contradictory emotional forces is clear. But the idiom and the linear semantic relationships are less easily accessible. One senses here the presence of the aforementioned "tunnels dérobés".

If Char uses dialogue to present the diverse conditions and qualities inherent in day and night, it is not done, I think, from an anthropomorphic view which, as in the case of Valéry, discovers patterns and qualities reminiscent of human behavior in natural objects. Rather it may be a way of dramatizing and of exploiting the flair of natural oratory, focusing the attention on the phenomenon the poet is considering. Perhaps too it gives them a certain symbolic stature.*5   Yet, one should not construe their voiced presence as an attempt to reconstruct their essence in philosophic sense. The author aims to "discover" reality; but it is a personal discovery without the pretension really to know objectively the thing-in-itself. It is more the report of a primitive intuition, "Participation mystique", with an admittedly strong admixture of external rational control.

The day's first two remarks almost have the force of exclamations so strong is their emotional impetus. There is a rapturously happy flair. "Tout ce qui peine m'accompagne, s'attache à moi, se veut heureux. Témoins de ma comédie, retenez mon pied joyeux." The remarks are all inclusive ("Tout ce qui peine... "), all-embracing actually by virtue of the verbal emphasis ("m'accompagne, s'attache à moi... "). The day addresses directly the people of its world, its audience as well as its inhabitants: "retenez mon pied joyeux." Both sentences end with a happy word, in the first case "heureux" which applies to the people and in the second case "joyeux" - its own emotional state, to which the poet gives a human touch by using the image of a foot, with implied movement, skipping or tripping from joy. The only contrary element so far is the word "peine" - acknowledging, naturally, that work and toil are the activities of its sphere.

The next two sentences have an equally positive overall tone but with a heightened tension reflected by the semantic nuances of "peine" and "J'appréhende midi et sa flèche méritée. Il n'est de grâce à quérir pour prévaloir à ses yeux." They circumscribe the moment of noon - no doubt against a suggested background of absolute light and heat. Negative elements appear rapidly in the words "appréhende", "flèche" and in the sense of the whole second sentence suggesting strong qual-

ity of mercilessness. Despite all this, a number of positive elements,
including the assurance with which the remarks are delivered, certainly do not communicate hopelessness and ultimately serve to maintain a positive equilibrium. For one thing, the word "appréhende" has
a double meaning as does its English equivalent: its commonplace
meaning is to fear; but the philosophical and psychological meaning is
to perceive and understand. The latter includes the idea of a desire
to know and of acceptance. In the word group "flèche méritée" the adjective is totally positive while the noun has multiple connotations.
One meaning is "arrow", which echoes the theme of pain and of fear.
But it has other meanings - pointer, church spire, the pole of a mast.
All of these have a vertical thrust which in Char's poetic world has
very positive psychological import. Picturing Beauty as "toute-droite"
in "Chaume des Vosges" is an example of the same imagery. Then,
although the total meaning of the second sentence is negative, three of
the words therein have a positive ring ("grâce", "quérir", "prévaloir")
which certainly attenuates the logically negative construction.

The final sentence completes a temporal trajectory from noon to
evening and reinforces, more gently, the day's all-inclusive embrace.
"Si ma disparition sonne votre élargissement, les eaux froides de
l'été ne me recevront que mieux." His people having finished their
tasks, released from work, day willingly accepts their freedom in exchange for his own disappearance. The last clause is interesting, although elliptical as an image. Possibly there is a visual source of sun
seen setting behind an expanse of river. In any case, the semantic
weight is certainly positive: the construction with a conditional "si"
clause followed by "ne...que" have a very positive sense; "recevront"
and "mieux" add unqualified acceptance. A first-hand experience also
suddenly revealed to me another side to that image. One sweltering
hot summer day, feet immersed in the cool swift waters of the river,
I realized how welcome indeed "les eaux froides de l'été" can be.

When night takes the center of the stage, he speaks <u>of</u> those who
pass through his domain instead of addressing them directly. "Ceux
qui m'offensent meurent jeunes." That pronouncement has a somber
cast: "m'offensent" and "meurent" by sense and by sound have a hollow, hostile resonance. But next he admits, albeit negatively ("Comment ne pas les aimer?"), that he too, of necessity, considers them
affectionately. Perhaps it is because he is bound with them throughout
the nocturnal expanse and slow temporal field. Indeed there is a reciprocal relationship indicated in an unusual syntactic sequence with
an apparent reversal of semantic connections. "Prairie de tous mes
instants, ils ne peuvent me fouler." The paradox consists of the phrase
"Prairie de tous mes instants" being presented in apposition to "ils":
they, the people are the field through which he passes. Yet the rest of
the sentence, "ils ne peuvent me fouler", indicates that they can not
trample or crush <u>him</u> (as if he were something underfoot), so that there
is a switch of the agent who is acting and the person acted upon. "Fouler" usually has physical sense of trampling on something (such as
grapes or grass). It also is used in a figurative sense to scorn, which
is comparable to the English figurative expression to be "crushed".
This relates to the verb of the first sentence "offenser". The last sen-

tence introduces another image, repeated, that of travel. "Leur voyage est mon voyage et je reste obscurité." It conveys in physical terms the notion of slow passage of time during the night, just as the image of the prairie suggests a similar expanse spatially. In both cases night equates his existence with that of his people. The last word, "obscurité", reiterates neutrally (without a hostile gesture) the black tone of the start.

Finally, the poet comments on their state of being, their relationship. The fashion in which he prefaces his remarks, "Il était...", carries the scene into a mythical realm, consistent with the way the speeches of night and day are presented ("Le jour disait... la nuit disait...") for such is the language of fairy-tales, a timeless imaginative conformation of reality. The first and most striking note is that of continued pain and opposition. "Il était entre les deux un mal qui les déchirait." The use of the imperfect tense reinforces the enduring nature of the conflict. The last line I find particularly moving. For first it establishes a thin yet strong continuous movement which immaterially bridges the gap. And then it reduces that to nothingness: "le vent ou rien, les pans de la rude étoffe et l'avalanche des montagnes, ou rien." The rhythm of the sentence lets the accent fall gently but firmly on "rien" as if the immaterial was so close to the quality of absence that it might well be nothingness, or that if the wind was not bridging the gap then nothing could. The wind and its alternatives - "les pans de la rude étoffe et l'avalanche des montagnes" - have interesting common features carefully chosen to highlight what is probably the main esthetic intent. All three, at first glance dissimilar, share an aura of things at home in the open air, simple, and with a certain roughness or force. The wind and the avalanche, natural phenomena, have in common high altitude, movement and power. The flaps of the rough cloth, which certainly refers to the title, "Chanson du velours à côtes", similarly evokes life in the outdoors, a rough vigorous quality. But, in contrast, it is human.

A collection of notes, Arrière histoire du Poème pulvérisé,*6 comments on the background or, more precisely, on the imaginative field surrounding the creation of the group of poems which includes "Chanson du velours à côtes". The passage concerning this poem is indeed more a poetic extension than an explanation.

> Le poète n'est-il pas ce montagnard qui récidive sans cesse et que l'assaut répété des sommets remet sur ses pieds? Poudré de neige, et l'été cerclé de mélèzes, il va d'un pic à un torrent. Il dort dans l'herbe du printemps. C'est tout son repos. Sur la râpe des crêtes et le vertige des aiguilles, s'exaltant, il prête au sourire. Cependant il meurt. Va poète, et que le velours te tienne, t'empêche de glisser... L'homme n'accomplit rien de franchement infructueux. Il ne perd pas ce qu'il se plaira ensuite à rechercher. L'intrigue, le désespoir sont sa lanterne, le poète est son baton.*

In the "Chanson" the poet, is audible only as a reticent final voice. The main elements of the poem are all natural: the speakers, day and night, the imagery and even if human beings are implicit in the speeches they are never mentioned as such directly. Natural tensions, contrasts, interactions form the web of the narrative, even though human moral judgments and emotions enter into the verbal structure ("peiner", "appréhender", "grâce à quérir", "offenser", "fouler"). The one concrete image, suggestive of man but not naming him directly, is in the title, referring to cloth (corduroy), which reappears unobtrusively but significantly at the end. Illustrating perpetual natural strife with its blend of affection and disaffection, the final note is to seek, perhaps fruitlessly, some immaterial key for fusion and comprehension. The poet, visible only behind the image of a rough-textured homely fabric, joins in that search.

NOTES

*1 Fureur et mystère, 210; in the subgroup entitled " Le Poème pulvérisé".

*2 "Fête des arbres et du chasseur" (Les Matinaux [Paris, 1950], 13-20) bears a resemblance, transcending differences of culture literary traditions, with "The Man with the Blue Guitar" of Wallace Stevens. In both cases there is a return to a formally simple lyricism but in both cases also the simplicity is deceiving for the underlying concern bears on the complex and potentially destructive relationship between the poet and reality.

*3 Fureur et mystère, 71-72.

*4 Fureur et mystère, 91.

*5 In a curious and difficult poem, "La Patience" (Fureur et mystère, 169-170) "Le Moulin" shares a place of preeminence as capitalized title of one of a number of curiously disparate stanzas along with "Vagabonds", "Le Nombre", and "Auxiliaires". Each have the force of a very real presence with clear symbolic stature.

*6 Arrière histoire du Poème pulvérisé (Paris, 1953), 54.

XV

"SEPT PARCELLES DE LUBERON"

Sept parcelles de Lubéron

I

Couchés en terre de douleur,
Mordus des grillons, des enfants,
Tombés de soleils vieillissants,
Doux fruits de la Brémonde.

Dans un bel arbre sans essaim,
Vous languissez de communion,
Vous éclatez de division,
Jeunesse, voyante nuée.

Ton naufrage n'a rien laissé
Qu'un gouvernail pour notre coeur,
Un rocher creux pour notre peur,
O Buoux, barque maltraitée.

Tels des mélèzes grandissants,
Au-dessus des conjurations,
Vous êtes le calque du vent,
Mes jours, muraille d'incendie.

C'était près. En pays heureux.
Elevant sa plainte au délice,
Je frottai le trait de ses hanches
Contre les ergots de tes branches,
Romarin, lande butinée.

De mon logis, pierre après pierre,
J'endure la démolition.
Seul sut l'exacte dimension
Le dévot, d'un soir, de la mort.

L'hiver se plaisait en Provence
Sous le regard gris des Vaudois;
Le bûcher a fondu la neige,
L'eau glissa bouillante au torrent.

Avec un astre de misère,
Le sang à sécher est trop lent.
Massif de mes deuils, tu gouvernes:
Je n'ai jamais rêvé de toi. *

Depersonalized, focused outside of the poetic self, the field of attention
in "Chanson du velours à côtes" contrasts sharply with that of "Sept
parcelles du Luberon, I" which touches the innermost depths of sensitivity. Although this poem dates from a later period, the difference
in focus does not represent exactly a chronological shift of emphasis.
Many poems from all periods (including the Surrealist epoch) are
molded of a material which is intensely subjective, some chiseled
with sharp edges of pleasure, others of pain. This one appeared first
in the collection Commune présence (1964) but its natural place is as
the opening poem in the sequence of Retour amont (1966), setting the
keynote of affliction and temporal perspective welded to the terrain.
In a sense, the direction of the esthetic inspiration lying behind it reiterates that of the "Chanson", namely the view of a poet whose inner
drive takes the form of an ascent to precipitous and barren, windswept
heights, a drive consisting of the hazardous quest for comprehension.*1

Intense sorrow, the central emotional content of "Sept parcelles, I"
communicates its force directly, unambiguously. The web of its components is however dense and elliptical. The main difficulty lies in the
extent to which the material and expression are subtle, deeply vital,
stringently succinct. This difficulty can not and should not even try to
be explained away. But two areas which present an obstacle to the
reader can be cleared up to some extent. Both have to do with references to people and places. One is characteristic of Char's style. To
varying degrees his poems have a particular basis in experience, with
a person, friend or acquaintance as the source - an event or a gesture
or the configuration of a relationship. In most cases the author discreetly does not name names, specify details of place, time or action.
So that although he will use personal pronouns carefully - singular,
plural, intimate, formal - the entire gamut of personal address, the
reader does not know exactly to whom they refer. The Arrière histoire
du Poème pulvérisé contains a number of explanations which show how
this is so. One poem of that group, "L'Extravagant", follows the steps
of a nameless person in a scene by moonlight with the air penetrated
by a frozen hell. Only in reading the commentary of that poem does
one learn that the subject is a friend's march to torture, one of many
horrendous human events witnessed by the author in the Resistance.*2
That the person is nameless and that the poetic narrative remains unidentified reinforces a conception of poetry as extracting a pure, general human essence from reality. In "Sept parcelles, I" this sort of
ambiguity is pervasive. One may speculate about the reference or origin but such speculations are not fundamental to grasp the poem's
deepest significance.

References to places and historical events, in contrast, are more
easily clarified. The title delimits in exact geographical terms the
physical setting. Luberon is a name of a chain of rocky, arid mountains in the Southern Alps slightly to the East and South of Avignon.
The poem has in addition a precise historical ground. On the southern
slopes of these hills, in the thirteenth century, lived a community of
heretics, the Vaudois, whose beliefs prefigured Calvinism. In the sixteenth century (February 1545), when such doctrines were anathema
to a royal power sensitive to the threat of the Reformation, an ex-

pedition decimated the population. Buoux was a fortified castle, high
on the crest of the range, today in ruins.

Although most of Char's poems have a free prose-style structure,
some are modeled in verse. Here, a musically tonal line, whose
rhythm proceeds from line to line and from stanza to stanza consistent
throughout the entire trajectory, is that of sustained lament. Briefly,
the first four stanzas sing of internal sorrow, involved in an awareness
combining present and past. The fifth verse is a dream-like isolated
summit of paradise lost. The final stanzas descend sharply, witness
to destruction.

The first stanza (as all five comprising the first part) contains three
lines which are descriptive and evocative; one must look to the fourth
for the subject. It is as if the poet is speaking softly, reflectively to
that subject rather than to himself or to a reader, with all his attention
and feeling absorbed therein. In the first verse, the "Doux fruits de la
Brémonde" may have some symbolic secondary reference but I think
rather they are simply the fruits of that land, although perhaps they
prefigure the subject of the second stanza, "Jeunesse". The first line,
"Couchés en terre de douleur", evokes the land, sorrow, and the first
word, bedded, suggests the enclosed, lingering self-absorbed atmosphere of the whole poetic focus. All three first lines are introduced
by past participles - "Couchés", "Mordus", "Tombés" - which indicate
states, lasting states, motionlessly sustained. Both the theme of the
earth and that of enduring time appear immediately, the latter in the
phrase, " soleils vieillissants". Easing the pain are simple mild elements: "grillons", "enfants","soleils", "doux fruits". This gentle tone
lingers, and more persistently, in the second stanza with the subject,
"Jeunesse, voyante nuée" ("youth, bright cloud") which offers a single
bright note of hope, an "élément futur"; and it conveys a sense of being
lifted above the earth. The first line of that stanza also appears positive in tone. This is clear in "bel arbre" but the meaning of the phrase
"sans essaim" (swarmless) is abstruse. Possibly it suggests absence
of tension, since the sound of swarming bees is nervously piercing.
In any case the s sounds introduced here, repeated in "languissez"
and "jeunesse" soften the tone. The two middle lines - "Vous languissez de communion, / Vous éclatez de division" emphasize conflict and
that familiar co-existence of contrary elements (communion/division).

The third stanza turns one's attention back in time. The poet addresses familiarly and with pity the vestiges of the fort Buoux. The
ship image proves doubly apt: offering the notion of shipwreck and
more particularly the possibility of an emotional guide, "un gouvernail
pour notre coeur". That line and the following, where the poet declares
that the ruins provide also "Un rocher creux pour notre peur" are
interesting because they closely associate emotions with the landscape
and in a poetically accurate way. The rock image calls for explanation.
The fort is made of rock, on a rugged, craggy site. Its hollow walls
are now caved-in ruins. Fear primitively suggests the search for a
place to hide, a cave or hollow. And "creux" may also have a figurative secondary sense of futility.

The fourth stanza is complex. Its main focus shifts from external
subjects to something more personal, "Mes jours", the poet's own

temporal experience. But the description brings in a number of other
elements. The "mélèzes grandissants", "le calque du vent", "muraille"
are parts of the natural setting connected with the fort, while "conjurations" and "incendie" prefigure the theme of massacre to be detailed
at the end. But for the time being the poet, his thoughts, his "days"
are removed from the past evils apparently protected by a wall of
flame.

Up to this point, the structure and rhythm of all the stanzas have
been the same. An eight syllable line predominates, the rhythm broken
into two separate short, excited statements. The first verb, in the
imperfect (for the first time), shifts the mental focus to the past, a
brief moment lost forever. The other verb "frottai", because of the
connotations of the past definite, marks something which happened
once for all and whose effects no longer have a real immediate psychological bearing on the present. It is an interlude of erotic ecstasy in
outline rather than substance. The way in which feelings are suggested
rather than specified by the phrase "le calque du vent" and by the
phrase "trait de ses hanches" indicates that the author must place a
high value on lines and transparencies, which are immaterial but carefully delimited and defined. This was the case also in the conclusion
of "Chanson du velours à côtes" where the effective tie was "le vent
ou rien..."

The aura of pleasure in that central stanza is sustained through the
first word of the last line, "Romarin", sweet in sound, in perfume,
and in figurative semantic resonance suggesting remembrance and
constancy. Only the last two words, curiously placed as an apposition
have the effect of a return to reality: "Lande butinée" (ravaged heath).

The last three stanzas, each with a separate thematic focus, are
devoid of images or thoughts which mitigate harsh reality. The sixth
stanza immediately solidifies the sense of inner, pained lucidity. The
ostensible subject is the razing of his home, possibly one of those
French country houses, century-old, thick-walled and built of the
stone and clay of the land. The idea of solid construction, and therefore slow demolition introduced by "pierre après pierre", is reiterated
on an emotional level by "J'endure" which combines the suggestion of
sustained pain with an internal semantic overtone in the syllable "dure",
homonym of the French word for "hard". In English actually the expressions "hardship" and "hard times" have a similar physical-
emotional force. The second sentence of the stanza, "Seul sut l'exacte
dimension / Le dévot, d'un soir, de la mort", is striking for its in-
voluted grammatical structure. The position of the words, I think,
depends mainly on a combination of desired sound and emphasis. The
word "sut" in that tense has a meaning both of knowing and suddenly
recognizing. "Le dévot", of course, is the subject, but "Seul", similar
in length and general phonetic impact, constitutes a dramatic opening.
Besides, "dévot" fits better in the last line since it adds to be triple
parallel phonetic rhythm: three disjunctive phrases each beginning
with d - "Le dévot, d'un soir, de la mort." And the whole line recalls
the situation of "Madeleine à la veilleuse". Death, an important semantic focal point of the sentence, whose sound in French has a definitive, somber sound falls suitably at the end of the line, sentence and

stanza. The central meaning of the sentence is conveyed by "Seul", "sut", "exacte dimension" and "d'un soir" all delineating a certain isolated, instantaneous recognition, in this case recognition of destruction and death.

Death, willed human destruction, the massacre of the Vaudois follows naturally as the subject of the next stanza introduced with an ironic twist, "L'hiver se plaisait en Provence." The execution is evoked discreetly but powerfully, with only one direct human reference in the form of the funeral pyre. What follows is not a description of passage from life to death, but a metaphorical sequence, reminiscent of Heraclitus, in which fire turns water from a solid to a liquid state, from snow and ice into boiling water which then slips into the rushing stream. The image is that of a violent but natural transmutation of natural elements from one condition to another.

Explicitly echoing, and with more resigned intensity, the theme of sorrow, "un astre de misère" of the last stanza recalls the initial "terre de douleur". Both phrases are placed similarly - at the end of the stanza's first line. The word "astre" broadens the field of natural phenomena from earth to heaven. Phonetically, it suggests prolonged suffering, the long first syllable, "astre", a prelude to the similar lengthened final syllable of "misère". The notion of long effects is expressed explicitly in the following line: "Le sang à sécher est trop lent,": centuries do not suffice to erase the moral damage. The earth, the imposing mountain range of the Luberon, dominates again at the end. "Massif de mes deuils, tu gouvernes..." But the ultimate sentence strangely modifies and mitigates, not only what immediately precedes, but the sorrowful tone of the entire poem. "Je n'ai jamais rêvé de toi." It is a very personal remark. The first person pronoun, "Je", is soft in sound just as the whole remark is uttered soft in tone. Yet it has a sure, confident cast. That entire sentence on the one hand recognizes and places solidly, permanently in the reality of an esthetic view, the ascendancy of the mountain witness to grief, and on the other hand with gentle insistence relegates that whole area of disturbed consciousness and conscience not to the realm of nightmare but to one of lucid unyielding awareness.

NOTES

*1 Retour amont (Paris, 1966), 9-10. That ascent whose goal is "au-dessus des sources", the author describes at length in an interview in Le Monde (28 mai 1966) entitled "René Char commente son 'Retour amont' ".

*2 Arrière histoire du Poème pulvérisé, 31.

XVI

L'INEXTINGUIBLE RÉEL INCRÉÉ

Les Sources

The land, friends, sights and sentiments - the raw material of Char's
poetry is close to home and down to earth. In a sense, as in the creative process of Péret, these ordinary experiences are a simple starting point; but instead of a springboard for adventure, their substance
is absorbed by the mind, enlarged upon, but not subject to travesty,
and retains its original form, solidity, and intrinsic qualities even
when transmuted and used as imagery. The esthetic transformation is,
I think, akin to that of certain Post-Impressionist painters and sculp-
tors, those whose final product retains some substantial formal attach-
ment to the objective world (Cézanne, Braque, Giacometti but not,
for instance, Klee, Chirico, Tanguy) - where visible elements of the
outside world subsist, reordered, rendered coherent, reduced to essential outline or frame, suffused with the lucidity of feeling and reflection. Char, speaking of the creative process, often describes it
as an ascension. A book of diverse essays and notes on this subject
covering the immediate World War II period is entitled Recherche de
la base et du sommet. The base is life. In the final paragraph of the
preface he says, "Je m'inquiète de ce qui s'accomplit sur cette terre,
dans la paresse de ses nuits, sous son soleil que nous avons délaissé.
Je m'associe à son bouillonnement..."*1 The summit is the lofty goal
of understanding upon which man sets his sights. A similar conception
provides the basis for the grouping of the poems in Retour amont, as
well as for an explanation of how for him a poem comes into being:
"...on est d'abord dans une matière absolue, puis tout, alchimique-
ment, se spiritualise. Ici, au fur et à mesure que l'on monte, les
lieux n'ont plus de nom..."*2
These two descriptions of the poetic process, poetic in themselves
in that they depend on the physical image of heights and ascension, do
not reveal all the complexity of the interrelationship of mind and matter in Char's poetry nor do they pretend to. Briefly to suggest some
of the forms in which experience enters into his poems, one can start
as does the poet himself by indicating the importance of the first and
simplest impressions. "L'aubépine en fleurs fut mon premier alphabet",
he states with the perspective of a long life behind him. And this immediate receptivity always appeared a source of poetic enchantment
and a store, no doubt, for future verbal reactions and resurrections.
A short passage from the wartime diary illustrates this sort of pervasive pleasure:

Le peuple des prés m'enchante. Sa beauté frêle et dépourvue de
venin, je ne me lasse pas de me la réciter. Le campagnol, la taupe,
sombres enfants perdus dans la chimère de l'herbe, l'orvet, fils du
verre, le grillon, moutonnier comme pas un, la sauterelle qui
claque et compte son linge, le papillon qui simule l'ivresse et agace
les fleurs de ses hoquets silencieux, les fourmis a assagies par la
grande étendue verte, et immédiatement au-dessus les météores
hirondelles...
Prairie, vous êtes le boîtier du jour.*3 *

This passage, as well as the succinct acclaim of the hawthorn, are
not poems but typical of an aphoristic style of simple thoughts expressed
poetically.

In the poems themselves the balance between reality, abstraction,
and imagery is more varied and subtle. Many poems no doubt had their
origin directly in a scene, a place or a representation thereof. There
are, for instance, several about a park, les Névons, a beloved natural
preserve: "Jouvence des Névons" and "Le Deuil des Névons",*4 written at different epochs but alike in a plaintive lyrical quality reminiscent of Verlaine, where the natural setting enters into the web of
the narrative, clear in outline but not so much a description as a
physical component woven into particular sentiments directly connected
with the place.

In other cases a place or a scene is the recognizable basis for inspiration and its configuration persists throughout the poem. Such is
the case in "Sept parcelles de Luberon, I". The mountain chain, its
rocky heights, its imposing presence, insects, sun, fruits, trees and
the aromatic herb, rosemary all contribute to give the work its concrete and particular body. However, it is not a question of just sketch-
ing in these natural phenomena as a background. They enter into the
poetic development rather because of a double spiritual force, the
reason no doubt lying in the type of the esthetic apprehension. On the
one hand, the poet is acutely and particularly conscious of the historical events which took place there and their residual effects, that is,
their inescapable persistence for anyone sensitive to and knowledgeable
about temporal realities. On the other hand, there is the personal
emotional reaction of the poet. At this particular moment he is not only
capable of sensing the accumulated grief of other human beings wedded
to that land but more particularly contains within himself - for a reason
perhaps quite personal and maybe even peripheral to the historical
events - the well of sorrow which emerges at that moment, expressing
itself but in close alliance with those hills bearing traces of wounds in-
flicted by that distant massacre. A résumé of this poem's core of
meaning should include integrally the real presence of the Luberon,
its past and painful temporal dimension and the poet's acute personal
pain momentarily pierced by a ray of ageless hope.

Elsewhere, a scene may similarly form the basis of the initial vision
for a poem but in the course of the esthetic development that concrete
substratum becomes less important thematically and tonally, forming
eventually a subdominant rather than dominant function. In "Déclarer
son nom" the sun, its intense heat, the river La Sorgue, the rooftops

of the village and the mill all are sharply defined in the memory relived. Yet they are secondary to the successive waves of feeling which
accompany the evocation. The focus is mainly subjective, starting from
the first statement, "J'avais dix ans", a simple, accurately naïve ego
affirmation. The next sentence, "La Sorgue m'enchâssait", is similarly within a personal optical field. There are indeed precise external
elements - the name of the river, the visual suggestion of sparkling
waters. The principal message however is one of feeling, priceless
spiritual treasures conveyed by the unusual verb "enchâssait". And,
although the statements which follow all have objective phenomena as
important grammatical elements (two are subjects, "le soleil" and "la
roue...du moulin", one is a predicate, "Avaient scellé le coq de fer
sur le toit des maisons"), it is the perception, visual and emotional,
of the child which dominates.

An even greater "spiritualisation" of matter, of a real place occurs
in a recent poem, "Tracé sur le gouffre":

Dans la plaie chimérique de Vaucluse je vous ai regardé souffrir.
Là, bien qu'abaissé, vous étiez une eau verte, et encore une route.
Vous traversiez la mort en son désordre. Fleur vallonnée d'un
secret continu. *

The waters of the Sorgue issue forth at the base of a towering cliff.*5
The level of the flow varies considerably from time to time and at the
moment this poem was written the stream was apparently low ("bien
qu'abaissé"). The water of the river is indeed a clear deep green -
"eau verte" is an accurate description and if anything an understate-
ment. At its source the streambed is filled with gigantic boulders, its
course gouged out of the cliff and the slopes immediately beneath. So,
various real characteristics underlie the idiom of this narrative: "plaie"
arises from the impression of the gorge, "abaissé" and "eau verte"
are direct details. The sentence, "Vous traversiez la mort en son
désordre", could likely have been suggested by the water flowing over
the black chaotic rocky slope. In the last sentence, "vallonnée" and
"continu" are again exact details while "Fleur" could be a pleasant
esthetic transformation of the green swirling current. But the extension of sense and feeling go far beyond simple sight and description.
The mind of the poet absorbs the physical details long familiar, sees
them as embodying an imaginative (but not absurd or fantastic) esthetic
scene. Perhaps even an esthetic or personal situation preceded the
choice of site in the composition of the poem. The imaginative extension is admitted or rather glorified at the start by the adjective "chimérique", and the emotional preoccupation is the same as in "Madeleine à la veilleuse" - contemplation of and empathy with suffering and
proximity to death. Suffering is announced by "plaie" and "souffrir".
Death is stated directly. The whole is conceived as a natural continuous path not without beauty. Much more than a simple symbol, the
scene, preserving all of its natural qualities and immediacy in the
poem, through the series of statements or reflections is transfused
with emotional vitality and subjective direction to become something
quite different and unique. This is perhaps what Char meant when he

described poetry as "apport de l'être à la vie".*6

From people alone can spring the warmth, the desire, and the complex of pleasure and pain which are necessary for the genesis of poetry. This is true of the simplest expression. In a series of reflections, "A la santé du serpent", where the common theme is independence, revolt, proud but sensitive challenge, the first statement reads thus: "Je chante la chaleur à visage de nouveau-né, la chaleur désespérée."*7 An infant, actually present only as an image, but still lifelike (really coming to life for the reader) characterizes that resurgent, vital emotional heat which engenders poetry as well as life. Char also says that for him, "un poème est toujours marié à quelqu'un".*8 This does not seem always to be the case - there are many poems which in their final form appear as either highly subjective dream-like sequences, bearing the traces of Surrealist expression or as abstract, complex configurations, their intellectual structure molded by feeling but purified of individual traces. Nevertheless it is true that many of his poems, among them the most moving, are either explicitly or implicitly addressed to people. The girl, "Madeleine à la veilleuse", even emerges as a real person. Sometimes the author not only speaks about but speaks to a literary or artistic figure, as in the poem "Tu as bien fait de partir Arthur Rimbaud!" Other people he names directly in the title (Giacometti, René Crevel) or in an epigraph. In "La bonne grâce d'un temps d'avril" there are two poems about little girls. Another entitled "La passante de Sceaux" relates another nameless chance encounter. There are many most beautiful love poems, about the act of love, about the intricate patterns of intentions, feelings, gestures which can equally bind couples together and differenciate them, happily or unhappily. These poems are frank and intimate. As was mentioned before, frequently the people who appear are, for us, anonymous. The nature of this anonymity is worth considering carefully. "Biens égaux" is a particularly interesting example:

> Je suis épris de ce morceau tendre de campagne, de son accoudoir de solitude au bord duquel les orages viennent se dénouer avec docilité, au mât duquel un visage perdu, par instant s'éclaire et me regagne. De si loin que je me souvienne, je me distingue penché sur les végétaux du jardin désordonné de mon père, attentif aux sèves... Moi qui jouis du privilège de sentir tout ensemble accablement et confiance, défection et courage, je n'ai retenu personne sinon l'angle fusant d'une Rencontre.

> Sur une route de lavande et de vin, nous avons marché côte à côte dans un cadre enfantin de poussière à gosier de ronces, l'un se sachant aimé de l'autre. Ce n'est pas un homme à tête de fable que plus tard tu baisais derrière les brumes de ton lit constant. Te voici nue et entre toutes la meilleure seulement aujourd'hui où tu franchis la sortie d'un hymne raboteux. L'espace pour toujours est-il cet absolu et scintillant congé, chétive volte-face? Mais prédisant cela j'affirme que tu vis; le sillon s'éclaire entre ton bien et mon mal. La chaleur reviendra avec le silence comme je te soulèverai, Inanimée.*9 *

Its inception is similar to "Déclarer son nom": memories of childhood, places clearly resurrected in imagination, the poet's father in the background. Then, in a moment of lucidity, of present awareness comes the statement "je n'ai retenu personne sinon l'angle fusant d'une Rencontre." This relegates to the past seemingly particular personalities, leaving their essence, specifically a "Rencontre", a meeting, a moment when two lovers find themselves face to face, perhaps by chance, perhaps by design. Once again one recalls the purely fortuitous encounter with Madeleine. This is indeed an open, direct view of life - valuing what may be unexpected, open to all that is positive in surprise or even shock (this, I think, is the sense of the expression "l'angle fusant").

The second paragraph speaks of the same country-side and of love, a nameless couple whom we meet in the first sentence introduced simply "nous avons marché côte à côte..." In the course of the love scene which ends in the present, the dominant atmosphere becomes more rarified ("L'espace pour toujours est-il cet absolu et scintillant congé... ?") and the end is simultaneously very intimate and still nameless: "...je te soulèverai, Inanimée."

On some occasions, thus, persons or places that are anonymous for the reader are certainly not for the author as in that poem, other love poems, works such as "L'Extravagant" where the tragic nature of the subject renders necessary the shelter of cristal essence. But even in those cases the unidentified pronouns and invented capitalized nomenclature (Rencontre, Inanimée) derived from esthetic motivations broader than that of personal discretion. For one thing, Char has an almost Oriental sense of delicacy, the conviction that a poet contemplating what is beautiful in reality should not venture too far in his contact or in his expression thereof. One short poem, "L'Alouette", ends in a gesture of withdrawal, "Fascinante, on la tue en l'émerveillant",*10 an indication that the author is aware of the extreme fragility of the thing and of the moment. Similarly in man's quest for knowledge, there are limits beyond which it is prudent not to venture. "Seule est émouvante l'orée de la connaissance. (Une intimité trop persistante avec l'astre, les commodités sont mortelles)".*11 This states directly the main thematic thread of two important works: "La Fête des arbres et du chasseur", where, against a choral background of guitars, a hunter's pursuit in the forest leads to total conflagration and a ballet, " L' Abominable homme des neiges", in which man's efforts to pierce the mystery of that strange creature whose presence was reported in the Himalayas as well as to scale the highest only lead to disappointment and disaster. So that, to name precisely, to fix exactly a time and a place would be to encroach on a plane of reality which resists indiscreet familiarity.

However, there is also a positive reason for unspecified pronouns, names such as "l'Inanimée", poems whose subject becomes rarified and spiritualized even though there may be a concrete base or integrated concrete imagery. It amounts to a deep intuitive sense that something invisible, tenuous, enduring is at the poet's fingertips, present in the real world, to be revealed esthetically. In the case of names emphasized, it is no doubt a question of extracting what represents the unique feature of the person or the occasion and literally naming that unique feature thus endowing it with a certain importance (but not the superhuman stature of Perse's Royal figures) and with a measure of permanence. Such is the power of words and more particularly names. In the case of a poem such as "Chanson du velours à côtes" one sees that ties which are immaterial but consisting of sometimes virtual sometimes actual energy are those which bind most effectively contrary realities - the wind, an avalanche, a poet whose presence is sensed behind the rough cloth and, in the end, "rien" - nothingness, given at least a verbal existence. In the case of a poem like "Tracé sur le gouffre" the title itself gives a clue as to what represents the core of the content - the outline, "tracé", first perceived and interpreted visually and then given spiritual substance. A late poem begins thus, "Permanent invisible aux chasses convoitées, / Proche, proche invisible et si proche à mes doigts..."*12 It is tempting, of course, to see in this the affirmation of some metaphysical principle or essence. If something of the sort is true, I think it might be related to Heraclitus' Logos - truth, verbal truth, lucid intelligence, something common to all yet containing an element of eternal mystery or to Whitehead's concept of endurance and eternality which is bound, as is Char's sense of the permanent, simultaneously to the real world (including a temporal dimension) and to man's experience of that world.*13

Rather than incorporate Char's thought in a philosophical framework, though, which he specifically avoids himself, it is more accurate to restrict interpretation to the poetic range. Maurice Blanchot does just this in an article where he emphasizes what he terms the "neutral" quality of Char's language and places it in the perspective of recognizing the value of the unknown - indeterminately future, present or past, positive or negative - which can best be suggested poetically, since by nature it must remain unspecified.*14 But if a certain neutral quality does recur in Char's formulations, there is equally a tendency to endow the invisible, the spiritual with life-like forms and voices. He does this in a sequence of poetic dialogues called "Les Transparents", whom he describes as "vagabonds luni-solaires", timeless wanderers each with an individual personality and name (Toquebiol, Eglin Ambrozane, Odin le Roc...) who stop to pass the time of day with the inhabitants of the country where they are traveling. In another prose poem the author muses over their function and their fate:

Pourquoi ce chemin plutôt que cet autre? Où mène-t-il pour nous solliciter si fort? Quels arbres et quels amis sont vivants derrière l'horizon de ses pierres, dans le lointain miracle de la chaleur? Nous sommes venus jusqu'ici car là où nous étions ce n'était plus possible. On nous tourmentait et on allait nous asservir. Le monde, de nos jours, est hostile aux Transparents. Une fois de plus il a fallu partir... Et ce chemin qui ressemblait à un long squelette nous a conduit à un pays qui n'avait que son souffle pour escalader l'avenir. Comment montrer, sans les trahir, les choses simples, dessinées entre le crépuscule et le ciel? Par la vertu de la vie obstinée, dans la boucle du Temps artiste, entre la mort et la beauté. *15*

They encompass the race of all poetic spirits. They are spirits yet
they are conceived humanly. If people engender Char's poetry, other
beings are often born within the land of the poem itself.

The ultimate source of all Char's creation nevertheless is quite
simply himself. Ensconced in his homeland, in constant contact with
people, the emotive force which informs his work comes from within.
The deceptively easy task the poet insists upon is "S'assurer de ses
propres murmures..."*16 In fact, such introspection yields fruit only
after long concentration. Feelings are not so much expressed as they
are perceived, contemplated, sounded to their very depths. Some are
fairly simple. In "Déclarer son nom", the vibrant, bright pleasure of
memory is sharpened by awareness of pain. In "Madeleine à la veilleuse", a profound sympathy weds the poet to the girl. In "Sept parcelles du Luberon, I" the emotive pattern is more complex; briefly
one could say that intense personal and eternal grief is fused in rock,
heath, and mind. A number of poems are built directly from an emotion
or an internal reflection and the narrative then constructs a verbal
equivalent thereof using both abstract and concrete imagery and semantic outline. "Marmonnement" illustrates the emotional and intellectual complexity of such ventures. In this poem a wolf image serves to
embody one of the obscure subconscious forces common to all with
which he engages in a compelling skirmish.

> Pour ne pas me rendre et pour m'y retrouver, je t'offense, mais
> combien je suis épris de toi, loup, qu'on dit à tort funèbre, pétri
> des secrets de mon arrière-pays. C'est dans une masse d'amour
> légendaire que tu laisses la déchaussure vierge, pourchassée de
> ton ongle. Loup, je t'appelle, mais tu n'as pas de réalité nommable.
> De plus, tu es inintelligible. Non-comparant, compensateur, que
> sais-je? Derrière ta course sans crinière, je saigne, je pleure, je
> m'enserre de terreur, j'oublie, je ris sous les arbres. Traque im-
> pitoyable où l'on s'acharne, où tout est mis en action contre la dou-
> ble proie: toi invisible et moi vivace... *17 *

Announced at the start is the triple will which motivates the protagonist - refusal to give in, desire to find himself, challenge. In the dark
reaches of a mental forest, two adversaries enter in contact - one lucid, determined, consciousness, the other a wolf, an ultimately unknowable psychological force. The two are "loyaux adversaires" - for
love and laughter ("je suis épris de toi...", "dans une masse d'amour
légendaire...", "je ris sous les arbres...") mitigate the formidable
elemental antagonism of their relationship. However, antagonism dominates: "Je saigne, je pleure, je m'enserre de terreur, j'oublie..."
Char's thirst for lucidity - in understanding the human mind (his own)
and in esthetic statement are as strong as those same motivations in
the case of Valéry. To these are added the Surrealist experience of
the mysteries and horror as well as a positive vital force of mental
activity. Personal in origin, such expression generates universal
truths.

L'Esprit

Revolt reigns from the start. The poems of <u>Le Marteau sans maître</u>, written mainly during the time Char frequented Surrealist circles, are distinctive for the violence of the images, for the vehemence of the social protest as well as implicitly for the conception of artistic creation as involving a similar wild, seemingly uncontrolled, force (witness the title of that first collection and the title of one poem therein, "L'artisanat furieux"). Even then, the revolt is not really angry but is tempered by the capacity for tenderness and sensitivity which become more apparent in later years. In <u>Moulin premier</u> (1936) appear the first serious reflections about the nature and aims of the artistic process. Although fascination with dreams and unconscious forces subsists, a new concern emphasizes the need for seriousness in poetry, the importance of reason, and focuses esthetic attention on reality (the word "surréalité" is now noticeably absent). One passage states, "J'admets que l'intuition raisonne et dicte des ordres..." But the initial poem of the series begins:

> La connaissance productive du Réel
> Aspirant vulnérable
> Ne se remporte pas d'après une mesure compliquée de larmes
> une construction joyeuse de ruses
> Mais est obtenue par une sorte de commotion graduée de fortune.*18 *

The rest of that poem as well as others of the same set establish limits, determine choice of values and particularly voice concern for esthetic coherence. From this collection also comes the message quoted at the start, "Transmettre ta part de merveilleux de rebellion de bienfaisance." That call to revolt recurs constantly. It appears, for instance as the last of three principal factors in an aphoristic definition: "L'essaim, l'éclair et l'anathème, trois obliques d'un même sommet." In addition to "anathème", the other two elements, "l'essaim" (signifying no doubt a certain fruitful uncommitted tension) and "l'éclair" (lucidity, comprehension), are again familiar forces in the esthetic process as experienced by the author. Just what is the nature of this revolt is an interesting question and one which cannot be answered simply.

At times, and particularly during the thirties, it is a challenge levelled at existing social values. The word "anathème" for example certainly has a strong moral force: That quotation comes from a volume published after World War II (in 1950).*19 But the general emphasis in the author's thought has then shifted from political protest to an affirmation of individual human values over constraints posed by social mores and particular other negative ethical attitudes. Yet, it is revolt without malice. "La vraie violence (qui est révolte) n'a pas de venin. Quelquefois mortelle mais par pur accident. Echapper aux orthodoxies. Leur conduite est atroce."*20

More basically, there is a sort of rebellion aimed at certain aspects of reality which appear inadequate. This was a characteristic he admired in other authors. Of Hölderlin, in a sequence entitled "Pour un Promethée saxifrage" he says, "La réalité sans l'énergie disloquante

de la poésie, qu'est-ce?" And of Heraclitus and George de la Tour:
"...je vous sais gré d'avoir de longs moments poussé dehors de chaque
pli de mon corps singulier ce leurre: la condition humaine incohérente...
d'avoir dépensé vos forces à la couronne de cette conséquence sans
mesure de la lumière absolument impérative: L'action contre le
réel..."*21 Against what is this battle waged? Against death, a theme
which recurs in Char's not usually so explicitly as in the case of "Madeleine à la veilleuse", never morbid but always with a lurking presence - something which resembles a gentle undercurrent of obsession.
Char felt a particular sympathy for Camus, dedicating to him the
Feuillets d'Hypnos and writing a prose poem on the occasion of the
latter's fatal accident. Whereas the latter's whole creative drive stems
from a philosophical and personal confrontation with mortality, in the
case of Char death remains a grievous fact, impossible to ignore. But
its absolute and therefore horrendous quality is attenuated by some
measure of afterlife - in art and in friendship: the cave paintings of
Lascaux seem particularly poignant to him for this reason; after Camus' death it was the grief he felt so strongly which provided the lasting existential tie - "la douleur, celle de compagnon à compagnon, que
l'archer, cette fois, ne transperce pas".*22
 There is also the desire to combat that which is imperfect in reality.
This is somewhat akin to the Surrealist aim of resolving contradictions,
replacing what is dull with a more satisfying substitute. Desire, hope
(exalted and inexhaustible psychic energy) are the forces which perceive what is lacking and correct or unify existing circumstances:

L'imagination consiste à expulser de la réalité plusieurs personnes
incomplètes pour, mettant à contribution les puissances magiques
et subversives du désir, obtenir leur retour sous la forme d'une
présence entièrement satisfaisante. C'est alors l'inextinguible réel
incréé.*23 *

This creative drive, then, amounts to correction rather than flight
from the real world or the substitution of a happier land of fantasy or
even the resolution of apparently contradictory states on a plane disconnected from external phenomena.
 To complete the forms of revolt, one should also include certain internal tensions. Essentially they represent revolt against self-satis-
faction, against simple emotional solutions, against reluctance to face
or to search for subconscious forces. I think that frequently the image
"essaim" is used to indicate this general order of tensions. More particularly they include doubt, self-doubts as well as general interrogations about life, and especially anxiety and anguish. Says Char in a
moment of self-dialogue: "Si tu ne libères rien de toi pour retenir plus
certainement l'angoisse, car sans l'angoisse tu n'es qu'élémentaire,
ni ne corriges pour rendre unique, tu pourriras vivant."*24 "Marmonnement" illustrates well this introspective type of revolt, dis-
stressing but tonic. The initial sentence in fact states that act of revolt - "Pour ne pas me rendre et pour m'y retrouver, je t'offense" -
and the figure thus challenged is the wolf, the mind's primitive un-
tamed energy. The emotions to which the hunter himself is prey in

that pursuit are indeed frightful – pain, sorrow, terror, a nightmare sensation of amnesia – but the outcome of the hunt is vital self-recognition ("nous bondissons par-dessus le frisson de la suprême déception pour briser la glace des eaux vives et se reconnaître là").

If the first attitude necessary for the inception of Char's poems is challenge or interrogation, which prepares the field, which opens up the vistas to be explored, then a multitude of psychological forces combine to form that new order, "l'ordre insurgé". These forces are not easily separated except by names. "J'admets que l'intuition raisonne", says the poet, unable honestly to distinguish pure abstract thought from the play of intuition and unknown subconscious forces. In practice, both reason and subjective insights are valued highly and brought into play in the elaboration of poetic forms and thoughts, a process which for Char is often long and difficult. The drive for comprehension, bringing sensations to the clear light of day was perhaps the most powerful, in a way similar to Valéry's compelling urge to understand and formulate except that for Char, the truth, since it was personal, could be very painful. "La lucidité est la blessure la plus rapprochée du soleil" is a statement which emphasizes the external ecstasy of grievous truth. "Produis ce que la connaissance veut garder secret, la connaissance aux cents passages..."*25 expresses an internal parallel – the need to disclose depths of feeling or thought which repressive forces seek to conceal and which once released may be disquieting and of a complexity impossible fully to grasp, those "tunnels dérobés" and "pistes captieuses". However will and reason can make inroads in that dark domain and more easily aid in verbal formulation of truths disclosed. And, besides exercising firm rational control in writing, carefully determining concepts, words, sentence structure and overall unity in the composition of his poems, Char certainly draws heavily on the resources of perceptive fields (mainly visual) and on the rich resources of dream and of memory. Many poems are overwhelmingly dream-like in atmosphere and visual and thematic sequence. Here are excerpts from one entitled "Pénombre":

> J'étais dans une de ces forêts où le soleil n'a pas accès mais où,
> la nuit, les étoiles pénètrent... Par endroit, le souvenir d'une force
> caressait la fugue paysanne de l'herbe. Je me gouvernais sans doc-
> trine, avec une véhémence sereine. J'étais l'égal de choses dont le
> secret tenait sous le rayon d'une aile... *26 *

It could be a dream, it could be the transcription of a mystical experience in the vein of Rimbaud, or it could be such an experience created imaginatively. In any case, such dream-like states were viewed (voluntarily or involuntarily), lived and transformed into words.

As for memory, Char envisages it as preserving feelings and maintaining them ready for immediate resurgence. He speaks of it as a subjective, emotional phenomenon. One poem, "A la désespérade", uses the image of a well (as did Valéry in "Le Cimetière marin") in the epigraph, "Ce puits d'eau douce au goût sauvagin qui est mer ou rien."*27 The main theme of the poem includes sensitivity to the variety of emotions contained therein constantly vibrating under the sur-

face with the wish that for the moment those remain held in check.
One line is particularly interesting, the last of the first stanza (the
subject is inverted as in the first section of "Sept parcelles I"): "Puits
de mémoire, o coeur, en repli et luttant." Of note is the fact that
heart and memory are in apposition - nearly synonymous, the fact that
they are withdrawn from surface consciousness and that they are constantly active, even aggressively so ("luttant"). Mention of memory
appears in another poem in a playfully sceptical tone:

> Que disais-tu? Tu me parlais d'un amour si lointain
> Qu'il rejoignait ton enfance.
> Tant de stratagèmes s'emploient dans la mémoire!*28 *

This is a particular case where the narrator questions the reality of
a statement regarding such far-reaching love. But I think he would
speak with equal reticence, perhaps not scepticism, concerning the
extent to which a person can judge accurately reality from imagination
in what comes to the mental surface in the cloak of memories. The
substance of two poems analyzed, "Déclarer son nom" and "Chaume
des Vosges", are a case in point. The latter is charged with recollections, events, and feelings covering a long period. It ripened intellectually and emotionally over many years before being published in its
definitive form. Some of the elements perhaps are distinct to a particular era, others singly or combined are a fusion of many sentiments
lived, relived, not only recreated but perhaps also created freshly by
a mental process in which memory was constantly active. In the former poem, the material is much more concentrated, evoking a clearly
defined moment, vibrantly resurrected. Yet, the atmosphere is such
that one wonders whether the poet himself knows or even cares greatly
whether the details and feeling were exactly such in the past reality.
What matters is the immediate poetic presence which is powerful.

A unique feature of the poetic process as conceived by Char is a
final spiritual explosion which he describes mainly with the verb "pul-
vériser". This is something which happens seemingly after the poet
has steeped himself in the feelings, the moment, the event which form
the subject and after the main verbal components have been, with effort, determined. It is a concept which, it seems, occurred to him at
the decisive moment in 1936 when discovering his own poetic principles.
The last lines of "Commune présence" are: "Essaime la poussière /
Nul ne décèlera votre union."*29 It is the final esthetic gesture whereby, reducing the elemental poetic substance to a fine dust and infusing
that dust with energy, the poem comes into being, unobtrusively coherent. A possible analogy which would clarify this unusual notion is
that of the basic elements of matter, reduced by contemporary science
into progressively more minute, dispersed, and neutral particles at
the base of which is pure energy. In another quotation Char suggests
that the final esthetic reduction takes place almost involuntarily or
miraculously. It is an isolated reflection: "Une poussière qui tombe
sur la main occupée à tracer le poème, les foudroie, poème et main."*30
A touch of the miraculous is indicated by the image of lightning divine
intervention. The final effect is positive, which one might not guess
from that statement. But it is clear in another more cogently presented

reflection, one which could be chosen from a number, representing inclusively one aspect of the author's esthetic credo.

> Pourquoi le poème pulvérisé? Parce qu'au terme de son voyage vers le Pays, après l'obscurité pré-natale et la dureté terrestre, la finitude du poème est lumière, apport de l'être à la vie.*31 *

After the initial urge to write (desire for a better world), after the intuitional formulation of content then rendered concrete and clear, the ultimate ingredient is the invisible pervasive breath of life. In a recent book of verse, no longer preoccupied abstractly with method and process, the author continues to embrace the same central value. Included in a sequence of thoughts under the title "Le terme épars" are the following words: "Petite pluie réjouit le feuillage et passe sans se nommer", gently evocative and in a way representing the return to an earthly touchstone. Here, instead of matter or thought violently reduced to small particles, it is a natural phenomenon, rain ("petite pluie..."), which by virtue of its fine, thinly dispersed liquidity can softly penetrate and please. The quality "dureté" no longer applies: for this phenomenon "douceur" would be a more appropriate nominative.*32

Le Poème

Parole en archipel, the title chosen for one considerable volume of verse, indicates that the poem itself, quite simply consisting of words, manifests a similar coherence, in this case the continuity is composed of separate, like entities. The image of an archipelago is apt as it combines a number of pertinent concepts - solid blocks of land (reality, perhaps) emerging from the sea (the heart and mind) related but with the chain of connection and creation hidden from the eye. It is also pertinent as it accurately emphasizes the linear nature of his style and the fact that each sentence within a poem, or each reflection within a series bound together by a common title, or whole groups of poems within a given collection, that each of these sequences consists of separate self-contained elements related by some "submarine" or subconscious common material. The archipelago is an original image. "Dentelles de Montmirail", the title of a short series of reflections reveals a similar inspiration. It is the name of a separated rocky peak in the Vaucluse; so it too includes an image of separate thrusts or outcroppings - geological in reality, intellectual in the poem. Another set of images reveals a parallel notion. Of these, one mentioned previously, "la ligne de vol du poème" is related, although less explicitly connected with verse, to the fascination for Char of a bird's trajectory. Another is the plain graphic term, "tracé". It figures of course in the title, "Tracé sur le gouffre", and with a slightly different field of connotations in the statement, "Un poète doit laisser des traces de son passage, non des preuves. Seules les traces font rêver."*33 One recalls that two images of the initial quotations - "tunnels dérobés" and "pistes captieuses" - have the same sense of linear direction.

"Chemin", a similar more general term, also frequently appears. These latter images emphasize the notion of line and forward direction, while "parole en archipel" includes also the important idea of sequence - distinct words related in linear form.

Judging by the nature of the finished product, I would surmise that the creative process for Char involves an initial vision or cohesive sensation of a situation or a scene, or an emotion, or a combination of those elements. The transposition of sensation and conviction then is elaborated into verbal form by groups of coherent thoughts, one following, one stemming from another until a terminal point is reached, where a verbal gesture reflects and emotionally resolves the whole. Changes, such as those in "Chaume des Vosges" would likely be within each group (phrase, sentence, line or stanza) altering not the concept but the form of its expression - from concrete to abstract, from image to direct statement, from human quality to some natural phenomenon which could be conceived as its equivalent. It seems doubtful that either the initial tonal core or the sequence of expression would be changed radically. Revision of the earliest poems involved reduction. His tendency to reduce poetic comment to the most concise and succinct proportions is striking and very characteristic. Many poems are only a sentence or two long, but their weight or subjective import is considerable, with an expanding longlasting effect on the reader. "Poètes, enfants du tocsin."*34 This short, isolated poetic definition is a case in point, where the image of the bell tolling disaster not only serves to suggest that esthetic creation is born of an urgent call to face crises but also prefigures the echoing effect such a brief remark has in the reader's mind. Similarly, the reflection, "La vie aime la conscience qu'on a d'elle", is warmly self-perpetuating.*35 Furthermore, in many cases, the title appears as a purified poetic residue, an esthetic equivalent of precious metals chemically refined. "Marmonnement", "Déclarer son nom", "Chaume des Vosges" have this intense, condensed quality.

Following closely the train of thought and the texture of several passages from the poems just analyzed should clarify the nature of Char's expression. Here, for ready reference, is the speech of night in "Chanson":

... Ceux qui m'offensent meurent jeunes. Comment ne pas les aimer? Prairie de tous mes instants, ils ne peuvent me fouler. Leur voyage est mon voyage et je reste obscurité.

The first line, as is the case with the speech of day, established the relation between night and the people of the earth. It is a direct statement, unambiguously expressing his position of domination and his ready hostility. The next sentence counteracts that prevailing distance and fraternity with death by showing another aspect of his character - a simultaneous immediate disposition to love them. The relative position of these two sentences is certainly necessary and inalterable considering the personality balance the author wishes to establish.

Next comes a statement ("Prairie de tous mes instants, ils ne peuvent me fouler") which is more complex in structure and in imagery. Recapitulating (but with a different emphasis) our first analysis, one notices that the apposition contains a reversal of actor and actions: in the first part, the prairie clearly refers metaphorically to the people; but in the second part the verb "fouler" paradoxically suggests that he, night, could be (but is not) scorned or trampled on. Night is thus connotatively paired with the broad field. So, the image of the prairie serves doubly - first directly allied with people and then with night, a reciprocal vision, set forth by the grammatical structure, no doubt intentionally. With an economy of words this establishes a relationship in which both night and people are unified to the point of having certain indistinguishable qualities (the same metaphor serving for both). As was noted before, the analogy of the prairie besides serving to relate the two subjects, also suggests a wide peaceful expanse and translates the slow temporal nocturnal pace into spatial terms. This illustrates well a special character of Char's imagery. Infrequently can it be interpreted as simple symbol or even as symbol with the regular component of poetic ambiguity. For its sense is inextricably bound in the particular thought sequence, grammatically dense, of each particular poem.*36

Another example is the image of grass in "Madeleine à la veilleuse": "Je voudrais aujourd'hui que l'herbe fût blanche pour fouler l'évidence de vous voir souffrir". As in the case of the prairie, it contains a very important visual element. In both poems there is relatively little in the way of a persistent and unified visual background (except for the picture of La Tour which enters in the poem but mainly without metaphorical extension). So the whitened grass and the soft, broad expanse evoked by the prairie represent points where the reader is apt to re-create for himself visually such grass and such a prairie. They are something of a concrete psychological perceptive tie between poet and reader. Besides that, whitened grass is an unusual and even realistically impossible idea (except if it were covered with frost; but I do not think that is the poet's intended reference). As was mentioned before, the image is of sufficiently unusual intensity effectively to erase, momentarily, the sight of the girl's distress. For this image also, its grammatical position determines the total impact: it is the result of a wish. Being subjunctive, that condition is grammatically as well as realistically in the realm of the hypothetical if not the impossible, which renders that desire all the more anguished.

The final sentence of the night's speech ("Leur voyage est mon voyage et je reste obscurité"), is much simpler. It continues the identification of night and the people but in more explicit terms ("Leur voyage est mon voyage"). It also suggests in a different way the temporal element introduced directly by "instants" in the preceding sentence with an imaginative extension spatially in "prairie". The concept of traveling includes by nature the concept of time. The last part of the sentence provides a final and appropriate note of an enduring state, "je reste" and affirms its basic characteristic, "obscurité".

Except for the initial address concerning their relationship with human beings, the day's speech and the night's speech do not exhibit a parallel structure. And in both speeches there is in a sense a free development of thought to the extent that certain transitions appear surprising or as non-sequiturs. Between "Comment ne pas les aimer?" and "Prairie de tous mes instants..." there is no logical liaison, although there is the continuity of the idea that the night is master. Also the change from direct statement to metaphorical statement is brusque. This is true of the day's speech too. Between "J'appréhende midi et sa flèche méritée" and "Il n'est de grâce à quérir..." the shift of attention is sudden and puzzling. However, despite the absence of logic, there is progression of description which in this case obeys an esthetic impulse. From the first two lines which emphasize the joyous, benign, and expansive nature of day, the line of the poem proceeds to a poetic climax - an equilibrium of noon and tension involving fear, lucidity, and acceptance, before entering into the final phase of welcomed disappearance. The line of that speech follows in part a temporal pattern from noon to night and partly a surge from pure joy to a tension of lucid apprehension to calm resolution.

Since the body of Char's work contains prose poems, free verse often divided into stanzas and also notes and reflections, the question arises as to what distinguishes the different forms, or rather what impulse leads the author to embody the initial inspiration in one or another verbal pattern. As for the latter, the notes and reflections, the explanation, I think, is not difficult. For they appear to be either answers to questions the author has been asking himself or brief subjective or objective insights or reflections. Throughout his work, evaluations and formulations of esthetic principles or ideas about the nature of poetry and the creative process accompany the collections of poems themselves. Sometimes they appear in a series published separately as is the case with A une sérénité crispée (1951) and the recent book "L'Age cassant" (1967) which contains also many direct reflections about his temperament and his life. Sometimes they appear as introductory notes to particular groups of poems, for example the "Argument" which introduces L'Avant-monde of Fureur et Mystère. Or the entire notebook Feuillets d'Hypnos which includes notes of experiences, sentiments, thoughts on art and beauty. All of these notes are "poetic" in that naturally Char employs imagery and elliptic phraseology as he does in regular poems. The quotation concerning the texture of poetry, ending with the portrait of the poet as one who establishes "... un ordre. Un ordre insurgé", is an example of this sort of expression. What distinguishes these notes from both the prose poems and the verse is a certain imaginative extension in the latter, a heightened sense of rhythm, sweep and an overall impact of form.

For the prose poems, such as "Déclarer son nom" and "Madeleine à la veilleuse", although their grammatical structure is regular (approaching that of ordinary discourse), have a very particular rhythm. In "Déclarer son nom" tonally speaking there are three parts: the first ("J'avais dix ans... le sage cadran des eaux") evokes contentment, bathed in the river and the sun; the second ("L'insouciance et la douleur... se supportaient ensemble") a sense of painful malaise rendered immobile by the heat; the third ("Mais quelle roue... incendie blanc") blinding emotional excitement. The first part contains three sentences: the first two are short and between them there is a marked pause in addition and in the respiratory reflex that would accompany the lines

read aloud. It is as if each thought contained such a depth of feeling
and memory that to be absorbed in full flavor those pauses are absolutely essential. The other two sentences are longer, each with a particular rhythmic sweep, and each with a lengthy sustained span of attention and expression. In the last sentence the emotional force gathers
momentum literally with the movement of the wheel image translated
structurally ("tournait plus fort, tournait plus vite") and terminates
in the burst of white fire.

"Sept parcelles de Luberon, I", is set in clearly defined and nearly
regular free verse. The balance between reflection (both intellectual
and emotive) and spontaneous and immediate lyrical outpouring is
weighted towards the latter. Less inwardly questioning, the feelings
and their verbal formulation appear closer to the surface and, at least
in the finished poem, seem to flow more freely. The division into separate stanzas is similar to the division into tonal and thematic groups
of the prose poems. And in both cases they either represent different
facets of the initial situation, scene or emotional experience or they
represent successive stages of thought embracing and penetrating,
step by step, in order to understand, the given situation. There is
rarely a temporal progression in Char's poetry, except to the extent
that thought is formulated and expressed not instantaneously but over
an interval of time. The subject matter, emotion or situation, is static
– a certain state presented in depth.

For a microcosmic view of the linguistic nature of his verse forms,
two stanzas from "Sept parcelles, I" should be enlightening, the fourth
stanza and the final stanza, the eighth. Here is the fourth:

Tels des mélèzes grandissants,
Au-dessus des conjurations,
Vous êtes le calque du vent,
Mes jours, muraille d'incendie.

As in all of the first four stanzas, which form a group, the subject appears at the end: "Mes jours". This is a stylistic trait common to
other poems. It places the subject in the context of the poem's particular terrain, defining it in a sense, not by simple description involving
realistic detail but rather by weaving together threads of analogy pertinent but whose source is a broader field. There are three separate
images, unrelated except by their common tie to the subject: "mélèzes
grandissants", "le calque du vent", "muraille d'incendie". The first
one, growing larch trees, suggests the temporal orientation, towards
the future, of growth and also a set of distinct but similar entities (individual trees / separate days). More importantly it is linked to the
mountain setting, flourishing on the heights above the scene of human
conflict. The wind also inhabits freely those heights and with that image, which includes the unusual word "calque" (the reproduction of a
design using tracing paper), the poet evokes a quality of transparency
which is nonetheless perceptible. Curiously, the word "calque" has a
substantial ring phonetically because of the two k sounds thus reinforcing a sense of reality albeit immaterial. "Muraille d'incendie" is quite
different. The first word of the image, wall, is as solid in fact as the
tracing of the wind is incorporeal. But it is a wall of fire, impenetrable

- not for concrete reasons (it, too, is insubstantial) but because of the heat. It is an image which closes the stanza and the first group of stanzas with vivid intensity. The images here are all natural, objective, and they qualify a human phenomenon - not just "days" but "my days", experienced subjectively. The other subjects of that first group of stanzas include "Fruits", "Jeunesse", and "Buoux". The first, fruits, is on the surface an object with perhaps an overtone of reference to the second one, youth. The latter subject is both human and abstract. Buoux is a fort, thus a real object but of human construction. The constant admixture, or coexistence on a common plane, or in parallel grammatical structures of objective and subjective, real and abstract, human phenomena and natural phenomena is most characteristic of Char's expression. It is not a question of style but of thought patterns. Perhaps it accounts for a certain measure of difficulty for the reader, since it involves having to be prepared for shifts of conceptual field and for the possibility of including together in the meaning one word or word group an objective sense with a separate metaphorical component. For instance in the line, "Un rocher creux pour notre peur", the hollow rock is simultaneously the real thing (which anyone can still see on the mountainside) and the perfect imaginative receptacle for fear. Enigma and depth are products of this conceptual flexibility and comprehensiveness.

Avec un astre de misère,
Le sang à sécher est trop lent.
Massif de mes deuils tu gouvernes:
Je n'ai jamais rêvé de toi.

The last stanza of "Sept parcelles, I" merits attention for other reasons. Its expression is much more direct. Rather than a definition of a unique subject by extended qualities, it expresses three emotive reactions. The dominant tone of deep sorrow is evident ("misère", "sang à sécher", "deuils"). Only one image appears, "astre". Its function, I think, is not so much visual and real in the poetic setting as it is phonetic, echoing and thus prolonging the length of suffering ("astre de misère...lent"); it also, of course, introduces a cosmic note. "Massif de mes deuils, tu gouvernes" situates the weight of grief externally, identifying it even with the mountain mass and stating its predominance, physical and spiritual. The last line is on the contrary totally subjective, "Je n'ai jamais rêvé de toi." It gently reiterates the close and intimate (the last word is "toi") nature of the relationship between the poet and his land. Gently, too, yet firmly it asserts a measure of independence by refusing to admit its entrance into the omnipotent world of dreams.

By the force of personal statement it resembles endings of many other poems. In all of the four poems analyzed the final gesture is a distinctly personal one. In "Déclarer son nom", the whole final sentence emerges from the past to propose an immediate commentary, an impassioned rhetorical question. In "Chaume des Vosges", the last line is oriented towards the future, offering a sure issue from present insecurity. In "Madeleine à la veilleuse", saying "...un peu d'huile se répandra par le poignard de la flamme sur l'impossible solution", the author discovers a means to alleviate the girl's distress. In all of these cases the poem is bound together in a decisive gesture, individual, as if the author felt an esthetic necessity to bring to a climax then to resolve the contradictions and tensions inherent in the situation from which the poem sprung. The essential coherence of this poetry would seem to consist of the attainment of a firm mental grasp of situations, humanly conceived, after penetration in depth, definition in objective and metaphorical extension, and throughout a reduction to verbal and emotional primary elements.

Although Char's concern for exact expression and exploiting to the full the weight and etymological resonances of each word is highly demanding, he nevertheless is aware of certain insufficiences of language. For one thing he feels strongly the need frequently and persistently to disassociate himself from the poetic world in its verbal, abstract field. Significantly, during the war he wrote: "Le poète ne peut pas longtemps demeurer dans la stratosphère du Verbe. Il doit se lover dans de nouvelles larmes et pousser plus avant dans son ordre."*37 There is a constant need to return to the source, to reestablish contact with people and places. The poems of Retour amont, despite the continued impetus towards spiritualization of matter manifest a clear firm hold on simple, immediate forms and objects. As the author remarked in an interview about that book, the last words of the last poem are "Content de peu est le pollen des aulnes"*38 (a tree which grows in valleys). So, reality - the base, the source - exercises a continuous pull.

In addition, the author is aware that language itself contains pitfalls. Words can sometimes be misleading. "Toute association de mots encourage son démenti, court le soupçon d'imposture. La tâche de la poésie, à travers son oeil et sur la langue de son palais, est de faire disparaître cette aliénation en la prouvant dérisoire."*39 In this case poetry hopefully (by virtue of perceptual frankness?) can reduce that danger. Another quotation, explaining the conception underlying a group of love poems, Dehors la nuit est gouvernée, sets the inadequacy of language against the clear gifts of objective and subjective perceptions and against the irrepressible urge to explore the ineffable. " Les poèmes du Dehors obéissaient dans mon esprit quand ils furent écrits, à l'exigence d'une marche dans l'indicible, avec, pour tout viatique, les provisions hasardeuses du langage et la manne de l'observation et des pressentiments."*40 Linguistic risks are as inevitable and necessary as other human risks.

The primal force underlying artistic reaction is the sense that there exists, within, a mine of what Char calls "certitudes distraites" whose origin and destination remain unknowable. Seemingly anterior to words and to gestures, and for that reason perhaps of a purer alloy, they exercise an attraction - asking, demanding to be grasped and confirmed. Besides, they urgently call for expression and the poet's function then becomes that of translating intention into act: "Le poète... traduisant l'intention en acte inspiré..."*41 Then, that which was in its original form silent and mysterious becomes less so, opens up hitherto inaccessible reaches of the mind and in addition reveals a multitude of new potentials. That quality of internal silence, mental phenomena transformed into voluble image and word is well illustrated by a note from

Rougeur des matinaux: "L'intensité est silencieuse. Son image ne
l'est pas. (J'aime qui m'éblouit puis accentue l'obscur à l'intérieur
de moi.)"*42 Viewed thus, the initial drive to write and the immediate
resulting satisfaction have to do with self-knowledge. Since the area
discovered and explored is the poet's own mind it is easy to see why
he should conceive of the web of the poem as consisting of hidden tunnels, harmonious rooms, a veritable spiritual labyrinth.

Once composed, the poem is invested with a reality of its own which
contains nevertheless a measure of possibilities yet undetermined.
Far from conceiving of poetry as having an absolute existence, abstracted from reality, it remains tied to that reality yet establishes
an individual existence. Thus, Char confirms, "La vitalité du poète
n'est pas une vitalité de l'au-delà mais un point diamanté actuel de
présences transcendantes..."*43 These "présences" are not however
confined to the present either in the spiritual matter of which they are
composed or in the overall, long-reaching effects and implications.
Since they spring from a personal subjective fount, they contain naturally the past, present and future, both imagined and real. The temporal color of Char's poetry contains a gamut of tones, shades, fusion
of tints and mellow progression from one to another. In "Déclarer son
nom" the imperfect past tense, consistent throughout, includes, of course,
the sense of continued states in the past, clear memories, with a sus-
picion of dream-like imaginative distortion. It carries with it also a
powerful flush of nostalgia.*44 And in the last sentence, although the
tense remains the same, there is an accent of the present - the past
recalled, relived, and rendered immediate through an impassioned
question. In "Sept parcelles, I" there is a progression from present
sorrowful revelations (in the first four stanzas) to a pure, distinct moment in the past, using the past definite which has the effect of clear
delimitation and finality. One suspects, still, that that moment is a
product of acute wishful thinking, a sort of memory-fantasy. The next
to last stanza, in contrast, relates to an objective past, a historical
event, the Vaudois massacre.

On an entirely different temporal plane, having to do not with the
internal time patterns of separate poems but with the general nature
of Char's poetry there is an unlimited extension towards the future.
This has to do with the implications of the adjective, "présences
transcendantes", of the preceding definition. The force of wish and
hope is a permanent factor underlying all his poetic production. "Le
poème est l'amour réalisé du désir demeuré désir."*45 This emphasizes the formative drive (elaborated in greater detail in the longer
quotation),*46 which is incomplete, aided by the magical and subversive force of desire, to transform the incomplete into fully satisfying
presences. The result is finally that "inextinguible réel incréé".

Throughout, the reader is not neglected. Quite the contrary, just
as Char conceives his poems from their inception as closely bound
with people close to him, friends and family, so he includes anyone
who ventures into his poetic world. The reader is a partner in the full
esthetic experience and the continued existence and sense of each poem
depends equally on full participation, inclusion of the reader's life in
the reality of the poem. Ultimately poet, poem, and reader are part-
ners in a renewed confrontation of the human condition.

```
            Touté vie qui doit poindre
                achève un blessé.
                  Voici l'arme,
                      rien,
           vous, moi, réversiblement
                    ce livre
                  et l'énigme
        qu'à votre tour vous deviendrez
        dans le caprice amer des sables. *47 *
```

NOTES

*1 Recherche de la base et du sommet (Paris, 1955), 2.

*2 "René Char commente son Retour amont", Le Monde, 28 mai, 1966.

*3 Fureur et mystère, 137-138.

*4 "Jouvence des Névons", Les Matinaux (Paris, 1950), 36; "Le Deuil des Névons", La Parole en archipel (Paris, 1962), 108.

*5 Retour amont, 13. The origin of the Sorgue is a truly dramatic natural phenomenon. The water comes from a subterranean source, below a high plateau, of which speleologists have not been able to penetrate all the mysteries. Both the cliff and the river bed strewn with massive boulders are of rugged gigantic proportions. The green shady forest at the base of the cliff and on the banks of the river provide a gentler attraction and form an appropriate site for recollections of Petrarch. It was in this region that the Italian poet met Laura and where he lived years later.

*6 "La Bibliothèque est en feu", La Parole en archipel, 73.

*7 Fureur et mystère, 203.

*8 "Partage formel", Fureur et mystère, 71.

*9 "Le Poème pulvérisé", Fureur et mystère, 179-180.

*10 La Parole en archipel, 33.

*11 A une sérénité crispée, 10.

*12 Dans la pluie giboyeuse, 36.

*13 Char's thought and expression, like that of Heraclitus, is enigmatic. So that a comparison between the two can only be tentative. I am not sure, for instance, that Char would subscribe to the idea of a transcendant spirituality which Heraclitus seems to suggest. The fragments of Heraclitus which bear on the question particularly are Fragments 1 and 2 and Fragment 42 (Wheelwright, Heraclitus, New York, 1964). Chapter V of Whitehead's Science and the Modern World discusses the notions of endurance and eternality.

*14 "René Char ou la pensée du neutre", L'Arc, no. 22 (Eté 1964), 9-14. Blanchot defines poetry in general thus: "...poésie, c'est-à-dire aussi la parole la plus simple, si parler est, en effet, où l'inconnu se désigne dans un rapport de présence autre que celui qui s'accomplit dans l'éclairement." To recognize a certain enigmatic base in poetry seems to me realistic; however to relegate categorically the poetic word to a field of obscurity not only is inaccurate (the poetic word is not really unclear, simply difficult or mysterious) but also renders critical commentary impossible.

*15 This prose poem appeared in De moment en moment (Alès, mars 1957) and was dated as written in 1948. The poetic dialogue, "Les Transparents", figures in Les Matinaux (27-35).

*16 Dans la pluie giboyeuse, 23.

*17 La Parole en archipel, 56.

*18 Le Marteau dans maître suivi de Moulin premier, 81.

*19 Les Matinaux, 84.

*20 A une sérénité crispée (1951), 23.

*21 "Pour un Promethée saxifrage", La Parole en archipel, 125; Fureur et mystère, 69.

*22 "L'Eternité à Lourmarin", La Parole en archipel, 125;

*23 "Partage formel", Fureur et mystère, 67.

*24 A une sérénité crispée, 21.

*25 Fureur et mystère, 136 and 204.

*26 Fureur et mystère, 166.

*27 Les Matinaux, 51.

*28 "L'Ordre légitime est quelquefois inhumain", Fureur et mystère, 162.

*29 Le Marteau sans maître suivi de Moulin premier, 98.

*30 "Le Risque et le pendule", La Parole en archipel, 58.

*31 "La Bibliothèque est en feu", La Parole en archipel, 73.

*32 For a sensitive discussion of pulverization, multiplicity, and unity in Char's work see the article by Georges Blin, "L'instant multiple dans la poésie de René Char", L'Arc, no. 22 (Eté 1963), 15-24.

*33 Dans la pluie giboyeuse, 84.

*34 Sur la poésie (Paris, 1958), 28.

*35 This simple truth appeared, anonymously adopted along with many others, on the walls of Paris during the student revolt in May 1968.

*36 Georges Mounin discusses certain of Char's images and points out the dangers of thematic criticism in his article, "Les Images de la vitre", L'Arc, no.22 (Eté 1963), 87-90. His commentaries of Char's work are most valuable. This article and others as well as his early study of Char's poetry have been reedited: Avez-vous lu Char? (Paris, 1969).

*37 "Feuillets d'Hypnos", Fureur et mystère, 95-96.

*38 "L'Ouest derrière soi perdu", Retour amont, 47.

*39 A une sérénité crispée, 15.

*40 Dehors la nuit est gouvernée... (Paris, 1949), 11.

*41 "Partage formel", Fureur et mystère, 77.

*42 Les Matinaux, 81.

*43 "Partage formel", Fureur et mystère, 78.

*44 This powerful affective force of the imperfect tense is also pervasive in A la Recherche du temps perdu. Proust was well aware of its expressive value and admired the use of that tense in Flaubert's works.

*45 "Partage formel", Fureur et mystère, 76.

*46 See page 189.

*47 This poem, set in italics, concludes Les Matinaux, 97.

POSTFACE

Radical diversity rather than uniformity or even simply common structures, themes and tones, this is the overwhelming final impression of
familiarity with the poetic spheres of Valéry, Perse, Péret and Char.
Admittedly, the choice of poets precludes resemblances on many
scores for reasons of personal background, temperament and interests.
However, even within the focus within which this study was begun -
their poetry conceived as reflecting mental activity - the divergency
is considerable.

To mention a few obvious comparisons, Valéry's poems trace patterns of subjectively oriented perceptions and sensations but reduced
to a pure impersonal, generalized substance in perfect contrast to
Péret's dramatically unique adventures suffused with the vivid emotions
of the dream world. The poetry of St. John Perse also portrays spiritual adventures, as does Péret's, but the expeditions of the former
are externalized, global against a poeticized historical and geographical tapestry. Péret also frequently explores the domain of personal
sentiment: the events and characters therein are above all fantastic.
Whereas Char ventures into the flickering and unfathomable shadows
of the human heart, he does so with generous honesty and in depth.

Similarly, their linguistic and formal structural characteristics -
the former deviant from ordinary verbal expression - are highly individual. Valéry's language is extremely elliptical but glows with a
pure transparent classical polish. His verse forms are traditional as
far as prosody is concerned, although their particular structural lines
follow often a specific temporal psychological sequence conceived as
and exemplifying shifts, changes of direction, attention and state, the
whole conceptually isolated and unified. Perse often phrases key passages elliptically (for instance the opening section of Anabase) but his
style includes a wide variety of verbal density from the succinct to the
prolix yet always with a clear esthetic aim. His vocabulary, his syntactic progressions and often the total real structure of the poetic entity typically pronounces, expresses or gives the impression of movement, but extrapolated from any ordinary recognizable temporal sequence. Péret composes sentences which are completely normal and
unambiguous from the point of view of the grammatical relationships
(including causal and qualifying constructions) but equally absurd in
their semantic progression. His forms also follow movements, actions,
rhythms including often expanding and contracting, upward or downward impulses either physically or emotionally based and completely

outside a recognizable temporal and spatial sphere. Char's verbal expression is perhaps the most difficult and the richest in the sense that it is connotatively extremely dense. Comparable to Valéry for his intellectual precision and carefully modeled grammatical formulations, its conceptual juxtapositions are original. The overall impression of his structure is static in a temporal sense, the fluid mental movements and extensions evolving around a given moment, a given impression or emotion.

This thumbnail sketch does not exhaust or even sharply define all their differences. Because what seems to me most interesting and fruitful are the implications of certain common qualities. Before examining these, a brief review of that key phrase "activité de l'esprit" is in order. I was initially struck by and then decided to use Tzara's distinction as the "point de départ" because it is concise and places the emphasis of thought and poetic thought as activity which has the advantage of suggesting desire or will, conscious or unconscious, directed or undirected, thus with a human angle. Breton's definition, "le fonctionnement réel de la pensée", while similar, seemed insufficient on two grounds: first, it has a mechanical cast and, second, it contains a metaphysical speculation ("réel") which it seemed more prudent to avoid. The word "activity" also includes the important notion of a process, taking place in time and usually involving the coordinated effort of several factors. Tzara's definition, as he elaborates it, contains some notions (genuinely his and perfectly suitable within his own view of artistic aims) which I would prefer to modify to apply more broadly to contemporary French poetry. "Activité de l'esprit" as he sees it follows dream-like thought patterns in that it is undirected. It is a sort of pure expression emanating from a nocturnal sphere. Preeminently alogical, it frees itself from language or/and its form ("se dégageant de la langue ou de sa forme") and even includes a certain sense of verbal inefficacy.*1 "Activité de l'esprit" he thus defines in contrast with "expression de l'esprit", which is logical and which, he says, expresses ideas and feelings. The emphasis on freedom from traditional linguistic forms and ordinary discursive logical presentations is certainly essential and accurate. Similarly the notion that it reflects thought which has an inward, introspective orientation is important. The parts of the definition which I would consider really inaccurate is first of all to separate poetry as being either mental activity or mental expression and, second, to relegate ideas and sentiments entirely to traditional poetry. Verbal formulation of any art, poetry or prose, involves mental activity (in the construction used, choice, and adaptation of vocabulary and syntax). It must also involve some sort of expression, if there is any content to it at all - expression of relationships, of concepts, of images, of emotions, of dreams or dream-like sensations in the case of Surrealist writing. My personal interpretation of Péret's poetry furthermore does not exclude either expression of feelings or concepts although the latter are obviously structured in his own way, in a personally derived "language". The definition, in my opinion, should be inclusive rather than exclusive - adding the resources of dreams and the unconscious, dissolving, an absolute distinction between the rational and the irrational which would then delimit a broader and more psychologically accurate field in the poetic material, in the creative process and in the content of the final product, the poem. Such fusion of mental categories is indicated when Perse speaks of "la logique du songe" and when Char states, "j'admets que l'intuition raisonne".

Without pretending to pursue fully the varieties of mental activity common to the poetry analyzed in this study, I would like to point out several interesting features which shed light on the nature of that poetry and can serve hopefully as a basis for further investigation. They have to do with the nature of the perceptions which prefigure the initial esthetic conception and which then influence the substance, linguistic structure, and form of that poetry, in fact, essentially determine its nature.

The first has to do directly with the type of perception of the outside world. In this respect, Alfred North Whitehead's study, Symbolism: its Meaning and Effect, presents three distinct modes of experience which bear interestingly on the problem at hand.*2 The three modes he calls presentational immediacy, causal efficacy, and conceptual analysis. Of these, the first two have to do with perception: they intersect on two grounds, they are based on sense-data and they involve locality. The sense-data, he explains have a double reference - they come from the outside and they are transmitted by an organ. The third mode, conceptual analysis, has no particular interest for us because it is exactly this - abstract thought, discursive reasoning with its linguistic elaboration in prose (also often determining the structure of traditional verse) - which is notably absent in the poetry of Valéry, Perse, Péret and Char.*3

As for the nature of what Whitehead terms presentational immediacy, it is present only in the experience of high-grade organisms, the sense-data involved depend on the percipient organism and its spatial relations to the perceived organisms and through it the contemporary world is exhibited as extended and as a plenum of organisms. Beyond disclosing the solidarity of actual things, the knowledge provided by it is "vivid, precise and barren" and to a large extent controllable at will. It is barren because one may not connect the qualitative presentations of things with any intrinsic characters of them. Pure presentational immediacy is neither delusion nor not-delusion, it contains no abstractions and simply has the result that things "are" objectively in our experience. What is most important for us is the point that its contents are vivid and that they promote imaginative freedom. The example he gives is the dog in Aesop's fable who loses its meat because it mistook the water image for the real thing. Presumably a poet would not "loose his meat": his impressions would rather have an imaginative or intuitive distortion or extension which would later be integrated in a poetic sphere.

The second mode posed by Whitehead, causal efficacy, is a primitive element in our experience and one which also functions (and functions well because it is not distracted) in low-grade organisms. Its function is to preserve that organism in its given environment and thus must accurately conceive the nature of that environment. One example he gives of a simple organism is a flower turning towards light. In human experience causal efficacy is a primitive element in our experience, concerned, as I understand it, with the preservation of the body and the ego. It has an extension in the past and the future - relating past experience with possible future events. And because of its close connection with preservation it is accompanied with emotions closely connected the primitive functioning of "retreat from" and "expansion towards": anger, hatred, fear, attraction, love, eagerness, massive enjoyment.*4 In conclusion Whitehead defines the bonds of causal efficacy as arising from without us, disclosing the character of the world from which we issue, an inescapable condition around which we shape ourselves and the bonds of presentational immediacy as arising from within us, subject to intensifications and inhibitions and diversions according as we accept their challenge or reject it.

The store of perceptions and acquired experience stemming from the mode causal efficacy, I would judge, furnishes raw material for all poetry, traditional and contemporary, since on the one hand it provides accurate information about scenes and events to be used in descriptions and settings and on the other hand it elicits the emotions which are after all the most basic poetic ingredient. The mode of presentational immediacy, however, appears most strikingly appropriate to characterize one distinctive feature common to the poetry of Valéry, Perse, Péret and Char. It has to do not with the inspiration of any given poem but rather with the type of perception which furnishes the scenes, objects, physical sensations from which the web of the poetic narrative is woven, the elements through which the tonal core is realized. Although the sense-data have their origin in the outside world, they are organized, colored, and enjoyed according to the mind's own will or inclination. As the philosopher pointed out, although they may not correspond to the external facts they are not delusions. Instead, they appear as imaginative interpretations or extensions.

Valéry elaborated this notion at length in his essay on Leonardo da Vinci where he urged that the artist, at a given moment, "look" with his eye rather than with his mind, excluding preconceived notions of what a thing ought to be or ought to look like. "La constatation est d'abord subie, presque sans pensée, avec le sentiment de se laisser emplir..."*5 The opening line of "Le Cimetière marin" contains just such an uninhibited visual impression: "Ce toit tranquille, où marchent des colombes..." The ocean, then motionless, actually looks like a solid, flat plane, a rooftop, and the boats floating on its surface appear to be doves. In "Les Pas" the perception involved is not visual but aural and the mistaken identity could be conceived as a near hallucination if it were not a sane person albeit a poet describing the sensations purposefully elaborating a possible confusion between analogous sounds. There the first impression and one which is developed dramatically is that of approaching footsteps. With masterfully prolonged suspense, the narrator divulges only in the last line, the last few words that the steps were fused in the sensation of his heartbeats. The perception in this poem thus enters into the main line of the structure as well as providing an essential part of the total dramatic setting - the narrator, his state of mind, his fantasies. It should be noted that in both "Les Pas" and "Le Cimetière marin" such perceptions are not immediate or in the near past experience of the poet. Instead they come from a mental store of similar real past experiences preserved in the memory upon which the poet draws, consciously, in the creation of an original esthetic situation. Also, there is a good measure of conceptual extension involved in many basically physical impressions, for instance in the sequence "Stable trésor, temple simple à Minerve, / Masse de calme et visible réserve, / Eau sourcilleuse..." (Strophe III). In the first noun group, "stable" reflects the sense-data while "trésor" is a poetic-imaginative value judgment. In "visible réserve", the adjective notes abstractly the sort of sensation and "réserve" combines both the physical impression of the water as a reservoir with a value overtone of conservation of something potentially desirable or useful. The key characteristic of such verbal formulations in the poetry of Valéry is their perceptual base free of preconceptions and their integration in the poetic narrative with an added complement of conscious lucid analytical judgment and conceptual extension.

An analogous process can be found in certain passages of Perse's works. Here is a sequence from Anabase (Strophe VII):

Chamelles douces sous la tonte, cousues de mauves cicatrices, que les collines s'acheminent sous les données du ciel agraire - qu'elles cheminent en silence sur les incandescences pales de la plaine; et s'agenouillent à la fin, dans la fumée des songes...

As in the first line of "Le Cimetière marin", the phenomenon viewed, in this case the contours of the hills, is presented in the text exactly as it could be (and likely was) apprehended subjectively, the undulating lines evoking naturally under the circumstances of desert life the shape of camels' backs, including the striations of the terrain seen full face resembling scars and folds of a camel's hide. The initial impression is extended, now consciously no doubt to include an idea of travel also natural considering the nomadic existence of desert peoples and the main action of the whole poem - an expedition. Perse even states explicitly the transition from scene viewed directly to an elaboration and diffusion of that scene in the imagination when he describes the vision as disappearing in "la fumée des songes".

In a completely different fashion, Perse makes use of immediate, sensitive, and disinterested sense impressions for poetic purposes in connection with a principal goal of poetry as he sees it: "elle [la poésie] devient la chose même qu'elle 'appréhende'... elle est, finalement, cette chose même, dans son mouvement et sa durée... " In this case the poet must first completely lose himself, identify himself with the phenomenon, I would gather, and then adapt his verbal formulation - succession of words and verse forms - to correspond to or evoke that initial impression. When, in the long poem, Vents, he writes "Et dispersant au lit des peuples, ha! dispersant - qu'elles dispersent! disions-nous - ha! dispersant... ", the repetition of the word "dispersant" and the exclamation "ha!" combined with the rhythm realized by the word groups all combine to recreate the sensation of wind. The word "dispersant" does so by virtue of its literal meaning; "ha!" by evoking a sudden gust (of breath, of air); the slightly irregular, broken word groups suggest successive wind currents. Here, the perception furnishes both the substance and the structure of the poetic expression or more accurately one should simply include the structure as an integral part of the meaning.

Péret, seeking to recapture the vitality and freshness of the primitive imagination, envisages not only his poetry but all poetry as rediscovering what he terms "la conscience poétique du monde". Rejecting rational constraints and habits, one should, he feels, seek and develop intuitive and sensitive reactions to all sorts of phenomena such as the melancholy roused by the sight of snow drowning all noises flake by flake, or the sense of enchantment aroused by the lily of the valley (a flower with special connotations for French people as it is the symbol of spring, the May Day bouquet). The introductory line "Soleil route usée pierres frémissantes... " is an example of such poetic perception and poetic use: it fuses a few components of a scene in one single perception directly transposed verbally without any explanations or conceptual extensions indicated directly, but conveying strongly the sense of stark natural fusion with emotional overtones of anxiety. Of note is the fact that this sort of perception does not particularly distort the shapes or conceptual significance of what is perceived but combines in the conception and the expression an instinctive emotional response which may or may not be reasonably justified. This is one sort of example he gives for the "merveilleux", source of poetry. Another example he mentions is quite different: that of the contents of a drawer whose ordinary contents (spools of thread, a compass, a liqueur spoon), can open up an extraordinary sequence of other things and events - a band of tulips coming forward in goose-step and in whose corolla are standing professors lecturing on the categorical imperative. For this poetic event to take place, he explains, one's mind must be in a state of vacation "en vacances". It is, of course, a sort of free association, in this particular case without a strong emotional response but rather leading to a dream-like nonsensical adventure. Péret uses such impressions and associations throughout all his poetry without any conscious control except sometimes to replace an ordinary noun or adjective with one less conventional or rationally predictable.

The perceptive resources in the poetry of Char are perhaps the most spiritually complex of all. As far as I can judge, immediate perceptions do not enter directly into his poetic narratives. However, his poems are particularly characterized by multiple visual and emotional resonances which assume a store of extremely acute and emotionally vibrant impressions. They reappear in diverse forms in the poem itself, retaining their original force and often their original substance, as is the case in the following lines: "... La Sorgue m'enchâssait... L'insouciance et la douleur avaient scellé le coq de fer sur le toit des maisons et se supportaient ensemble." In the first sentence, the original perception has an emotional substratum which reaches far into the past but whose physical properties can be and probably were verified at any time. The expression "m'enchâssait" derives in part from the emotional recollection of a unique and precious instant, in or near the river and in part from the brilliance of the water sparkling in the summer sun. In the second sentence the physical perception coming

from external sources includes the simple sight of the weather vanes
on the rooftops, stated directly, and the intense heat which however is
transformed first into the sensation of their being fixed, "scellé", a
slight irrational distortion easily understandable and secondly into an
emotional apprehension of carelessness and pain whose source is really unknown. It is difficult to separate (and probably foolish to attempt)
what is past perception from what is immediate or nearly immediate,
what is imaginatively distorted or emotionally realistic or unrealistic
as a reaction. One can state with certainty that all of Char's poetry is
built on a vast accumulation of sense-perceptions woven into the poetic
sequence in an entirely unique fashion.

This brings us to the second feature of the mental process underlying the expression of these four poets and has to do with the way these
immediate, inwardly born, and inwardly integrated sense-data are
translated into language and combined in the linguistic sequence of the
poem. The essential evidence is that the traditional notion of image
and metaphor as involving clear cut components of tenor, ground and
vehicule, or "signifié" and "signifiant", no longer exist neatly as such.
Whatever each particular poet may be speaking of, expressing, it is
not a simple description of an idea, an event, or an emotion. It is
rather a subjective reconstitution or an invention and thus can no longer
always simply qualify the elements of its narrative analogically or replace a recognizable objective element by a simple symbol.

This does not mean that some images will have a recognizable and
fairly limited symbolic import. "Le Rameur" de Valéry for example
is easy to recognize, the poetic mind, seen as an introspective wanderer (or navigator). The wolf in "Marmonnement" by Char, similarly
appears to represent an obscure primitive psychological force. Yet,
even there, the image is so essentially a part of the nightmarish drama
- a flight and confrontation in a mental forest between a conscious,
combative narrator and a legendary, hostile yet compellingly attractive enemy - that the wolf's semantic value as symbol is overshadowed
by the immediacy, the emotional complexity, the spiritual ambiguity
of the chase itself.

In Char's poetry particularly there is an everpresent semantic tendency to include in one expression meanings both concrete and abstract,
subjective and objective. In "Sept parcelles de Luberon, I", the line,
"Un rocher creux pour notre peur", combines the very real and concrete rock of the fort Buoux on the range of Luberon, a reference to
the real setting, with an imaginative extension suggesting a solid pro-
tective hollow, a hiding place, figurative of course, a spiritual shelter
in a moment of fear. "Massif de mes deuils" in the last stanza of the
poem is again the massive mountain range seen by the poet as still
bearing the scars and embodying the Vaudois massacre in a real but
distant historical past and in addition the poet's own towering present
of personal grief. This double semantic content of a single word or a
single expression in Char's idiom also leads to a linear juxtaposition
of human qualities with natural phenomena ("L'insouciance et la douleur
avaient scellé le coq de fer... ") with the result that the reader must be
ready to encompass conceptual overlay and shifts of attention.

Both in Perse's and in Valéry's expression what might often easily be mistaken for metaphor is really a simple perceptive reaction expressed in the poem as such. The initial vision of the ocean transcribed "Ce toit tranquille où marchent des colombes" in " Le Cimetière marin" and the sequence from Anabase starting "Chamelles douces sous la tonte..." are intended I think not to be simple images but rather the reconstitution of a perception real or possible. "Le Cimetière marin", "La Jeune Parque", and "Narcisse" of Valéry, which represent a nucleus of his most important poems, all follow moment by moment the thought process of the protagonists including perceptions coming from the outside world, reactions, ideas and fantasies. After Anabase, the imagery of Perse becomes more elaborately constructed, less directly reflecting a given possible experience. Instead of translating imaginatively a possible real scene, he creates a whole new world whose source in reality can be discerned behind its people and gestures but where exists in its own right a poetic kingdom extrapolated from real time, real space. Although the waves of the tide erasing patterns on the sand are apparent in the background of the line from Exil IV, "L'officiant chaussé de feutre et ganté de soie grège efface, à grand renfort de manches, l'affleurement des signes illicites de la nuit", the priest, his clothing and his gestures are more than an extended metaphor, they belong to the whole dramatic sequence as character and as ritual action.

Péret's use of imaginative figures represents an even more drastic departure from conventional notions of imagery and metaphor. On the one hand the natural phenomena, the objects, the rare people in his poetic world (with the exception of the political satire) can hardly be construed as symbols, as images, as "signifiants" which refer to something or idea other than themselves. In the poem "Soleil route usée..." the "rues molles comme des gants / les gares aux gestes de miroir", although fantastically conceived, represent an imaginatively real background for that particular phase of the narrative. "Les voyageurs parfumés / voyageurs sans secousses" are indeed travelers. "Le pain blanc" who reappears in the course of events as a main actor appears simply to be a loaf of white bread come to life. On the other hand Péret's use of simile - frequent and conventionally stated (using "comme", "semblable à", "pareille à") - takes on an entirely different function from what one would expect. For instead of principally indicating a relationship or having a descriptive value, it introduces a new element to the narrative which then either acts out its role or is developed to a desired effect and then replaced in turn by another image. This does not mean that there may be no semantic connection, a complete absence of "ground". For instance, in the sequence "l'orage aux yeux de paon glisse sous lui / comme un serpent qui dort sa queue dans son oreille" the word "glisse" leads into the idea of a snake. But this snake is not sliding, it is asleep (a sort of paradox which Péret clearly enjoys presenting) and its presence, instead of elaborating the nature of the storm, appears to have an important function of its own, adding a note of menace, of potential evil to the atmosphere.

Enlarging on the notion of image, metaphor or more broadly language as symbolic expression, one might consider that the poem as a whole is a sort of symbol subjectively conceived, made up of a coherent complex of perceptions and feelings verbally structured.

The perceptions which serve as a store of raw material for these poets are initially, and consciously, valued not for their practical consequences or for their factual content (for their external accuracy) but for their immediate imaginative distortion and for the emotional reaction which accompanies them. The nature of the inspiration for a given poem varies immensely from poet to poet, but in each case the orientation is introspective – for Valéry an exploration of the configurations of sensations, thought processes, capacities and phases of the human mind; for Perse ambitions and explorations of the human spirit on a universal scale; for Péret the world as experienced poetically to enjoy fully the unlimited possibilities of uninhibited imagination and dream venture; for Char a life-time of individual experiences, affective ties with places and people, subjected to the explosive force of thought and feeling in order lucidly to recreate.

Ordinary discourse is inadequate for this since it has a logical base and an orientation towards the outside world: in content as description or explanation or judgment of natural of social phenomena, in aim (primary aim) as a means of speaking directly to a particular person or audience.*6 Thus, a new sort of language, a new sort of symbolic expression becomes necessary. Since a completely different language would be incomprehensible to others, a familiar vocabulary and syntax is used which adjusts the forms of usage to fit the poetic purpose. The individual word retains its normal signification but inclusively: the whole variety of literal, figurative meanings plus a connotative field whose range would depend on the poet's and on the reader's experience. For instance in the line from "Sept parcelles de Luberon, I", "Jeunesse voyante nuée", the abstract noun "jeunesse", carries with it (in French) a sense of lightness, life and innocence. Or the expression "Camphre de la corne" from Anabase VII has multiple exotic overtones including sensuality, abundance, Oriental riches.

The flexibility of syntactical expression is greater. Without pretending to explore fully the possibilities, one can discern certain atypical (but not ungrammatical) usages which are useful poetically. The frequent use of ellipsis is one notable feature of the work of Valéry, Perse, and Char. The opening of Anabase is striking in this respect: "...Etranger. Qui passait. Et voici qu'il est bruit d'autres provinces à mon gré...Je vous salue, ma fille, sous le plus grand des arbres de l'année." The first two sentences clearly lack ordinarily essential parts – the first has no predicate, the second no main clause. There are also the ellipsis marks of punctuation separating the next two sentences. Their function? A break in thought? An unstated thought? A passage from reflection to remark? The latter I would think. And finally, there is a general elliptic cast to the presentation in that none of the characters is clearly identified, neither the Stranger nor the narrator nor the girl. The latter appears later in apposition to the narrator's spirit (thus no doubt is an incarnation of his spirit) but to have mentioned that first would probably not reflect accurately the narrator's real chain of thought.

Another common syntactic "distortion" is the frequency of impertinences. Péret does this especially with relative clauses and adverbial expressions often simply to expand an unfolding adventure, sometimes

to create a causal framework peculiar and unique but essential for the
given situation. Char's semantic impertinences are of an entirely different order. They have to do with the conceptual versatility and fluidity of his thought. When he says, "L'insouciance et la douleur avaient
scellé le coq de fer sur le toit des maisons..." using carelessness and
pain as the subject, although completely impossible agents for the
predicate in a realistic sense, they indicate no doubt the emotions of
the child, identifying his feeling with the sight of the weather vane's
physical immobility and with the sensation of intense summer heat.
Or in the sentence "Mais quelle roue dans le coeur de l'enfant tournait
plus fort, tournait plus vite que celle du moulin dans son incendie
blanc", the wheel is pertinent in the second part of the sentence but
technically impertinent in the first. It could be construed in the latter
case as metaphor but I think its use there transcends the idea of metaphor as analogy. Wittgenstein presents the notion that a word used for
its secondary or figurative sense is not really a metaphor because it
is the only possible way to say what you mean. He also expresses a
similar opinion concerning ellipsis - that we call a sentence elliptical
not because it leaves out something we think but in comparison with a
particular paradigm of grammar.*7 In both cases syntax described in
conventional grammatical terms as special cases or deviants are not
so, practically; rather they reflect simply a particular mental situation expressed verbally. The poetic language is thus a heightened and
personally structured case of this same sort, designed to transmit
accurately a particular mental configuration.

   This analysis has other interesting applications particularly relevant
in the case of poetry. One is that the mental situation by nature includes not only thought but subjective reactions and feelings. This being the case then, indeed, all of the explicit tonal elements in a given
poem are essential to the content and cannot simply be construed as a
sideproduct of style or as destined for effect superficially conceived.

   The affective values of rhythm repetitions, sound patterns, and
modulations represent one set of factors reproducing a tone. "Les
Pas" is an example in miniature of such carefully constructed modulations of feelings, sound patterns, and semantic nuances.

   Ne hâte pas cet acte tendre,
   Douceur d'être et de n'être pas,
   Car j'ai vécu de vous attendre,
   Et mon coeur n'était que vos pas.

The last stanza repeats three times the very word "pas" with the reiterated sound suggesting footsteps and with the resonance of different
semantic references - the first two indicating negation, which is part
of the theme of something not real or not realized, and the last naming
the footsteps which echoes the beginning of the poem. And the modulation of feeling from start to finish of the whole poem is also carefully delineated, another essential factor in the ultimate sense, progressing from silent interested awareness to mystical delight to excited expectancy to a final suspension and pleasure in something un-
fulfilled - all trace patterns of feeling connected with lucid expectancy.

   In addition, the tonal content of a poem can be built up by sets of words or phrases which have no particular syntactic relationship within themselves but which all exhibit some common characteristic. In the case of Péret this, along with rhythmic variations, appears to be the main source of the content. For instance in the love poem "On Sonne" the following grammatically unrelated phrases - "un saut de puce", "une brouette dansant", "la projection pulvérisée du soleil", "ce petit insecte qui t'a chatouillée", "cet éphémère de sucre irisé", "un navire en dérive", "une île plantée d'arbres bleus" - all of these have a similar emotional content of light, bright happiness.

Also extremely important, although less tangible and harder often to discern, is the feeling or mental attitude which prefigures and underlies a given statement, whose existence is implicit but nonetheless real. Wittgenstein's thought is also pertinent in this respect for he considers the intention behind an expression as part of its meaning. He states for instance that a significant sentence is one which can not merely say, but also think. He considers also that a feeling gives a sentence, but not each word, meaning and truth. His example for this is the simple exclamation, "Oh, if only he would come!"*8 There, I gather, the impact and meaning are measured by the force of wish and desire felt by the person who said or wrote those words. The same is also true for many types of poetic expression. The subtle but insistent impressive force of the last line of Char's "Sept parcelles de Luberon, I" - "Je n'ai jamais rêvé de toi" - coming after the long lament and the sense of grief wedded to the mountain mass, derives from the sad but calmly controlled sense of gently resistant embrace which underlies the statement. Thus, this sort of expression can be considered an act, a mental gesture which takes on a real external existence and is communicable to others through language.

Including partial elements, non-discursive and some even non-verbal, such as rhythm, sound, semantic resonances and extensions, implicit feelings or intentions and structural lines as important factors in the total sense of a poem implies that the poem itself must be considered as a conceptual totality and as a coherently cohesive statement. This is not an unrealistic notion. There is no reason why a set of sentences should not stand for a single comprehensive representation, an act of cognition (but not knowledge, as it is inwardly based). The nature of that representation would not be essentially analytical or descriptive in an "objective" sense since the raw material consists of sense-data with a considerable and usually willed, subjective form of apprehension and since the determining inspiration or conceptual core behind a given poem is equally subjective - an event internal or external - is similarly inwardly viewed, colored and verbally shaped. If this is indeed the case, then it is not surprising that an individual poet's creations, taken as a whole, relate in some measure to experience common to all human beings but also disclose a unique world, different in content and structure from the real world and simultaneously different from the worlds of other poets. Each poet thus creates a world apart.

NOTES

*1 Tristan Tzara, "Essai sur la situation de la poésie", Le Surréalisme au service de la révolution, no. 4 (1931), 15-23.

*2 Alfred North Whitehead, Symbolism: its Meaning and Effect (New York, 1958).

*3 The case of Valéry is complex and rather unusual. While the linguistic expression and overall structure of his poems diverge from the patterns of discursive reasoning, his life-long reflections (highly intellectual and intellectual in nature) on the nature of psychological phenomena certainly determined preoccupations and even in an indirect way some of the formal characteristics of his verse.

*4 Interestingly, Proust experienced and described the form of involuntary memory which preserved and conveyed esthetic sensations as including also such primitive emotions but only those of a positive sort (love, eagerness, warmth).

*5 Paul Valéry, Introduction à la méthode de Léonard de Vinci, OEuvres I, 1164.

*6 In poetry, certainly, there is also a desire to communicate but the overriding drive is to be faithful to the inner configuration of inspiration.

*7 Ludwig Wittgenstein, Philosophical Investigations, 10e.

*8 Philosophical Investigations, 146e.

APPENDIX: TRANSLATIONS OF POEMS AND LONG QUOTATIONS
(marked with asterisk in text)

p. 2   The eye must reach the structure but only reach it by the de-
       tour of a group of movements of incidents and deviations which
       end well and conduct it to the goal not abruptly but as a system
       of ducts and canals conduct water from the mountain to the
       sea, having been completely utilized.

                    Paul Valéry, Cahier VI, 1916-1918. My translation.

p. 3   Born of my voiceless time, your steps
       Slowly, ecstatically advance:
       Toward my expectation's bed
       They move in a hushed, ice-clear trance.

       Pure being, shadow-shape divine -
       Your step deliberate, how sweet!
       God! - every gift I have imagined
       Comes to me on those naked feet.

       If so it be your offered mouth
       Is shaped already to appease
       That which occupied my thought
       With the live substance of a kiss.

       Oh hasten not this loving act,
       Rapture where self and not-self meet:
       My life has been the awaiting you,
       Your footfall was my own heart's beat.

                    Paul Valéry, "The Footsteps", trans. C. Day Lewis,
                    Selected Writings (New York: New Directions,
                    1950; rpt. 1964), 75.

pp. 9- This quiet roof, where dove-sails saunter by,
   13   Between the pines, the tombs, throbs visibly.
        Impartial noon patterns the sea in flame -
        That sea forever starting and re-starting.
        When thought has had its hour, oh how rewarding
        Are the long vistas of celestial calm!

        What grace of light, what pure toil goes to form
        The manifold diamond of the elusive foam!
        What peace I feel begotten at that source!

When sunlight rests upon a profound sea,
Time's air is sparkling, dream is certainty -
Pure artifice both of an eternal Cause.

Sure treasure, simple shrine to intelligence,
Palpable calm, visible reticence,
Proud-lidded water, Eye wherein there wells
Under a film of fire such depth of sleep -
O silence!... Mansion in my soul, you slope
Of gold, roof of a myriad golden tiles.

Temple of time, within a brief sigh bounded,
To this rare height inured I climb, surrounded
By the horizons of a sea-girt eye.
And, like my supreme offering to the gods,
That peaceful coruscation only breeds
A loftier indifference on the sky.

Even as a fruit is absorbed in the enjoying,
Even as within the mouth its body dying
Changing into delight through dissolution,
So to my melted soul the heavens declare
All bounds transfigured into a boundless air,
And I breathe now my future's emanation.

Beautiful heaven, true heaven, look how I change!
After such arrogance, after so much strange
Idleness - strange, yet full of potency -
I am all open to these shining spaces;
Over the homes of the dead my shadow passes,
Ghosting along - a ghost subduing me.

My soul laid bare to your midsummer fire,
O just, impartial light whom I admire,
Whose arms are merciless, you have I stayed
And give back, pure, to your original place.
Look at yourself... But to give light implies
No less a somber moiety of shade.

Oh, for myself alone, mine, deep within
At the heart's quick, the poem's fount, between
The void and its pure issue, I beseech
The intimations of my secret power.
O bitter, dark, and echoing reservoir
Speaking of depths always beyond my reach.

But know you - feigning prisoner of the boughs,
Gulf which eats up their slender prison-bars,
Secret which dazzles though mine eyes are closed -
What body drags me to its lingering end,
What mind draws it to this bone-people ground?
A star broods there on all that I have lost.

Closed, hallowed, full of insubstantial fire,
Morsel of earth to heaven's light given o'er -
This plot, ruled by its flambeaux, pleases me -

A place all gold, stone, and dark wood, there shudders
So much marble above so many shadows:
And on my tombs, asleep, the faithful sea.

Keep off the idolaters, bright watch-dog, while –
A solitary with the shepherd's smile –
I pasture long my sheep, my mysteries,
My snow-white flock of undisturbed graves!
Drive far away from here the careful doves,
The vain daydreams, the angels' questioning eyes!

Now present here, the future takes its time.
The brittle insect scrapes at the dry loam;
All is burnt up, used up, drawn up in air
To some ineffably rarefied solution...
Life is enlarged, drunk with annihilation,
And bitterness is sweet, and the spirit clear.

The dead lie easy, hidden in earth where they
Are warmed and have their mysteries burnt away.
Motionless noon, noon aloft in the blue
Broods on itself – a self-sufficient theme.
O rounded dome and perfect diadem,
I am what's changing secretly in you.

I am the only medium for your fears.
My penitence, my doubts, my baulked desires –
These are the flaw within your diamond pride...
But in their heavy night, cumbered with marble,
Under the roots of trees a shadow people
Has slowly now come over to your side.

To an impervious nothingness they're thinned,
For the red clay has swallowed the white kind;
Into the flowers that gift of life has passed.
Where are the dead? – their homely turns of speech,
The personal grace, the soul informing each?
Grubs thread their way where tears were once composed.

The bird-sharp cries of girls whom love is teasing,
The eyes, the teeth, the eyelids moistly closing,
The pretty breast that gambles with the flame,
The crimson blood shining when lips are yielded,
The last gift, and the fingers that would shield it –
All go to earth, go back into the game.

And you, great soul, is there yet hope in you
To find some dream without the lying hue
That gold or wave offers to fleshly eyes?
Will you be singing still when you're thin air?
All perishes. A thing of flesh and pore
Am I. Divine impatience also dies.

Lean immortality, all crêpe and gold,
Laurelled consoler frightening to behold,

220

Death is a womb, a mother's breast, you feign -
The fine illusion, oh the pious trick!
Who does not know them, and is not made sick -
That empty skull, that everlasting grin?

Ancestors deep down there, O derelict heads
Whom such a weight of spaded earth o'erspreads
Who are the earth, in whom our steps are lost,
The real flesh-eater, worm unanswerable
Is not for you that sleep under the table:
Life is his meat, and I am still his host.

'Love', shall we call him? 'Hatred of self', maybe?
His secret tooth is so intimate with me
That any name would suit him well enough,
Enough that he can see, will, daydream, touch -
My flesh delights him even upon my couch
I live but as a morsel of his life.

Zeno, Zeno, cruel philosopher Zeno,
Have you then pierced me with your feathered arrow
That hums and flies, yet does not fly! The sounding
Shaft gives me life, the arrow kills. Oh, sun! -
Oh, what a tortoise-shadow to outrun
My soul, Achilles' giant stride left standing!

No, no! Arise! The future years unfold.
Shatter, O body, meditation's mould!
And, O my breast, drink in the wind's reviving!
A freshness, exhalation of the sea,
Restores my soul... Salt-breathing potency!
Let's run at the waves and be hurled back to living!

Yes, mighty sea with such wild frenzies gifted
(The panther skin and the rent chlamys), sifted
All over with sun-images that glisten,
Creature supreme, drunk on your own blue flesh,
Who in a tumult like the deepest hush
Bite at your sequin-glittering tail - yes, listen!

The wind is rising!... We must try to live!
The huge air opens and shuts my book: the wave
Dares to explode out of the rocks in reeking
Spray. Fly away, my sun-bewildered pages!
Break, waves! Break up with your rejoicing surges
This quiet roof where sails like doves were pecking.

Paul Valéry, "The Graveyard by the Sea", trans.
C.Day Lewis, Selected Writings (New York: New
Directions, 1950; rpt. 1964), 41-49.

p. 17   Jeannie did receive your dates. I'm the one who's eating them.
I have a great weakness for that sticky fruit whose sugar, half
liquid and almost pulpy, is impregnated with a special silk
covering a bone, designed for mouths.

One ought to classify fruits like letters of the alphabet.
There are palatals, there are some which hurt the teeth, d's
and t's. Dates are liquid and labial.

p. 21   O Vanity! Very First Cause!
The Other who reigns in the Heavens,
With the word that was light itself
Opened the spacious universe.
As though bored with the pure theater
Of Self, God broke the barrier
Of his perfect eternity:
He became He who fritters away
His Primal Cause in consequences,
And in stars his Unity
. . .
Faced with your own funereal image,
Glory of my darkling glass,
So profound was your distress
That when you breathed over the clay
It was a sign of hopelessness!

> Paul Valéry, "Silhouette of a Serpent", trans.
> David Paul, Poems (Princeton: Princeton Univer-
> sity Press, Bollingen Series XLV.I, 1971), 187;
> 189.

p. 29   I said: sense of a universe. I meant that the poetic state or
emotion seems to me to consist in a dawning perception, a
tendency toward perceiving a world, or complete system of
relations, in which beings, things, events, and acts, although
they may resemble, each to each, those which fill and form
the tangible world - the immediate world from which they are
borrowed - stand, however, in an indefinable, but wonderfully
accurate, relationship to the modes and laws of our general
sensibility... They become... musicalized, somehow commen-
surable, echoing each other.

> Paul Valéry, "The Art of Poetry", trans. Denise
> Folliot, (New York: Pantheon Books, Bollingen
> Series XVI, 1958), 198.

p. 30   ...a little stream which was seeking a bed in the sand, hesitating, flowing back, carrying and depositing minuscule pieces
of flint...
- Yet another problem, my friend, he said: it's the drama of
this stream which is having a hard time with its little pebbles...
Let's consider our stream anthropomorphized. How would you
define his story right now?... we would have to condense the
story in one word, in an ambiguous epithet which would show
at the same time the material side of the thing: the stream,
what? pebbly?
(he adds laughing, shingly?) - and the side, what shall I
call it, moral? of this stream seeking its way, hesitating and

clearing its path and to do that places, displaces, feels, re-
places its tiny stones, following some deep-seated expediency,
obeying rigorously its laws... That's our true writer's task.
(M. Fabre proposes "scrupulous".)

He straightens up, delighted: - "Bravo", he says, "Scru-
pulus, little pebble. So the word did exist!...

Lucien Fabre, Paul Valéry vivant. My translation.

p. 31   The actors in this drama are mental images, and it is easy to
understand that if the peculiarities of these images be eliminated, and if only their succession, frequency, periodicity, their
diverse capacities for association, and, finally, their duration,
be studied, one is at once tempted to find analogies in what is
called the material world, to compare them with scientific
analyses, to give them an environment, a continuity, properties
of displacement, of speed, and then mass and energy.

> Paul Valéry, Fragments from "Introduction to the
> Method of Leonardo da Vinci", trans. Thomas
> McGreevy, Selected Writings (New York: New
> Directions, 1950), 97.

p. 34   The mind is at the mercy of the body as blindmen are at the
mercy of those who can see and who help them. The body
touches and does everything; begins and finishes everything.
From it emanate our true lights, and even our only ones, which
are our needs and our appetites, by which we have a sort of
perception "from a distance" and "superficial", of the state of
our intimate structure. "From a distance" and "superficial",
aren't those the characteristics of visual sensation? That's
why I used the word: light.

> Paul Valéry, Tel Quel. My translation.

p. 36   Unseen unknown
Hazard or genius?
Hardly come
The task is done!

Neither read nor understood?
How many errors promised
To the best spirits!

> "The Sylph," trans. Lloyd Alexander,
> Selected Writings (New York: New
> Directions, 1950), 73.

p. 39   Tough pomegranates half-opening
Yielding to your intemperate seeds,
I see you as brows of sovereign minds
Bursting with their discoveries!

> Paul Valéry, "Pomegranates", trans. David Paul,
> Poems (Princeton: Princeton University Press,
> Bollingen Series XLV. I), 207.

p. 39   ... The soul lets through
Its responsive eyelids, its sensitive suns,
When, in the movement that covers me with stones,
I plunge in defiance of all this idle blue.

> Paul Valéry, "The Rower", trans. W. J. Strachan,
> Selected Writings (New York: New Directions,
> 1950), 62–65.

p. 44   You embarass me with your questions... What I remember is
to have tried to maintain constant musical conditions, that is
to say that I have endeavored to submit, at each moment, the
meaningful content to the will or the intention to satisfy the
auditory sense.
    Rhythm, accents, tone–quality must be in my opinion, fac-
tors at least as important as the abstract element of poetic
language.

> Paul Valéry, interview with Fernant Lot, "Regard
> sur la prosodie de Paul Valéry", La Grande Revue
> (mars 1930), 93. My translation.

p. 46   We walk in time, and these
Our dazzling bodies
Have steps ineffable
That mark in fable...

> Paul Valéry, "Song of the Columns", trans. Vernon
> Watkins, Selected Writings (New York: New Di-
> rections, 1950), 56–61.

p. 47   All action is a brief madness.
Man's most precious moment is a brief attack of epilepsy.
Genius is an instant flash.
Love is born of a glance and a glance is enough to kindle life-
long hatred.
If we are worth anything it is only because we have been, or
have the power to be, "beside ourselves" for a moment. That
tiny moment outside myself is a seed or strewn like a seed.
And all time to come develops it – or lets it die.

> Paul Valéry, "Rhumbs", trans. Stuart Gilbert,
> Analects (Princeton: Princeton University Press,
> Bollingen Series XLV.14, 1970), 179–180.

When the sky, color of a cheek,
At last lets my eyes enjoy it,
Turning gold at the moment of dying,
Time plays among the roses,

> Paul Valéry, "The Cincture", trans. C. F. Mac-
> Intyre and J. Laughlin, Selected Writings (New
> York: New Directions, 1950), 71.

p. 48   To see, Oh miracle, see my mouth faintly shaping,
Betray...limn on the water a blossom of thought,
And what events to be, glittering in the eye!

> Paul Valéry, "Fragments of the Narcissus",
> trans. David Paul, Poems (Princeton: Princeton
> University Press, Bollingen Series XLV.I, 1971),
> 151.

Oh, admirable! that vibrant head!
How she, like slow fiber-thread
Partitioning its time of growth,
Divides without let or halt
The burden of the starry vault,
The fascination of the earth!

> Paul Valéry, "Palm", trans. Denis Devlin,
> Selected Writings (New York: New Directions,
> 1950), 51.

p. 51   But in myself I am no more mysterious
     Than the simplest among you

   ...

It is from you I drew the obscurity that tries you,
Who strays within himself discovers me at once...

> Paul Valéry, "The Philosopher and the Young
> Fate", trans. David Paul, Poems (Princeton:
> Princeton University Press, Bollingen Series
> XLV.I, 1971), 267; 269.

p. 56   The Anglo-Saxon mind for a long time has been accustomed to
the discursive method of English poetry - poetry of ideas, thus
of definition and of elucidation, always explicit and logical,
since the source is rational, therefore lending itself to the formal sequence of an intellectual and ethical system.
...[French poetry's ultimate goal is to] integrate its living self
with its object, between the poet and the poem. Doing more
than witness or depict, it becomes the thing itself that it "ap-
prehends", that it evokes or engenders...it is, finally, that
thing itself, in its movement and duration.

> Saint-John Perse, letter to George Huppert. My
> translation.

pp. 59-   We shall not dwell forever in these yellow lands, our
60   pleasance...

The Summer vaster than the Empire hangs over the tables
of space several terraces of climate. The huge earth rolls on
its surface overflowing its pale embers under the ashes - Sul-
phur colour, honey colour, colour of immortal things, the
whole grassy earth taking light from the straw of last winter -
and from the green sponge of a lonely tree the sky draws its
violet juices.

A place of stone of quartz! Not a pure grain in the wind's barbs. And light like oil. - From the crack of my eye to the level of the hills I join myself, I know the stones gillstained, the swarms of silence in the hives of light; and my heart gives heed to a family of crickets...

Milch-camels, gentle beneath the shears, sewn with mauve scars, let the hills march forth under the facts of the harvest sky - let them march in silence over the pale incandescence of the plain; and kneeling at last, in the fantasy of dreams, there where the peoples annihilate themselves in the dead powder of earth.

These are the great quiet lines that disperse in the fading blue of doubtful vines. The earth here and there ripens the violets of storm; and these sandsmokes that rise over dead river courses, like the skirts of centuries on their route...

Lower voice for the dead, lower voice by day. Such mildness in the heart of man, can it fail to find its measure?... "I speak to you, my soul! - my soul darkened by the horse smell!" and several great land birds, voyaging westwards, make good likeness of our sea birds.

In the east of so pale a sky, like a holy place sealed by the blind man's linen, calm clouds arrange themselves, where the cancers of camphor and horn revolve... Smoke which a breath of wind claims from us! the earth poised tense in its insect barbs, the earth is brought to bed of wonders!...

And at noon, when the jujuba tree breaks the tombstone, man closes his lids and cools his neck in the ages... Horse-tramplings of dreams in the place of dead powders, O vain ways swept away by a breath, to our feet! where find, where find, the warriors who shall watch the streams in their nuptials?

At the sound of great waters on march over the earth, all the salt of the earth shudders in dream. And sudden, ah sudden, what would these voices with us? Levy a wilderness of mirrors on the boneyard of streams, let them appeal in the course of ages! Erect stones to my fame, erect stones to silence; and to guard these places, calcades of green bronze on the great causeways!...
(The shadow of a great bird falls on my face.)

> Saint-John Perse, Anabase VII, trans. T. S. Eliot, Collected Poems (Princeton: Princeton University Press, Bollingen Series LXXXVII, 1971), 123-127.

pp. 68- Strange was the night, when so many breaths were lost at
69 the crossways of the room...
And who is that wandering before dawn at the ends of the earth, crying out for me? Which tall repudiated girl has gone, on whistling wings, to visit other thresholds, which girl, tall and crossed in love, has gone.

At that hour when the lapsing constellations, whose language changes for the men of exile, sink into the sands in search of a place of purity?

World-wanderer was her courtesan's name among the priests, in the Sibyl's green caves, and morning knew how to erase the tracks of naked feet from our sill, among sacred writings...

Serving girls, you served, and in vain you held out fresh linens to catch the chance fall of one pure word.

With the plovers' complaints departed the plaintive dawn, departed the showery hyades in search of the pure word,

And on most ancient shores my name was called... The ghost of the god dwelt among the smoking embers of incest.

And when this day's pale substance had dried into the sands,

Fragments of beautiful stories adrift in spirals, in the sky full of errors and erring premises, went turning around to the scholiast's delight.

And who was it there that flew away? And so who was it, that night, who, against my will, stole from my stranger's lips the practice of this song?

Turn over with your stylus, on the table of the shores, O Scribe, the wax impressed with the empty statement.

Waters of the deep, the waters of the deep on our tables will wash away the year's most beautiful numbers.

And it is the hour, O Beggarwoman, when on the shut faces of great stone mirrors exposed in the caves

The celebrant, shod in felt and gloved in raw silk, with a great sweep of his sleeve wipes away the illicit signs of night.

So goes all flesh to the hairshirt of salt, ashen fruit of our vigils, dwarf rose of your sands, and the spouse of a night shown out before the dawn...

Ah! all is vain in the winnowing of memory! all insane among the fifes of exile: the pure nautilus of free waters, the pure mover of our dreams,

And night's poems disowned before the dawn, the fossil wing entrapped in great amber vespers...

Ah! let them burn, let them burn on the sand-capes, all this refuse of feather, fingernail, dyed hair, impure linen,

And the poems born yesterday, ah! the poems born one evening in the lightning's fork, what's left of them is, like ash in women's milk, but the faintest trace...

And I, from all winged things for which you have no use, composing a language free of usage and pure,

Now I have once more the design for a great, delible poem...

> Exile, trans. Denis Devlin, Collected Poems
> (Princeton: Princeton University Press, Bollingen
> Series LXXXVII, 1971), 153-157.

p. 75   In you, moving, we move, and we pronounce you the unnamable Sea: mutable and movable in her moultings, immutable and immovable in her mass; diversity in the principle and parity of

Being, truth in the lie and betrayal in the message; all presence and all absence, all patience and all refusal - absence, presence; order and madness - licence!...

Saint-John Perse, "Seamarks", trans. Wallace Fowlie, Collected Poems (Princeton: Princeton University Press, Bollingen Series LXXXVII, 1971), 551.

p. 77 Stranger, whose sail has for so long moved along our coasts, (and at times, in the night, we hear the creaking of your pulleys),
 Will you tell us what torment is yours which prompts you, one evening of great warmth, to set foot among us on the custom-ridden land?
 "In bays of black marble streaked with white wings in the breeding season,
 The sail was of salt, and light was the mark of the talon on the water. Then was so much sky a dream for us?
 Scale, soft scale taken from the divine mask
 And the smile far at sea, of the great sacred ills...

 Freer than the feather which is cast from the wing,
 Freer than love leaving with the departing evening,
 You see your shadow, on the mature water, free at last of its age,
 And you let the anchor make the law in the undersea eclogue.

 A white feather on the black water, a white feather towards glory
 Has done us suddenly this great hurt, of being white and so strange, before evening...
 Feathers drifting on the black water, spoils of the strongest,
 Will they tell you, O Evening, who was fulfilled there?

 The breeze blew from the highlands, with that taste of areca nut and dead hearths which for a long time travels.
 The illustrious Ladies, on the capes, opened to the fires of the evening a nostril pierced with gold.
 And gentle again was the sea in the steps of greatness.
 Will the stone hand of destiny be offered us again?...

 It is the criste-marine, on your beaches, which was ripening again
 This taste of flesh, of all flesh the happiest,
 And the earth crying out on its porous banks amidst the avid brambles and live roses
 Of the foam, was for us a light thing, a more costly thing
 Than women's linen in dreams, than the soul's linen in dreams.

Saint-John Perse, Seamarks, trans. Wallace Fowlie, Collected Poems (Princeton: Princeton University Press, Bollingen Series LXXXVII, 1971), 447-449.

228

p. 82   Noon, its red lions, its famines, and the Sea Year at its highest
over the table of the Waters...
--What black and blood-stained girls go over the violent sands,
passing by the effacement of things?
Noon, its people, its strong laws... The bird, vast as its circle,
sees man free of his shadow, at the limit of his weal.
But our brow is not without gold. And our scarlet steeds are
still victorious over the night.

Thus the Horsemen in arms, on the cliffs, at Continents' end,
make the round of peninsulas.
--Noon, its forges, its great order... The winged headlands in
the distance open up their routes of blue-white foam.
The temples shine with all their salt. The gods awaken in the
quartz.
And the man on watch, high above, amidst his ochre clays and
fawn-coloured chalks, sounds red noon on his iron horn.

Noon, its lightning bolt, its omens; Noon, its red lions in the
forum, and its cry of a sea eagle over the deserted road-
steads!...
--We who perhaps one day shall die, proclaim man as immortal
at the flaming heart of the instant.
The Usurper rises from his ivory chair. The lover washes
himself of his nights.
And the man with the golden mask divests himself of his gold
in honour of the Sea.

> Saint-John Perse, <u>Seamarks</u>, trans. Wallace
> Fowlie, <u>Collected Poems</u> (Princeton: Princeton
> University Press, Bollingen Series LXXXVII,
> 1971), 575.

p. 86   My work, entirely one of "recreation", has always evolved outside of place and time: as studied and memorable as it is for
me in its incarnations, it intends to escape from all reference,
historical or geographical; similarly, although "lived" for me
rather than "abstracted", it intends to escape from any personal repercussion. In this respect the second part of my published work no less than the first part inclines towards transpositions, stylizations and creations of an absolute order.

> Saint-John Perse, letter to Roger Caillois. My
> translation.

p. 87   ... For in the morning, on the pale meadows of the naked Water,
all along the West, I saw Princes walking, and their Kinsmen,
men of high rank...

> Saint-John Perse, "Praises", trans. Louise Varese,
> <u>Collected Poems</u> (Princeton: Princeton University
> Press, Bollingen Series LXXXVII, 1971), 31.

p. 87   Under the bronze leaves a colt was foaled. Came such an one
         who laid bitter bay in our hands. Stranger. Who passed. Here
         comes news of other provinces to my liking...

> Saint–John Perse, "Anabasis", trans. T. S. Eliot,
> Collected Poems (Princeton: Princeton University
> Press, Bollingen Series LXXXVI, 1971), 101.

p. 88   Exile is not of yesterday! exile is not of yesterday!
         ... "O vestiges, O premises",
         Says the Stranger on the sands, "the whole world is new to
         me..." And the birth of his song is no less alien to him.

> Saint–John Perse, "Exile", trans. Denis Devlin,
> Collected Poems (Princeton: Princeton Univer-
> sity Press, Bollingen Series LXXXVI, 1971), 149.

p. 89   And, on all the shores of the world, the ghost of the god in
         smoke abandons his bed of asbestos.
         The spasms of lightning are for the delight of Princes in
         Taurida.

> Saint–John Perse, "Exile", trans. Denis Devlin,
> Collected Poems (Princeton: Princeton Univer-
> sity Press, Bollingen Series LXXXVI, 1971), 147.

We step over the gown of the Queen, all of lace with two
grey stripes (and how well the acid body of a woman can stain
a gown at the armpit).

> Saint–John Perse, "Anabasis", trans. T. S. Eliot,
> Collected Poems (Princeton: Princeton Univer-
> sity Press, Bollingen Series LXXXVI, 1971), 107.

p. 93   Divine fire appeared to me already in the immediate presence
         of the world. I had need of no intercessor, other than those of
         which our earthly universe is constituted. That is why I have
         never been able to feel completely Christian; like the true chil-
         dren of the Islands, I was "saved" at birth.

> Saint–John Perse, in an article by Claude Vigée.
> My translation.

p. 94   A fine poem always has the stamp of the absolute. If you be-
         come the theme, you live it; language plays a role in the cre-
         ative process, you attain the center. If you become the sea,
         the wind, you have breadth. One page tomorrow will suffice
         for me to be lightning, light, if I take these themes. One can
         treat all these themes on a single page, the same length. In
         that case they are rhythmic definitions.

> Saint–John Perse, from an article in Arts by
> Christian Gali (8 novembre 1960). My translation.

230

p. 95 ...May we no longer have, between the crowd and you, the unbearable radiance of language:
"...Ah! we had words for you and we did not have enough
words,
And behold, love makes us one with the very object of these
words,
And words for us they are no longer, being no longer signs
or adornments,
But the thing itself which they signify
...
In you, who move, we move also, in you, living, we keep
silence, and we live you at last, sea of alliance..."

> Saint-John Perse, "Seamarks", trans. Wallace
> Fowlie, Collected Poems (Princeton: Princeton
> University Press, Bollingen Series LXXXVII,
> 1971), 565-567.

...Narrow are the vessels, narrow our couch.
Immense the expanse of waters, wider our empire
In the closed chambers of desire.
...
In vain the surrounding land traces for us its narrow confines.
One same wave throughout the world, one same wave since
Troy
Rolls its haunch toward us. On a far-off open sea this gust
was long ago impressed...
And the clamour one evening was loud in the chambers:
death itself, blowing its conches, could not have been heard!

> Saint-John Perse, "Seamarks", trans. Wallace
> Fowlie, Collected Poems (Princeton: Princeton
> University Press, Bollingen Series LXXXVII,
> 1971), 451.

p. 96 Increasing and whistling thus at the turn of our time, they
came down from the high passes with this new whistling
wherein no one has known his own race.
And scattering on the bed of the peoples, ha! scattering -
let them scatter! we were saying - ha! scattering...

> Saint-John Perse, "Winds", trans. Hugh Chis-
> holm, Collected Poems (Princeton: Princeton
> University Press, Bollingen Series LXXXVII,
> 1971), 235.

...Farther on, further up, where the thin men go on their
saddles: farther on, further up, to where the thin mouths
are, with sealed lips.
For a long time westward-faced...

> Saint-John Perse, "Winds", trans. Hugh Chis-
> holm, Collected Poems (Princeton: Princeton
> University Press, Bollingen Series LXXXVII,
> 1971), 267.

p. 96-   None has surprised, none has known, at the highest stone
97   frontal, the first alightning of this silken hour, the first light
touch of this thing, fragile and so trifling, like a fluttering of
eyelashes. On bronze revetments and on soaring chromium
steel, on heavy blocks of mute porcelain and on thick glass
tiles, on rocket of black marble and on white metal spur, none
has surprised, none has tarnished

    that mist of breath at its birth like the first shiver of a
sword bared... It snowed, and behold, we shall tell the wonder
of it: how dawn silent in its feathers, like a great fabulous owl
under the breath of the spirit, swelled out in its white dahlia
body. And from all sides there came upon us marvel and festival. And let there be salutation upon the surface of the terraces, where the Architect, that summer, showed us the eggs
of nighthawks!

> Saint-John Perse, "Snows", trans. Denis Devlin,
> Collected Poems (Princeton: Princeton University
> Press, Bollingen Series LXXXVII, 1971), 199-201.

p. 98   ...and we ourselves with her, in a great flow of people and a
great trampling of the crowd, in our festival dress and our
light tissues, like the final recitation after the strophes and
the epode, and with this same dance step, O crowd! which towards the strong wide sea, a drunken sea, leads the docile
grave land, a drunken land...

> Saint-John Perse, "Seamarks", trans. Wallace
> Fowlie, Collected Poems (Princeton: Princeton
> University Press, Bollingen Series LXXXVII,
> 1971), 559.

p. 99   Under the bronze leaves a colt was foaled. Came such an one
who laid bitter bay in our hands. Stranger. Who passed. Here
comes news of other provinces to my liking. - "Hail, daughter!
under the most considerable of the trees of the year."

> Saint-John Perse, "Anabasis", trans. T. S. Eliot,
> Collected Poems (Princeton: Princeton University
> Press, Bollingen Series LXXXVII, 1971), 101.

p. 101   Ah! all is vain in the winnowing of memory! all insane among
the fifes of exile: the pure nautilus of free waters, the pure
mover of our dreams,
    And night's poems disowned before the dawn, the fossil wing
entrapped in great amber vespers...

> Saint-John Perse, "Exile", trans. Denis Devlin,
> Collected Poems (Princeton: Princeton University
> Press, Bollingen Series LXXXVII, 1971), 157.

p. 102   The incorporeal and very real, imprescriptible; the irrecusable
and undeniable and unappropriable; uninhabitable, frequentable;

immemorial and memorable - and what, O what, O what else, unqualifiable? The unseizable and inalienable, the irreproachable irreprovable...

> Saint-John Perse, "Seamarks", trans. Wallace Fowlie, Collected Poems (Princeton: Princeton University Press, Bollingen Series LXXXVII, 1971), 553.

p. 102 --and erect on the shining edge of the day, on the threshold of a great land more chaste than death,
the girls made water straddling and holding aside their print gowns.

> Saint-John Perse, "Anabasis", trans. T.S. Eliot, Collected Poems (Princeton: Princeton University Press, Bollingen Series LXXXVII, 1971), 133.

p. 103 A white feather on the black water, a white feather towards glory
Has done us suddenly this great hurt, of being so white and so strange, before evening...
Feathers drifting on the black water, spoils of the strongest, Will they tell you, O Evening, who was fulfilled there?

> Saint-John Perse, "Seamarks", trans. Wallace Fowlie, Collected Poems (Princeton: Princeton University Press, Bollingen Series LXXXVII, 1971), 447.

p. 111 Man discovers circular poetry
He sees that it rolls and pitches
like botanical tides
and periodically prepares its ebb and flow

> Benjamin Péret, "Le Mariage des feuilles", Le Grand jeu. My translation.

p. 113 Doorbell

A flea hop like a wheelbarrow dancing on the cobblestone's knees
a flea who melts into a staircase where I would live with you dear
and the sun like a bottle of red wine
turned itself into a nigger
whipped slave
But I love you as the shell likes its sand
where someone will unearth it when the sun has the shape of a bean
which will begin to germinate like a stone showing its heart in a cloudburst
or of a sardine can opened up
or of a sailboat whose jib is torn

I would like to be the projection of the sun pulverized on the
    ivy adorning your arms
that little insect that tickled you when I first knew you
No
that may-fly of iridescent sugar doesn't look any more like
    me than mistletoe looks like oak
which now just has left a crown of green branches where a
    pair of robins live
I would like to be
for without you I am barely the crack between the stones of
    the next barricades
I have your breasts so much in my chest
that two smoking craters are drawn there like a reindeer in
    a cavern
to receive you as the armor receives a nude woman
awaited in the depths of its rust
liquefying itself like the window panes of a house which is
    burning
like a castle in a big fireplace
resembling a ship drifting
anchorless rudderless
towards an island planted with blue trees which make me
    think of your navel
an island where I would like to sleep with you

> Benjamin Péret, "On Sonne", Un Point c'est tout.
> My translation.

p. 120   Half Way

The old dog and the ataxic flea
happened to meet on the tomb of the unknown soldier
The old dog stank like a dead officer
and the flea said
Isn't it too bad to pin little bits of shit with red ribbons
on your chest
Formerly rotten leeks didn't blush about being rotten
coughing and spitting bits of wood made very respectable
    hearses
with a poisonous odor of church mushrooms
and the mustache was only used for sweeping
Now springs of old hair burst forth from between cobblestones
and you simply adore them old general
for they come from the skull of a priest
who hasn't any bones
who hasn't any eyes
and who watches himself dissolving in a holy-water basin

> Benjamin Péret, "A Mi-chemin", Je ne mange
> pas de ce pain-là. My translation.

p. 125- Sun rough road shuddering stones
126 A storm's spear hits the frozen world
It's the day when liquids curl up
liquids with suspicious ears
whose presence is hidden under the mystery of triangles
But now the world stops being frozen
and the storm with peacock's eyes slides under it
like a snake sleeping with its tail in its ear
because everything is dark
streets soft as gloves
stations with mirror-like gestures
canals whose banks try vainly to greet the clouds
and the sand
the sand which is frozen like a pump
and projects far out its tentacles of cristal
All its tentacles will never succeed in transforming the sky
    into hands
For the sky opens up like an oyster
and the hands only know how to grasp beams of the sea
which soil the blue glances of the sharks
perfumed travelers
unshaken travelers
who skirt eternally the warning whistles of the willows
tall red pepper willows which are falling on the ground like
    feathers

If some day the earth ceases to be a willow
the big swamps of blood and glass will feel their bellies swell
and cry Nettles Nettles
Throw the nettles in a nigger's gullet
one-eyed as only niggers can be
and the nigger will become a thistle
and his lost eye a cassock
meanwhile a long bar of copper will stand up straight as a flame
so far so high that the nettles will no longer be his children
but fatal convulsions of a great body of foam
greeted by a thousand hooks of seething waters
which the white bread throws
that bread so white that next to it black is white
 and that the bitter rocks devour slowly the ankles of the
    mahogany dancing girls
but the nettles oh mosaic the nettles tomorrow will have
    donkey's ears
and feet of snow
and the nettles will be so white that the whitest bread will
    be forgotten in their labyrinths
Their cries will resound in the thousand agate tunnels of
    morning
and the landscape will sing One Two Three Four Two Three
    One Four
crows have church gleams
and drown every night in God's gutters

But be quiet heap of bread the landscape is lifting its long
    feather arms
and the feathers fly off and cover the tail of the hills
and now the bird from the hills finds itself in the water cage

But feathers stop for the landscape is now hardly more than
    a short straw
that you pull
So it's you girl with breasts of sun who will be the landscape
the hypnotic landscape
the dramatic landscape
the frightful landscape
the glacial landscape
the absurd white landscape
which goes away like a beaten dog
to curl up in the mail boxes of the big cities
under hats of the winds
under oranges of the mists
under ravaged lights
under the hesitant and sonorous steps of madmen
under the shining rails of women
who follow from afar the will-o'-the-wisps of the tall herons
    of the day and of the night
the tall herons with lips of salt eternal and cruel
eternal and white
cruel and white

> Benjamin Péret, "Soleil route usée...", Immor-
> telle maladie. My translation.

p. 127   Q: Where are you going?
A: They will take me... off to where men are falling dead, dead,
as snow falls.
Q: What did you see there?
A: A great blue wave... a great blue wave, rolling, rolling...
(From that moment Péret's face takes on an ecstatic expres-
sion which continues until he wakes up. He is most astonished.
He wears a beatific smile.)

> Benjamin Péret, "Récit de sommeil hypnotique".
> My translation.

p. 133   Pure psychique automatism by means of which we propose to
express either verbally, in writing, or in some other fashion,
what really goes on in the mind. Dictation by the mind, unham-
pered by conscious control and having no aesthetic or moral
goals.

> André Breton, First Manifesto, passage translated
> by Herbert S. Gershman, The Surrealist Revolution
> in France (Ann Arbor: University of Michigan
> Press, 1969), 35.

p. 134   This drawer which I open shows me, among the spools of
thread and the compasses, an absinthe spoon. Through the
holes of that spoon a band of tulips marching the goose-step
come to meet me. In their corolla are standing philosophy
professors airing their views about the categorical imperative.

> Benjamin Péret, in his introduction to Anthologie
> des mythes, légendes et contes populaires d'Amé-
> rique. My translation.

p. 135   Long live the sixth of February
grumbles the tobacco juice
dressed in shit adorned with fleur-de-lis
How fine it was
Buses were burning like heretics in the old days
. . .
Long live the sixth of February
and long live the seventh
I shouted for two days
Death to Cachin Death to Blum
And I stole everything I could in the stores
whose windows I broke

> Benjamin Péret, from Je ne mange pas de ce
> pain-là. My translation.

His fate was as short as a sweat
My sister
have you seen my pipe
My pipe is dead
and my wide eye is dull

> Benjamin Péret, "Le Quart d'une vie", Le Grand
> jeu. My translation.

p. 136   When the mountains suckle the snakes which are smothering
them
and the thoroughbreds summon the electricity
to go hang itself somewhere else
the dust amalgamated on the new-born infants
splits from top to bottom

> Benjamin Péret, "S'Ennuyer", De Derrière les
> fagots. My translation.

p. 139   It [the box] is full of a light cotton
which flies off at the slightest sound
which crackles at the slightest breeze
which is bored at the slightest rain
and which kills at the slightest whim

It can't go on like this
On the foot of the man next to me is falling
a moss of clouds

which is green
It's spinach
On the head of the woman next to me are falling
pebbles of fur
which she delights in
They are mice

> Benjamin Péret, "La Boîte aux lumières", Le
> Grand jeu. My translation.

p. 141 May the black wheat die if the sparrow's teeth
don't attract the sky-larks
if the lights of the white wine don't obscure the old mirrors
if the shoelaces don't guide the butterflies in the evening
when the rain falls like a hanged-man
whose rope has broken
because the neighbor was fighting with his wife
because of a clock which insisted on laughing before striking
in order to let its owners know that the world is upside-down
that the streams tomorrow will hunt the huntsmen

> Benjamin Péret, "A Demain", De Derrière les
> fagots. My translation.

p. 142 Centuries of coal lanterns of dry paste
losses of time waterfalls
follow one another and are lost in the gray path which leads
to the bloody islands
there is no longer any more time than water

> Benjamin Péret, "Une île dans une tasse", Le
> Grand jeu. My translation.

...the song of the kettle in love with the tropics
was fading away as noon
sweeps away its midnight sputtering with centuries beyond
    memory

> Benjamin Péret, "Dernier malheur dernière
> chance". My translation.

p. 143 From the depths of the granite which hides its secret of lichen
under a glitter of showmen
surrounding a team of fighters stiff with cold
under their garments of tweezers
emerges a sad gas-lamp's gleam which would be a cat
watching for the breathless scars of the wall
bearded hermit whom a vast plain planted with sea-shells
reunites with the tree-trunks which banished him
but isolates from the banks whose bells he doesn't hear
haunt his sleep peopled with hips
floating in a dawn wind which returns to him mat satins

> Benjamin Péret, "Mille regrets", Feu central.
> My translation.

p. 144   if I love you it's because the sun is square
and time too
and yet I'll never go all around time
because time turns like a roulette wheel
...
Tides of my errors where did you put our winds
...
o my dear
you who are my tide my ebb and flow
you who go down and come up like the thaw...

Benjamin Péret, "Nue nue comme ma maîtresse",
Dormir dormir dans les pierres. My translation.

p. 146   ...I cut out man from a prune. He was still minuscule but I had
confidence in time which would let him grow, besides he had
promised me. Man had barely begun to breathe when he stood
up and shouted "And my wife? Where is she?" "It's up to you
to find her," I told him. And having collected some honey which
was dripping from a hive, he formed his wife.

Benjamin Péret, Histoire naturelle. My translation.

p. 147   I mean by suicide that sudden consciousness of self which makes
us wish to become a turnip or a coal-shovel, although I picture
inadequately the metamorphoses a person who has committed
suicide might undergo in order to reach the definitive stage of
a turnip or a coal-shovel.

Benjamin Péret, La Brebis galante. My translation.

p. 148   It [the analogical image] moves, between the two attendant
realities in a fixed direction, which is absolutely not reversible.
From the first to the second, it marks a vital tension turned to
a degree towards health, pleasure, quietude, grace rendered,
established usage.

André Breton, La Clé des champs. My translation.

p. 150   Nothing gave one to suppose that one day harmony would reign,
when the sky seemed to clear up and the storm disappeared...
a rain-bow sparkled above the fascinated earth. The vegetation
understood and, in good grace, each plant occupied noiselessly
the corner for which it was destined.

Benjamin Péret, Histoire naturelle. My translation.

p. 152   The true mission of the artist - painter or poet - has always
consisted of rediscovering in himself the archtypes which underlie poetic thought, of charging them with a new affectivity, so
that, between himself and his fellow-men will circulate a cur-

rent of energy so intense that his archtypes made real will appear as the most obvious and the newest expression of the milieu which conditioned the artist.

> Benjamin Péret, "Wilfredo Lam", Médium (jan. 1955). My translation.

p. 152 Obviously, these people [Mayan] did not maintain simple relations of necessity with the outside world, but each man adhered with every fiber of his being, which he had not dreamed of dissociating to the exclusive benefit of reason.

> Benjamin Péret, Le Livre de Chilám Balám de Chumayel. My translation.

p. 158 Within the poem's fabric must be found an equal number of hidden tunnels, harmonious rooms, at the same time as future elements, havens in the sun, misleading paths and beings who call out to one another. The poet is the ferryman of all that which forms an order. And an insurgent order.

> René Char, A une sérénité crispée. My translation.

p. 160 To State One's Name

I was ten years old, enchased by the Sorgue. The sun sung the time on the waters' wise dial. Heedlessness and pain had sealed the weathercock on the rooftops and bore with each other. But what wheel in the heart of the watchful child was turning harder, turning faster than the mill in its white fire?

> René Char, "Déclarer son nom", Fureur et mystère. My translation.

p. 164 Thatch in the Vosges

Beauty, most upright, on such sordid roads,
at a haven of lamps and snug courage,
May I fall benumbed and may you be my December wife.
My future life - is your face, asleep.

> René Char, "Chaume des Vosges", Fureur et mystère. My translation.

p. 166 Madeleine with the candle

I would like the grass to turn white today to crush the evidence of seeing you suffer: I would not look beneath your hand, so young, at the hard, unstuccoed shape of death. One peremptory day, others, less eager however than I, will remove your cotton blouse, will occupy your alcove. But when they leave they will forget to quench the night-light and some oil will spread by the dagger of the flame over the impossible solution.

> René Char, "Madeleine à la veilleuse", Fureur et mystère. My translation.

240

p. 171 Corduroy Song

Day said: Everything that comes with me, clings to me, wants to be happy. Witnesses of my comedy, retain my joyful foot. I apprehend noon and its deserved spear. No request for mercy will prevail in its eyes. If my disappearance rings your release, the cold waters of summer will receive me all the better.

Night said: Those who offend me die young. How can one help liking them? Meadow of all my instants, they cannot crush me. Their journey is my journey and I remain obscurity.

There was ill between the two, rending them. The wind went from one to the other; the wind or nothing, the flaps of the rough cloth and a mountain avalanche, or nothing.

> René Char, "Chanson du velours à côtes", Fureur et mystère. My translation.

p. 174 Is not the poet that mountaineer who returns ceaselessly and whom the repeated assaults on the summits put back on his feet? Powdered with snow, and in summer surrounded by larch trees, he goes from peak to torrent. He sleeps in the spring grass. That is his only rest. On the rough file of the crests and the vertige of needle-like peaks, in exultation, he makes one smile. However he dies. Go ahead poet, and may velvet hold you, keep you from sliding... Man accomplishes nothing clearly fruitless. He does not lose what he will take pleasure later in seeking. Intrigue, despair are his lantern, the poet is his staff.

> René Char, Arrière histoire du Poème pulvérisé. My translation.

p. 176 Seven Plots in Luberon

I

Bedded on ground of pain,
Bitten by crickets, by children,
Fallen from aging suns,
Sweet fruits of Brémonde.

In a fine swarmless tree,
You languish in communion,
You burst in division,
Youth, bright cloud.

Your shipwreck has left nothing
But a rudder for our heart,
A hollow rock for our fear,
O Buoux, ill-treated boat!

Like growing larch trees,
Above conspiracies,
You are a tracing of the wind,
My days, wall of fire.

It was close. In a happy land.
Raising her cry to pure delight,
I rubbed the line of her hips
With the stubs of your branches
Rosemary, foraged heath.

Stone by stone, I endure
The demolition of my home.
Only he, devout, one evening
Saw the exact dimension of death.

Winter enjoyed Provence
Under the black stare of the Vaudois;
The pyre has melted the snow,
Water slipped, boiling, into the torrent.

With a star of misery,
The blood is too slow drying.
Mount of my grief, you govern!
Never have I dreamed of you.

> René Char, "Sept parcelles de Luberon, I", Retour
> amont. My translation.

p. 182   Field folk enchant me. Their beauty, frail and devoid of
venom, I never tire of telling about it. The field-mouse, the
mole, dark children lost in the myth of grass, the slow-worm,
son of glass, the cricket, as frisky as anything, the grasshopper
who claps and counts his linen, the butterfly who feigns to be
drunk and pesters the flowers with his silent gasps, ants
sobered by the wide green expanse, and right overhead the
swallow meteors...
    Prairie, you are day's watch-case.

> René Char, "Feuillets d'Hypnos", Fureur et mys-
> tère. My translation.

p. 183   In the chimerical wound of the Vaucluse I have watched you
suffer. There, although low, you were a green water, and yet
a road. You were crossing death in its disorder. Flower undulating with a continuous secret.

> René Char, "Tracé sur le gouffre", Retour amont.
> My translation.

p. 184   I am enamoured by this tender bit of country, by its arm-rest
of solitude, where storms come to break loose gently, on whose
mast a lost face, momentarily lights up and reaches me. As
far back as I can remember I can see myself leaning over the
vegetables in the untidy garden of my father, heeding the saps...
I who had the privilege of feeling all together despondency and
confidence, desertion and courage, I have remembered no one
except the spurting angle of an Encounter.
    On a road of lavender and wine we walked side by side in a
child-like setting of thorny-throated dust, each knowing himself

loved by the other. It was not a man with his head in the clouds
whom you kissed later behind the mists of your faithful bed.
Here you are, naked, and, of anyone, the best only today when
you pass through the exit of a rough hymn. Space forever, is
it this absolute and sparkling holiday, weak about-face? But
predicting that, I affirm that you live; the furrow brightens
between your well-being and my ill. Warmth will return with
silence as I will lift you up, Inanimate.

> René Char, "Biens égaux", Fureur et Mystère.
> My translation.

p. 186   Why this path rather than the other one? Where does it lead to
attract us so strongly? What trees and what friends are living
behind the horizon of its stones, in the distant miracle of
warmth? We have come this far for there where we were it
was no longer possible. They were tormenting us and were
going to enslave us. The world in our day, is hostile to Transparent Ones. Once more we have had to leave... And this path
which resembled a long skeleton lead us to a country which had
only its breath with which to scale the future. How can one
show, without betraying them, the simple things, traced between the twilight and the sky? By virtue of obstinate life, in
the loop of the artist Time, between death and beauty.

> René Char, De moment en moment. My trans-
> lation.

p. 187   So as not to yield and so as to find myself again, I challenge
you, but how enamoured I am of you, wolf, whom they wrongly
call funereal, filled with the secrets of my hinter-land. In a
mass of legendary love you leave the pure bare footstep pursued
by your claw. Wolf, I call you, but you have no nameable reality. Besides, you are unintelligible. Non-comparing, compensating, how do I know? Following your flight without mane,
I bleed, I cry, I am seized with terror, I forget, I laugh under
the trees. Pitiless hunt where one persists, where all is
brought into action against the double prey: thyself invisible
and myself vigorous.

> René Char, "Marmonnement", La Parole en ar-
> chipel. My translation.

p. 188   Productive knowledge of the Real
vulnerable aspirant
Is not achieved by means of a complicated measure of tears
  a joyous construction of ruses
But is obtained by a sort of progressive upheaval of fortune.

> René Char, Moulin premier. My translation.

p. 189   Imagination consists of expelling from reality several incomplete persons, putting to work the magical and subversive

powers of desire, in order to obtain their return in the form
of an entirely satisfying presence. Then it is the inextinguish-
able pre-existent real.

> René Char, "Partage formel", <u>Fureur et mystère.</u>
> My translation.

p. 190   I was in one of those forests where the sun has no access but
where, at night, the stars penetrate... In places the memory
of a force was caressing the peasant flight of the grass. I was
self-composed without doctrine, with a serene vehemence. I
was the equal of things of which the secret was to be found
under the ray of a wing.

> René Char, "Pénombre", <u>Fureur et mystère.</u>
> My translation.

p. 191   What were you saying? Your were telling me of a love so
     distant
That it went back to your childhood
So many stratagems are used by one's memory!

> René Char, "L'Ordre légitime est quelquefois in-
> humain", <u>Fureur et mystère.</u> My translation.

p. 192   Why <u>pulverized poem</u>? Because at the end of its trip towards
the Land, after pre-natal obscurity and earthly severity, the
limit of the poem is light, bringing life into being.

> René Char, "La Bibliothèque est en feu", <u>La Pa-
> role en archipel.</u> My translation.

p. 200   All life which is to dawn
       dispatches one wounded
         Here is the weapon
           nothing
yourself, myself, interchangeably
       this book
      and the enigma
that in turn you will become
in the bitter caprice of the sands.

> René Char, <u>Les Matinaux.</u> My translation.

SELECTED BIBLIOGRAPHY

1. Primary Sources

a. Paul Valéry

Correspondance d'André Gide et de Paul Valéry, 1890-1942 (Paris: Gallimard, 1955).
Lefèvre, Frédéric, Entretiens avec Paul Valéry (Paris: Le Livre, 1926).
Mondor, Henri, Propos familiers de Valéry (Paris: Grasset, 1957).
Paul Valéry vivant (Marseille: Cahiers du Sud, 1946).
Valéry, Paul, Cahiers, 29 vols. (Paris: CNRS, 1957-1961).
_____, Charmes, commentés par Alain (Paris: Gallimard, 1929).
_____, Le Cimetière marin, preface by Henri Mondor (Grenoble: Le Cercle des universitaires bibliophiles, 1954).
_____, "Cours de poétique" (notes prises par Georges le Breton), Yggdrasil (1937-1938).
_____, La Jeune Parque, ed. by Octave Nadal (Paris: Le Club du meilleur livre, 1957).
_____, Lettres à quelques-uns (Paris: Gallimard, 1952).
_____, OEuvres, 2 vols (Paris: Gallimard, 1957-1960).
_____, Réponses (Paris: Au Pigeonnier, 1928).

b. Saint-John Perse

Honneur à Saint-John Perse (Paris: Gallimard, 1965).
Saint-John Perse, Anabasis: A Poem by Saint-John Perse, translation and preface by T.S. Eliot, 1st ed. (London: Faber & Faber, 1930).
_____, Collected Poems (Princeton: Princeton University Press, Bollingen Series LXXXVII, 1971).
_____, OEuvre poétique, 2 vols. (Paris: Gallimard, 1960).
_____, Oiseaux (Paris, Gallimard, 1963).

c. Benjamin Péret

Péret, Benjamin, "A travers mes yeux", Littérature, no.5 (oct. 1922), 13.
_____, Anthologie de l'amour sublime (Paris: Albin Michel, 1956).
_____, Anthologie des mythes, légendes et contes populaires d'Amérique (Paris: Albin Michel, 1960).
_____, Le Déshonneur des poètes (Paris: Pauvert, 1965).
_____, Le Gigot sa vie et son oeuvre (Paris: Le Terrain vague, 1957).

_____, Histoire naturelle (Ussel: Manosque, 1958).
_____, Le Livre de Chilàm Balàm de Chumayel, translation and pref-
ace by B.Péret (Paris: Denoël, 1955).
_____, Mort aux vaches et au champ d'honneur (Paris: Arcanes, 1953).
_____, OEuvres complètes, 2 vols. (Paris: Losfeld, 1969-1971).
_____, radio interview with Pierre de Boisdeffre and Philippe Sou-
pault, Arts, 878 (18 juillet 1962).
_____, "Récit de sommeil hypnotique", Littérature, no.6 (nov. 1922),
1-16.
_____, "Ruines: ruines des ruines", Minotaure, nos.12 & 13 (mai
1939), 57-61.
_____, "Le Sel répandu", in Le Surréalisme en 1947 (Paris: Ed.
Pierre à Feu, 1947), 21-14.
_____, "Wilfredo Lam", Médium, no.4 (janvier 1955), 1.
Péret, Benjamin et al., Toyen (Paris: Ed. Sokolova, 1953).

d. René Char

Char, René, A une sérénité crispée (Paris: Gallimard, 1951).
_____, L'Age cassant (Paris: Corti, 1967).
_____, Arrière histoire du Poème pulvérisé (Paris: Jean Hugues,
1953).
_____, Art bref, suivi de premières alluvions (Paris: GLM, 1950).
_____, Artine et autres poèmes (Paris: Tchou, 1967).
_____, Le Chien de coeur (Paris: GLM, 1969).
_____, Commune présence (Paris: Gallimard, 1964).
_____, Dans la pluie giboyeuse (Paris: Gallimard, 1968).
_____, Dehors la nuit est gouvernée, précédé de Placard pour un
chemin des écoliers (Paris: GLM, 1949).
_____, Fureur et mystère (nouvelle ed. Paris: Gallimard, 1962).
_____, Le Marteau sans maître suivi de Moulin premier (Paris:
Corti, 1945).
_____, Les Matinaux (Paris: Gallimard, 1950).
_____, La Parole en archipel (Paris: Gallimard, 1962).
_____, Recherche de la base et du sommet (Paris: Gallimard, 1955).
_____, Retour amont (Paris: Gallimard, 1966).
_____, Sur la poésie (Paris: GLM, 1958).
_____, Trois coups sous les arbres (Paris: Gallimard, 1967).
Mora, Edith, "René Char commente son Retour amont", Le Monde
(28 mai 1966).

2. Critical Works

a. Paul Valéry

Austin, L.J., "Paul Valéry compose 'Le Cimetière marin'", Mercure
de France, nos.1076-1077 (avril & mai 1953), 577-608; 47872.
Bémol, Maurice, Variations sur Valéry (Paris: Nizet, 1959).
Cain, Lucien J., Trois Essais sur Valéry (Paris: Gallimard, 1958).
Dragonetti, Roger, Aux Frontières du language poétique (Gand: Romanica
Gandensia, 1961).

Duchesne-Guillemin, Jacques, Etudes pour un Paul Valéry (Neuchâtel: A la Baconnière, 1964).

Gelsey, Elisabeth A., "L'Architecture du 'Cimetière marin' ", RHL, no.63 (juillet-sept. 1963), 458-464.

Georghe, Ion, "Les Idées de Paul Valéry sur le langage poétique", RSH 139 (juillet-sept. 1970), 423-431.

Guiraud, Pierre, Langage et versification d'après l'oeuvre de Paul Valéry (Paris: Klincksieck, 1958).

Henry, Albert, Langage et poésie chez Paul Valéry (Paris: Mercure de France, 1952).

Hytier, Jean, La Poétique de Paul Valéry (Paris: Colin, 1953).

Ince, W. N., The Poetic Theory of Paul Valéry (Leicester: Leicester University Press, 1961).

Lawler, James, Form and Meaning in Valéry's "Le Cimetière marin" (London & New York: Cambridge University Press, 1959).

_____, Lecture de Charmes (Paris: PUF, 1963).

Lot, Fernand, "Regard sur la prosodie de Paul Valéry", La Grande Revue CXXXII (mars 1930), 84-99.

Mackay, Agnes, The Universal Self (Toronto: University of Toronto Press, 1961).

Mathews, Jackson, "The Poetics of Paul Valéry", Romanic Review XLVI, 3 (Oct. 1955), 203-217.

Noulet, E., Paul Valéry (Bruxelles: La Renaissance du livre, 1951).

Robinson, Judith, L'Analyse de l'esprit dans les Cahiers de Valéry (Paris: Corti, 1963).

Walzer, P.O., La Poésie de Paul Valéry (Genève: Pierre Cailler, 1953).

Weinberg, Bernard, "An Interpretation of Valéry's 'Le Cimetière marin' ", Romanic Review XXXVIII, 2 (April 1947), 133-158.

b. Saint-John Perse

Bosquet, Alain, Saint-John Perse (Paris: Seghers, 1961).

Caillois, Roger, Poétique de Saint-John Perse (Paris: Gallimard, 1954).

Charpier, Jacques, Saint-John Perse (Paris: Gallimard, 1962).

Fabre, Lucien, "Publication d'Anabase", Les Nouvelles littéraires, août 1924 (rpt. Honneur à Saint-John Perse, 406-407).

Gali, Christian, "Quatre heures avec Saint-John Perse", Arts, 8 (novembre 1960).

Garaudy, Roger, D'un réalisme sans rivages (Paris: Plon, 1963).

Henry, Albert, "Amers" de Saint-John Perse: Une poésie de mouvement (Neuchâtel: A la Baconnière, 1963).

Honneur à Saint-John Perse (Paris: Gallimard, 1965).

Knodel, Arthur, Saint-John Perse (Edinburgh: Edinburgh University Press, 1966).

Little, Roger, Word Index of the Complete Poetry and Prose of Saint-John Perse (Durham: 1965).

_____, Supplement "A" to the Word Index of the Complete Poetry and Prose of Saint-John Perse (Southampton: University of Southampton Press, 1968).

_____, "The Image of the Threshold in the Poetry of Saint-John Perse", MLR 64 (Oct. 1969), 777-792.

Mauriac, François, "Bloc-notes", L'Express, 8 décembre 1960.
Parent, Monique, Saint-John Perse et quelques devanciers (Paris: Klincksieck, 1960).
Saillet, Maurice, Saint-John Perse: poète de gloire (Paris: Mercure de France, 1952).

c. Benjamin Péret

Bédouin, Jean-Louis, Benjamin Péret (Paris: Seghers, 1961).
Caws, Mary Ann, "Péret - Plausible Surrealist", YFS, no. 31 (May 1964), 105-111.
_____, The Inner Theater of Recent French Poetry: Cendrars, Tzara, Péret, Artaud, Bonnefoy (Princeton: Princeton University Press, 1972).
Courtot, Claude, Introduction à la lecture de Benjamin Péret (Paris: Losfeld, 1965).
"Hommage à Benjamin Péret", Arts, no. 742 (30 sept.-6 oct. 1959), 34.
de Mandiargues, A.P., "Le Temps, comme il passe", La Nouvelle revue française XIV (nov. 1959), 931-934.
Matthews, J.H., "Mechanics of the Marvellous: The Short Stories of Benjamin Péret", L'Esprit créateur, Vol. VI, no. 1 (spring 1966), 26-30.
Mazars, Pierre, "L'OEuvre et la mort de Benjamin Péret", Le Figaro littéraire, 26 sept. 1959, 3.
Mayoux, Jehan, "Benjamin Péret, la fourchette coupante", Le Surréalisme même, nos. 2 & 3 (1957).
Patri, Aimé, "Légende et réalité de Benjamin Péret", Preuves IX (décembre 1959), 83-84.
Paz, Octavio, "Péret", Les Lettres nouvelles, 7 octobre 1959, 26-27.
Soupault, Philippe, "Benjamin Péret: audace, fidélité, surréalisme", Arts, No. 766 (16-22 mars 1960), 4.

d. René Char

Benoit, P.A., Bibliographie des oeuvres de René Char de 1928 à 1963 (Paris: Le Demi-jour, 1964).
La Charité, Virginia A., The Poetics and the Poetry of René Char (Chapel Hill: University of North Carolina Press, 1968).
Mounin, Georges, Avez-vous lu Char? (Paris: Gallimard, 1969).
Onimus, Jean, "Poétique de l'aphorisme en marge de René Char", Revue d'Esthétique, no. 2 (1969), 113-120.
René Char, L'Arc, no. 22 (Eté 1964).
René Char's Poetry: Studies by Maurice Blanchot, Gabriel Bounoure, Albert Camus, Georges Mounin, Gaeton Picon, René Menard, James Wright (Rome?: Editions de Luca, 1956).

3. General Sources

Alquié, Fernand, La Philosophie du surréalisme (Paris: Flammarion, 1955).

Aragon, Louis, Traité du style (Paris: Gallimard, 1928).

Balakian, Anna, "Metaphor and Metamorphosis in André Breton's Poetics", French Studies XIX (January 1965), 34-41.

Breton, André, "Lettre à Renéville", NRF, 1 mai 1932 (ret. Le Point du jour, Paris, 1934).

_____, La Clé des champs (Paris: Pauvert, 1967).

Champigny, Robert, "Analyse d'une définition du surréalisme", PMLA XXXXI, 1 (March 1966), 1939-144.

Cohen, Jean, Structure du langage poétique (Paris: Flammarion, 1966).

Hartmann, Geoffrey, The Unmediated Vision (New Haven: Yale University Press, 1954).

Manifestes du surréalisme (Paris: Pauvert, 1962).

Picon, Gaeton, L'Usage de la lecture (Paris: Mercure de France, 1961).

Poulet, Georges, Le Point de départ (Paris: Plon, 1964).

Raymond, Marcel, De Baudelaire au surréalisme (Paris: Corti, 1952).

Richard, Jean-Pierre, Onze études sur la poésie moderne (Paris: Ed. du Seuil, 1964).

Tzara, Tristan, "Essai sur la situation de la poésie", Le Surréalisme au service de la révolution, no.4 (déc. 1931), 15-23.

Vigée, Claude, Révolte et louange (Paris: Corti, 1962).

Whitehead, A.N., Science and the Modern World (1st ed. 1926; rpt. Cambridge: Cambridge University Press, 1953).

_____, Symbolism: its Meaning and Effect (New York: Macmillan, 1958).

Wittgenstein, Ludwig, Philosophical Investigations, translated by G.E.M. Anscombe (2nd ed. New York: Macmillan, 1967).

Weinberg, Bernard, Limits of Symbolism (Chicago: University of Chicago Press, 1966).

ACKNOWLEDGEMENTS FOR POEMS ANALYZED IN THE TEXT

Paul Valéry, "Les Pas, " OEvres, I (Paris: Ed. Gallimard, 1957).
Paul Valéry, "Le Cimetière marin, " OEuvres, I (Paris: Ed. Gallimard, 1957).
Saint-John Perse, Anabase, Strophe VII, OEuvre poétique, I (Paris: Ed. Gallimard, 1960).
Saint-John Perse, Exil IV, OEuvre poétique, I (Paris: Ed. Gallimard, 1960).
Saint-John Perse, Amers VIII, OEuvre poétique, II (Paris: Ed. Gallimard, 1960).
Saint-John Perse, Amers, "Dédicace, " OEuvre poétique, II (Paris: Ed. Gallimard, 1960).
Benjamin Péret, "On Sonne, " OEuvres complètes, II (Paris: Losfeld, 1971).
Benjamin Péret, "A Mi-chemin, " OEuvres complètes, II (Paris: Losfeld, 1971).
Benjamin Péret, "Soleil route usée . . . , " OEuvres complètes, I (Paris: Losfeld, 1969).
René Char, "Déclarer son nom, " La Parole en archipel (Paris: Ed. Gallimard, 1962).
René Char, "Chanson du velours à côtes, " Fureur et mystère (Paris: Ed. Gallimard, 1962).
René Char, "Chaume des Vosges, " Fureur et mystère (Paris: Ed. Gallimard, 1962).
René Char, "Madeleine à la veilleuse, " Fureur et mystère (Paris: Ed. Gallimard, 1962).
René Char, "Sept Parcelles de Lubéron, I, " Retour amont (Paris: Ed. Gallimard, 1966).

385 582